W9-ADD-402

Love Without Calculation

Other Works by David Power

Christian Priest: Elder and Prophet. Burns and Oates, 1972.

The Eucharistic Mystery: Revitalizing the Tradition. Crossroad, 1992.

Gifts That Differ: Lay Ministries Established and Unestablished. Pueblo, 1980; 2nd ed. 1985.

Irenaeus of Lyons on Baptism and Eucharist: Selected Texts with Introduction, Translation, and Annotation. Alcuin/GROW, 1991.

Ministers of Christ and His Church: A Theology of the Priesthood. G. Chapman, 1969.

Sacrament: The Language of God's Giving. Crossroad, 1999.

The Sacrifice We Offer: The Tridentine Dogma and Its Reinterpretation. Crossroad, 1987.

Unsearchable Riches: The Symbolic Nature of Liturgy. Pueblo, 1984.

"Word of the Lord": Liturgy's Use of Scripture. Orbis, 2001.

Worship: Culture and Theology. Pastoral Press, 1991.

Love Without Calculation

A Reflection on Divine Kenosis

"He emptied himself,
taking the form of a slave"
—Philippians 2:7

DAVID NOEL POWER, O.M.I.

A Herder and Herder Book
The Crossroad Publishing Company
New York

The Crossroad Publishing Company
481 Eighth Avenue, Suite 1550, New York, NY 10001

Copyright © 2005 by The Crossroad Publishing Company

All rights reserved. No part of this book may be reproduced, stored in a retrieval system, or transmitted, in any form or by any means, electronic, mechanical, photo-copying, recording, or otherwise, without the written permission of The Crossroad Publishing Company.

This book is set in 10/12 Sabon.
The display type is ITC-Mendoza Book.

Printed in the United States of America

Library of Congress Cataloging-in-Publication Data

Power, David Noel.
   Love without calculation : a reflection on divine Kenosis, "He emptied himself, taking the form of a slave," Philippians 2:7 / David Noel Power.
      p. cm.
   "A Herder and Herder book."
   Includes bibliographical references and index.
   ISBN 0-8245-2283-4 (alk. paper)
   1. Church. 2. Incarnation. 3. Catholic Church—Doctrines. 4. Jesus Christ—Mystical body. I. Title.
BX1746.P69 2005
230'.2—dc22

                                                          2005003907

1   2   3   4   5   6   7   8   9   10   09   08   07   06   05

*To the Seminarians of 2001 to 2003
at Our Lady of Pentecost, Tahiti,
where this work was begun
and largely written*

Contents

⚜

Acknowledgments

With the production of this book, there are several people who had some part in it whom I would like to acknowledge.

First, I mention the seminarians and the staff who were at the Seminary of Our Lady of Pentecost while I was teaching there. Though much of the time they did not even know what I was writing, they provided hospitality, environment, much patience with one so "uncultured," as well as the incentive of an encounter with diversity and a young Christianity. The people too of different communities in Tahiti and Fakarava were always most welcoming of my presence and preaching on the Scriptures, and in many ways "made me think."

Second, I am grateful to Father David Kalert, O.M.I., who during his time as provincial superior allowed me the freedom of the ministry of teaching and writing, and gave me every encouragement. All my Oblate confreres as well, even when bemused, have been very considerate.

Third, I thank Dr. John Jones of Crossroad Publishing Company for his ready acceptance of the manuscript and for guiding it to publication.

Most of all, I am thankful to Dr. Michael Downey, without whose interest and initiative the manuscript would have remained in a drawer of a filing cabinet, along with some other unpublished material. I am also appreciative of the kind and insightful, if unduly praiseworthy, preface that he has written to the work.

Introduction

My acquaintance with David Noel Power, O.M.I., dates to 1977. I was a graduate student in theology at The Catholic University of America in Washington, D.C., and he had just arrived from Rome to take up a teaching post in the Department of Theology. How fortunate we were. It is impossible to calculate the extent of his influence on both students and colleagues during his tenure at Catholic University. The same might be said of his earlier years in Ireland and in Rome.

Since retiring from Catholic University and becoming Professor Emeritus of Systematic Theology and Liturgy, David Power has continued teaching and writing at Catholic University and around the world—in Ottawa, San Antonio, Tahiti, and elsewhere. Called upon to provide an introduction to the work of the one who has over many years been mentor, guide, colleague, and friend, I am mindful above all that I have been and shall always be a student alongside so many others of different generations throughout the world, whose debt to an extraordinary teacher can never be repaid. Our testament to him is to do as he has done, living freely and responsibly with, in, and from the gift we have received, and passing it on so that others might have life to the full.

Of gifts received and lessons learned, two stand out. The first is that we must always attend to the "thought thought" but, even more importantly, we must probe what Power speaks of as the "thought being thought." This entails much more than simply grasping what a thinker has said or a writer has written. It requires a discipleship in thinking with the thinker as the thoughts are being thought and, in so doing, giving rise to yet further thought. Such discipline brings us to the threshold where we might learn a second lesson. And this is learned only by those willing to go deep. In seeking to discern the Word beneath all words, to hear the speaking of the Name that deafens all naming in the bottoms of a blue-green-black vast silence of unknowing, or allowing ourselves to be gazed upon by the Love beyond all measure whose measure alone is Love itself, we are being plunged into the very life of God known in the self-emptying of Christ.

This volume, begun while David Power was teaching at a small seminary in French Polynesia, is different from his other works in at least two significant ways. First, more than any of his previous publications, this one provides autobiographical clues—from his youth in Blackrock near Dublin, the years as a student in Rome, the long months of meandering on a dot-of-an-island in the far reaches of the Pacific—that help us grasp his abiding concern for the poor of the earth, a concern expressed in the motto of the religious congregation to which he committed himself while still a teenager: "To evangelize the poor he has sent me; the poor are being evangelized." Second, this work takes the form of theological reflection drawing from the storehouse of memory, rather than a project of systematic research and presentation. Here as elsewhere there is no lack of order and precision in Power's reflection on liturgical, scriptural, and theological texts. But in these pages his prose is quite often poised on the brink of the poetic.

His thinking here centers on two points. First, there is the call of the Church to live poverty according to the Gospel so that it might be truly the Church of the Poor. Second, taking a cue from John Paul II's encyclical *Fides et Ratio* and homing in on an image given considerable attention in recent theologies, Power looks to the *kenosis* found in the Letter to the Philippians (2:4-11) as key to understanding (1) the gift of God given to the world through the sending of the Word and the Spirit; (2) the identity of the Church and the realization of its mission; (3) the very life of God, the Divine Trinity.

Some forty years after the Second Vatican Council, David Power endeavors here to let us know what he really thinks, or how his thoughts are being thought, by probing the connection between the self-emptying of Christ and the Church's call to be poor. For Power, the Church is called to conform itself to Christ in loving service and poverty in its internal life and self-understanding, as well as in its manner of carrying out its mission—both as an extension of the mystery of Christ understood from the vantage of *kenosis*.

In its current weakened state, brought on by external forces and by its own sinfulness and failure, the Church is being invited to consent to a poverty that is not of its own choosing and, in so doing, to enter freely into the *kenosis* of Christ. The way of self-emptying takes the form of living in evangelical poverty, becoming the Church of the Poor who know that life and the life with God are given freely, without calculation. It is the truly poor who know how to wait with boundless hope for such a gift that is always and everywhere on offer.

The gift comes to those whose self-emptying makes room enough to receive. Living the mystery of *kenosis* is living for eternal life—a life we cannot fully imagine, the life that God alone gives through the *kenosis* of Christ *and* of the Church. This life, the very life of God, is where Power's thoughts being thought will take those daring enough to go deep, pushing out into the vastness of an ever-widening, never-to-be-exhausted circle of generosity.

In *Love Without Calculation* David Power is thinking through the un-say-able. He invites us to join him in wondering, pondering, beholding, praying from a heart branded by gratitude for such a generous descent by which we have knowledge of God in Christ through the gift of the Spirit calling us into the depths of *kenosis*, learning anew what it might mean to be the Body of Christ in our own time and place.

MICHAEL DOWNEY
Professor of Systematic Theology and Spirituality
Saint John's Seminary, Archdiocese of Los Angeles

Foreword

This book has a rather odd genesis. After some forty years of teaching theology in Ireland, Rome, and Washington, I retired as emeritus professor at the Catholic University of America and went to teach in a small seminary in French Polynesia, where the Oblates of Mary Immaculate had promised to supply some teachers for yet a little while. As things stood there, I was not in a position to do library research, the seminary library being stocked mostly by books that were the leftovers of seminaries in Europe or North America. This in effect prompted me to take up the challenge sometimes put to me by confreres, a bit exasperated by my books, to write "what you really think." Thus I set about putting down some theological reflections, fueled by the storehouse of memory, product of many years of teaching and research. When I first showed some of these to a friend, I referred to them as Pacific meanderings, or doing theology in recline, away from the pressure of university demands. Since then I have put more order and coherence into the work, but it bears the mark of such a beginning and is still more theological reflection than research.

Looking out over the infinite blue, green, and black of the South Pacific Ocean from a veranda on the side of a hill on the French Polynesian island of Tahiti, I knew that whatever I wrote there would bear the imprint of this seascape, with its multi-hued sunrise and sunset, blinding mid-day light and star-studded night. Putting together much of this manuscript in this oceanic setting, while teaching seminarians of the mixture of ethnic backgrounds that resulted from colonization and that was a living trace of history, I felt how much the imagination brought to an understanding of divine revelation was set on edge by memories and situation.

The people of Polynesia are always in the process of coming to terms with a history that even in modern times owes as much to oral as to written tradition. Living memory mixes mythic seafarers of uncertain provenance, island dwellers deeply attached to their atoll, Spanish, English and French explorers, and Chinese immigrants brought by colonials to supply labor. Common lore mingles stories of an age of kingdoms and tribes often at odds with each other, idyllic memories of a golden past, the still-bleeding remembrance of subjection to foreign powers and more lately the record of putting together the structures of a quasi independence that remains hard won and insecure. In its own miniscule way this reflects the muddled and even disturbed remembrance that many today across the world carry of their past.

It was not at all my intention to do a "Polynesian" theology, not having done the field work that this would require and being there as a foreigner and stranger. However, the situation in its own way provided metaphors that enlighten whatever theology is written in this century. Disturbed and fragmented memory is the sign of an epoch when the imagination is profoundly deranged by what is recalled or recorded of the tragedy and atrocity of a passing century. One of the vivid and frightening memories that I retain from my teens is picking the morning newspaper off the floor where it had been deposited by the newsboy and opening it to the first photographs taken when Allied troops entered the Nazi concentration camps. There was an appalled silence in the breakfast room when I brought in the paper to show it to my parents. Ireland had maintained its fringe neutrality during World War II, but even then these pictures bespoke an evil that nobody could stand back from. How little I suspected what other pictures of atrocity I would see in newspapers and on screen during the next sixty years.

Several generations now have been witness to such things. In the telling of time, peoples are disturbed by terrifying recollections, by the sound of the clash of war, by the smell of seemingly unconquerable disease, by ideologies of massive injustice that knows little respite despite the efforts of many, and by bleak fears of a bleak future, affecting earth, sea, and sky as well as humankind. The very hopes of building a new world order, which humanity and especially Western countries entertained in the nineteenth and twentieth centuries, are confounded by the recollection of two world wars and a variety of local hostilities, of the holocaust of the Jewish people and other genocides, of famines and epidemics that are left uncontrolled, and at present by a breakdown of international organizations intended to construct a new coalition of peoples. Even the tentative network of nations created since 1947 has dissolved in face of claims to military power and the righteousness of nations. God's name is invoked in justifying terrorism and in justifying punitive onslaught. The aphorism of John Paul II, "no justice without peace, no peace without pardon" has little claim on those who determine what seems to them desirable for the balance of power.

The Churches write and speak these days quite eloquently of the eschatological hope that promises a more just earth as well as a future infinity of divine blessings. In its preaching of the Gospel, however, and its counsels for the moral order, the Catholic Church in particular is in a very different position to that in which it was one hundred or even fifty years ago. In many respects, it has become a weak voice. It is weakened internally by failure to live according to the testimony of Christ and by some resounding scandals. It is weakened externally by reason of its inability to engage effectively with those who pursue other paths to truth. Despite its past strong claims to being source of truth it is called to open its heart and its mind to others and to other religions, and indeed to purify its own memories, an exercise that requires a new foundation for an internal spiritual and institutional reform. How then is it to capture anew the voice of God, to promise a future of hope not just for an absolute future but for times to come within the range of human history? How is it to let God's revelation show forth?

If we are not to fall prey to the expectation of the Rapture that many entertain, compiling the index of calamities that foretell a drastic end, we have to look to the sources and developments of Christian faith and tradition, though even in that we are in a parlous condition. Compared with what they were at one time, doctrine and theology are much less homologous. This reflects the tensions and struggles and even divisions within the communion of the pilgrim people of God.

Being of the generation of theologians who lived through the period of the Second Vatican Council and its aftermath, trying to come to grips with what it asked of theology, my theological work has been marked by that need. Catholics are still in fact in the process of appropriating what was said and what was done at and by the Second Vatican Council.[1] Out of a longer past of ecumenical encounters, other Churches, one with Catholics in the Body of Christ, match or outstrip the Catholic Church in openness to dialogue as they deal with many of the same issues, but also bear the bruises of internal divisions. The Second Vatican Council left Catholics with a mass of documents, documentation, and unsorted historical memories. Those who read between the cracks are left with a sharp awareness of the variety of choices and orientations at work within the body of those who claim to represent the apostolic tradition. Inherent in every human statement there is a question lurking and for all its efforts to reach consensus the Council could not hide the questions and the tensions that refused to be suffocated by words. One can read documents purely analytically or one can think from them, attentive to the questions that beg for adequate formulation before they can be pondered. The latter way is imperative.

Though this is not a work on the Council, it is under the influence of the theological and pastoral enterprise of which the Council was a part. Like many other elders, from having lived a while on the margins I have a living memory of this synodal gathering that made the sixties not just a new decade but another eon. During its latter sessions I was doing doctoral studies in Rome. By the good graces of an Irish bishop, Dr. Peter Birch, in whose diocese I had worked, I was actually able to enter the Aula for a short period and catch the aura of the internal dynamic of debate and corridor discussion and hear the banter of the coffee bar, where I was admonished by a Curial Cardinal to consider all persons equal when it came to getting to the urn. Naturally, many of those studying together at the time traipsed around Rome to conferences of the Catholic Church's theological "greats" and of the observers from other Churches. With faces put on them, names like Rahner, Congar, Schillebeeckx, Chenu, Küng, Nissiotis, Thurian, Moorman became household words that students tossed around with vague familiarity.

There was no doubt that the *aggiornamento* asked by Pope John XXIII was not understood in the same way by all. For some it meant spelling out faith and doctrine in such a way that it would address the inroads of creeping secularization. For others it meant bringing the Gospel more effectively to people who lived with the memories I have mentioned and preaching it more faithfully to peoples who did not share a European heritage. The consensus formulated in the documents voted by large majorities was real but it was also in some measure a compromise rather than a coherent convergence. All in all, memory and study of history and documents allow us to distinguish three orientations in what went on at the time. Similar currents of thought, action, and feeling have played their part in the impact that the Council has had on the Church and in how it was assimilated into the life of the faithful. I briefly outline the three because I want to cue in chiefly to the third in writing these reflections.

First, the orientation of the Church under previous papacies remained alive during the Council. While a new openness to the world and its evolution, as well as a concern with justice and peace, left its mark during the papacies of Pius XI and Pius XII, the prevailing interest seemed to be the need to keep intact the deposit of faith through doctrinal formulations and through clarifying the inner identity of the Catholic Church in its institutions and distinctive practices. This was seen as the best way of serving the modern world and of countering tendencies that alienated society from God. Though theological studies had made great strides and masses of the faithful had their role in liturgy, in mission and in Catholic Action, internally a hierarchical and sacral vision of the Church underlay such a formulation of the conciliar mission. During and after the Council, this remained the concern of many bishops and many Catholics, even among those who favored most of what the Council wrote. When bishops went home, it was many times found that this viewpoint still swayed their pastoral action. The Sambuca and the Strega, the cappuccino and the pasta, were left behind, with the exhilaration that they fueled and celebrated.

Second, there was the tendency to think that in preaching the Gospel, the world itself needed to be taken not as norm but as barometer. The Gospel had to be proclaimed and witnessed in ways that touched humanity and its history, both where it hurt and where it showed most promise. This conviction prompted bishops and their advisers to be more historically conscious and to ask that we read whatever signs the times give us of deeper aspirations, as well as of failure and despair. It was hoped that better scriptural studies and better acquaintance with God's Word on the part of all the baptized would help. This current left a clear imprint on the life of the Church, on its formulation of belief and on its active openness to the ecumenical movement, to cultures and to dialogue with other religions, not exclusive of a readiness to contemplate some change in ecclesiastical structures. In some respects, one might say that such a perspective was later given succinct formulation in the repeated saying of John Paul II: the Gospel must take root in cultures and cultures need to be challenged and enriched by hearing the Gospel.[2] For theology in particular, this means crossing over the distinctions between Churches in study and reflection, as it also increasingly means situating oneself in appreciative relation to cultures and religions and vast human movements.

Third, there was a specific desire that was shared by a number but expressed most strongly in the conciliar grouping that called itself The Church of the Poor.[3] This desire was to look to the Beatitudes as ethical charter of the disciples of Christ and foundation for the reign of God in the world. The partisans of the group saw the effort to bring justice to the poor as obedience to God's Word and an avenue along which one could bring the Gospel to the world. This meant seeing work for peace and justice as inherent to evangelization. In the internal life of the Church, this would exact greater simplicity, more conscious evangelical poverty, and greater involvement of all the baptized.

Some trace of this third current of thinking is found in the early part of the Constitution on the Church (no. 8), when a specific connection is made between the self-emptying and poverty of the Son incarnate on the one hand, and the poverty of the Church in its service of the poor on the other. There it is recalled that "Christ carried out the work of redemption in poverty and persecution," that he who was rich became poor for our sake, and took on the form of a slave, emptying himself out for the salvation of the world. The Church, the document says, must follow the same route in its service, especially in its service to the poor. It is to embrace the poor and the suffering and to do this faithfully it will often need to be purified.

This commitment to the option for the poor and to evangelical poverty exercised an influence on the papacy of Paul VI when he described the development of peoples as an intrinsic factor in evangelization,[4] when he journeyed to such places as Uganda and India, when he renounced wearing the papal tiara and when he made his pilgrimage to Israel with the Patriarch Athenagoras. That only those who are themselves poor can speak among the poor was given poignant symbolic expression at his funeral rites: according to his wishes a plain wooden coffin was placed in the middle of Saint Peter's Square, Bible atop, its leaves fluttering in the wind that blew across the piazza, opening the book at random wherever the spirit prompted.

We still need to discern these three movements at work in the Church and in our own hearts. Fifty years after the Council it is the third trend that has to be taken more seriously and thought about more fully, reflecting in a particular way on the connection between the self-emptying of Christ and the Church's call to be poor. The Catholic Church and all those represented in the World Council of Churches have indeed given much thought and action to the mission among the poor of the world but are always in need of coming to grips with the implications for their own innermost identity and way of life. This also has consequences for our approach to God, for the way in which God reveals the divine design and the divine self. Indeed Pope John Paul II in the encyclical on *Fides et Ratio* (no. 93) has invited theologians to ponder the mystery of *kenosis* as key to the knowledge of the Holy Trinity and of the salvation that is given to the world through the sending of the Word and the Spirit.[5]

In a theological reflection concerned with the faith and mission of Christ's Church, we should not think of theology purely in terms of Magisterium or of professional theologians, with academic qualifications. It is the Church as the body of believers and disciples that is on the move, listening to the Word and the Spirit, and sorting things out for itself. Considering that all hear God's Word at liturgy, looking at how an ecclesial and missionary movement so often has its roots among the baptized, some have fostered the theological axiom that all the faithful are "theologians." Thinking back over fifty years, it is vital to see how the laity has influenced the reception of the Council in the Catholic Church and how this has in effect changed the Church's living profile. This does not mean that there is convergence among all the committed faithful or that they all see their ministry in the same light. However, whichever of the three orientations mentioned, or mix thereof, they share, their involvement in the last fifty years has changed the face and the action of the Church in quite extraordinary ways. Symptoms of this change can be numbered. There is participation in the liturgy, in both traditional and innovative fashion. There is involvement in ministry, with the diversity found from continent to continent. There is considerable work for charity and for justice, often going hand in hand with new style movements and communities, following different orientations. Working together may mean doing so through organizations as varied as Opus Dei, Communion and Liberation, the Catholic Worker Movement, the Focolarini and the San Egidio Community, or through more makeshift sharing among those who feel called to lives of simplicity linked with the work of evangelization. In short, one cannot simply look to bishops and priests and professional theologians to find out what the Church's horizons are, or how the experience and texts of Vatican II are being appropriated. One has to see this from within the company of all the baptized.

Even in weakness, reflecting on the faith we start with the knowledge that we are loved and that God has opened the eternity of his holiness to our view, not face to face for now but darkly, as in a mirror. It is both the intimacy and the amplitude of this love that is overwhelming and even at times casts us into the kind of terrifying darkness into which Abram was thrown at the very moment when Yahweh struck covenant with him (Gen 15:12). The knowledge of God's embrace of humanity comes to us through the remembrance of event and the play of language. As we find ourselves as Church situated in the events of our own time while looking back on the events of covenant and its renewal, we are struck dumb and have to learn to speak anew. As the horizons of the Church are expanded beyond its own institutional boundaries, it needs to reconsider all its wonted expressions in order to encompass the immensity of the love that gives it life and yet is not confined within its confines. Its whole way of being, acting and thinking is affected. In such a movement, language itself is deeply touched, whether it be the language of the imagination, the language of doctrine, the language of rite, the language of devotion, the language of law, the language of theology or the language of prayers babbled half-consciously.

It is within this movement of faith that the endeavour is engaged in this work to say where Christian trust lies, or how to appropriate the Word of God and the breathing of the Spirit, as well as liturgical and doctrinal traditions, to formulate what one "may truly believe." Always conscious of the limits of expression, when I got to thinking about the work as project I found that initially my thoughts centered on the two points brought together in no. 8 of *Lumen Gentium*. On the one hand, there is the call for the Church to live poverty according to the Gospel. On the other, there is a strong current of spiritual and theological response to the image of the *kenosis* of the Son of God found in the Letter to the Philippians, 2:4-11, as it was later proposed for reflection by John Paul II and has been frequently employed in recent theologies. Perhaps it is just an accident that we both belong to the same missionary congregation, but a confrere of mine, Lucien Richard, has already written a book on what Christ's *kenosis* means for Christology, the Church and the theology of God.[6] There is, however, room for a further set of reflections on this and while I have learned much from his book, the approach taken here is rather different to that of Richard.

I risk some use of the first person singular because the work I present here is more theological reflection than a concerted effort at systematic presentation. Without access to rich library resources, I drew upon the storehouse of memory, even in my references to authors cited. I have of course verified a number of matters since, put in footnotes, enlarged the manuscript with additional thoughts, shepherded language, and taken good advice from friends and editors. I have even inflicted greater order on the text to give it inner coherence, but I have not tried to alter the book's character as reflection rather than research and I have allowed the tensions of thinking through the unsayable to remain. Supplying footnotes does not reflect further research: rather they are deference towards and acknowledgment of those from whom I learned and I trust some help to readers who want some basic information about where to look beyond the page.

With all of this, I have ended up with three parts and a postlude to the work, though in fact the material was not written in this order, given the sequence of my Pacific meanderings. In the first part I offer liturgical, scriptural and theological reflections on the mystery of Christ's self-emptying. In the second part, there is a follow-up on this in a reflection on the mystery of his Body, the Church, which in its mission is called to conform itself to Christ in loving service through poverty and persecution. In the third and in itself most crucial part, it is from this ground that I offer reflection on the mystery of God, known through the *kenosis* of Christ and Church. God is to be known, loved and served through the way in which divine compassion and divine love enter the world and the history of humanity; hence we access this through the mystery of Christ and Church, here presented under the sign of *kenosis*. The postlude is on the prayer of the Church. The order of presentation, however, should not prevent readers from starting with whichever section of the book they please.

If the final chapter is on prayer, this does not mean that it comes only at the end. Studies in liturgy and theology, as well as experience, have convinced me more and more that the celebration of worship is the ground of theology. Grasp of what occurs in liturgy may enable communities and theologians to formulate what can be called fundamental theology. That is to say, it offers us the foundation on which to stand, it gives us an orientation in faith for all theological expression. Grounding one's thought in the prayer and movement of liturgy also means turning more and more to interest in the forms of language used to express the faith, to the play of imagination and so to cultural and hermeneutical issues. Given the power of poetic forms, I am persuaded of the crucial role that liturgical traditions have in theological research and reflection and of their importance in the appropriation of scriptural revelation and apostolic faith.

PART ONE

THE KENOSIS OF CHRIST

Theology is by definition the talk of God, God's Word spoken, transposed into talk about God. We laud and praise the divinity for the mighty works of creation and of salvation and for releasing the human race from the grip of sin and death. In Jesus Christ, proclaimed as Son of God and Word made flesh, we acknowledge the gift of God, the Son to whom we are to listen, the priest in whom we have access to the Father, the Lord in whom we may reign in peace and justice, even in this world, him with whom we are made one by the power of the Spirit. For Christian believers, faith and hope are evoked by looking upon Christ and by listening to the Word of scriptural revelation. But is it possible to sustain such confidence in the midst of both the turmoil and the religious indifference of our times?

When we simply listen to how the name of God is being used around us we note that these days when people talk of God, odd things get said. We have heard God invoked in order to justify conflict and killing, and this is shocking and dangerous to humanity, to say nothing of blasphemy. Divine truth and the divine name are often more endangered by their invocation than by atheism's denials. If in turn we try to speak more justly, both philosophical and theological discourse about God are disrupted by terrifying memories and by a knowledge of a world situation that defies all that has been said about the divinity. We are really pressured by too much evil to be coherent. Minds are darkened by remembrance of such events as the Shoah, the genocidal massacres of Rwanda, the impieties of the South African regime of apartheid, the slaughters in Vietnam and Cambodia where great powers and local powers in hostile collusion inflicted their punishments, the sufferings of emigrants and refugees on high seas or dry land, and terrorist attacks in sundry places.

To talk of the times one could borrow the imagery of the circles of hell from the German scholar Jürgen Moltmann.[1] Together with others, he has described the infernal regions to which many are condemned in our world in situations that seem to worsen rather than improve. Because it is too much to bear, we turn our gaze away from the incomprehensible condemnation to poverty of the majority of the world's population on an earth that is rich in resources, but we still see it out of the corner of the eye. The proliferation of arms makes us ever conscious of the possibilities of a nuclear holocaust; countries and communities continue to be subjected to a violence that runs the range from terrorist activities which do not shrink before the destruction of the innocent, through ethnic conflict and massacre, to the sophisticated justification of the death penalty and self-righteous bombardments in faraway places. The instinct to violence even finds domestication in the battering of women and children, something now available upon the Internet, inclusive of pornographic violation put on view to circles of the perverted. Whatever the vaunted claims of advance in the promotion of human rights, millions suffer discrimination, from the alienation and distancing of any who seem to be different, to a racial, cultural and gender casting of character. While we are told by scholars that most religions and peoples retain some notion of a divine creation, we are plumb in the middle of an enormous disregard for creatures that are not of the human race. Much of the richness and wonder of the world and of the cosmos is under threat owing to its exploitation for profit. Government plans are devised to address issues of youth and old age but by themselves they do little to block out the fact that we see many forced by the circumstances of their lives to a youth or an old age resigned to meaninglessness. They are entrapped in a cycle of cynical exploitation by those who find the absurd profitable.

We are bidden nonetheless to listen to God's word, to turn to the one whom he has sent into the world to bear the burden of sin and to reconcile humankind with the God whom he names Father. When millenniums crisscross and memories are disturbed by recall of events that spell out the chaos of humanity's efforts to be perfect according to its own terms, we still place confidence in the Word of the Lord and in the Spirit of truth. Whatever the awareness of multiple interpretations across the ages we still ask that what was spoken and written be let to resonate within our chaos. As we heed this God of unfailing covenant, we sense that we are passing through the circles of hell, led not by Dante or Virgil but by Christ himself. As Christ entered the tomb to be among those who dwelt in the absence of God, so it is in passing through hell, the place of the dead, that we hear God speak and we hear the word of Jesus who speaks to us of the one of whom he is Son—of the God who is Father, not Judge or Almighty, or Law—and who has given the divine Spirit without calculation of any sort to those whom he chooses to call children (John 3:34). Through his death upon the Cross and through his descent into hell, Jesus subjected himself at the Father's bidding to the utmost limits of death and being dead, not simply to save us but to reveal God's true name to us.

While the collapse of that to which human ambition had aspired, with all its great potential to construct a world and a new humanity, is a formula for despair and calls for the loud voice of lamentation, it is in Christ that Christians find hope. The hope is oddly kindled by the witness that it is in infernal circles that some have continued to name God. Is it there that we are to hear God's voice, the divine claim to a name? There is the love that survives the death. If God says, as he did to Moses, "I am who I am," we must pay close attention: God is here in weakness, the one talking to you, the one bidding the hearer to act out of trust in a covenant of liberation, justice and love. You will not find my name, God seems to say, by making comparisons, by a simple reasoning based on indicators of providence found here and there. No, it is in attention to what God says of the gift made to creation that we may come to know divine reality, as we follow Christ through the regions of the hell that humanity has made of earth.

As a particular way of attending to the divine revelation given in Christ and in the divine Spirit, we have been reminded by Pope John Paul II in his encyclical on *Faith and Reason* (no. 93) that theology has a task today to penetrate the mystery of divine *kenosis*, to see how in this manner the Divine Trinity has come among us and to what destiny we are being led. It seems a particularly apt expression to speak of the passage of the One declared Son in the Spirit through hell. Indeed, in recent decades quite a few writers have sought to probe the meaning of this term. It might then be possible to take this metaphor and image as a key to listening to what the scriptures say to us of the sending of the Son into the world and even into the realm of death by the Father, and of the gift of the Spirit.

In presenting Christ to the world today, or in rendering an account of the hope that is within us, there are several levels of discourse, marking a kind of dialogical progression that remains always faithful to Christian belief but also seeks communion in the truth with persons of other beliefs. As John Paul II has put it in his encyclical on the Mission of the Redeemer, humankind is caught up in a search for unity, for reconciliation, and is trying to move towards a common destiny. Speaking of Jesus Christ needs to be respectful of other convictions, convincing of what belief in Him brings, yet faithful to our own tradition.

First, we may speak of Christ the way that anyone interested in truth and overcoming evil, and in the reconciliation of those who are at odds, might see him or hear his story. From the Gospels, we may tell of how Jesus related to the world and to God and of how what he made manifest still lives among us. Human destiny as Jesus presented it is one with the destiny that God has given his dealings with the world. To love God is to love neighbour, even to the point of forgiveness, and to love neighbour in this way is to open minds and hearts to the message of a divine fatherliness that is unique in the preaching of Jesus. In him, who presents himself as the Son of God in his way of living human life, we see the compassion of the divine and the place given in this compassion to the suffering, the weak, the lowly. We also see how Jesus stands before the powers of this world, religious and temporal, inviting them to share such solicitude and faith but uncompromising with their ambitions to lord it over others, ready indeed to submit himself to opprobrium on account of the truth. Human authority exists for only one purpose: to serve all that Jesus teaches humanity about those whom Jesus calls blessed in the reign of God.

On a second level, we speak of him "as necessary to salvation," not in the sense of an obligation imposed but as a way through the turmoil of evil and sin, as a way to life that confronts evil and that fulfills aspirations and needs. This is the meaning given to necessity by medieval theologians when they wrote of something that is fitting, appropriate, strikingly suited to the need to be met. For humankind to be united in one, with a sense of common destiny, the web of hatred, injustice, and sin has to be broken: this is "necessary." Humans need to know how to face death in the hope of life, be it personal, generational or cultural. In self-giving, in being for others, in seeking freedom from a global Babel, belief in both human community and in transcendent gift are needed and possible. In Jesus Christ we are given a way to be free from evil, a way to pass to life through death lived as self-gift and witness. We find in him a way of deep solidarity with sinful humanity, with those who suffer from sin and even with those who need to be forgiven their sin. As the Letter to the Hebrews puts it, Jesus learned from suffering, became perfect in his love of God and sinner through suffering, and thus is given to us as the way to truth (Heb 2:10, 18; 4:14-16).

The third level of discourse is thus introduced by the second. In the fullness of Christian faith, we proclaim Christ as the Son whom God gives to the world, the one in whom the plenitude of the Divine Spirit reposes. It is our belief that in him God offers his own justice to the world, along with the grace of forgiveness, healing and reconciliation. We see in Christ and the Spirit in whom he is anointed the presence of God in human life and history, the pledge of divine love and fidelity. He is God's compassion, God's way of involving the divine self in humanity's struggle with sin, evil and suffering, and in humanity's search to follow the way of reconciliation that opens to eternal life.

On any of these levels, the metaphor of *kenosis* is operative and is indeed integral to all discourse. Whether Jesus Christ is an example, a way of salvation, or truth itself, can be known only through penetrating the mystery of his self-emptying, in obedience to the exigencies of the kingdom to which he testified.

The first section of this book is therefore on the mystery of Christ seen as *kenosis*. Its aim is to relate liturgical tradition, scriptural reading and theological reflection in the pursuit of the meaning of such a mystery.

1

Christ's Kenosis: Liturgical Interpretations

---------------------- ✠ ----------------------

Liturgy or common worship is sometimes called the primary place where the Word of God is heard, interpreted and appropriated. What is made of scriptural texts in that setting provides a foundation for further theological reflection. Therefore, to begin these theological reflections, I will look at the text of the hymn in the Letter to the Philippians where the term *kenosis* is found and then see how its citation plays out in liturgy. There we will see how in Christian faith this term serves as a key to an interpretation of the mystery of Christ that is celebrated by the community. This metaphor is first noted in the Anaphora of Basil the Great in the Byzantine Liturgy, but most attention will be given to its place in the Holy Week Liturgy of the Roman Rite. Both the text itself and its liturgical use provide a foundation for ongoing theological consideration.

Christ's *Kenosis*: Philippians 2:6-11[1]

Writing to the Church in Philippi, Paul finds that there is some disunity among them. He praises their faith quite lavishly and recalls his own sufferings for Christ's sake and his desire to come among them again. However, there seems to be in his mind the fear that there are some false brethren, some rivalry, some ambition that disrupts a life shared in faith. He reminds them therefore of the attitudes they ought to have towards each other, at the core of which is love. This love, however, is modeled on that of Jesus Christ. In the end, they will behave among themselves according to the way they think of Christ, encouraged by their faith to follow his example. It is at this point that he turns to a hymn that was probably sung among them as part of their common worship. He wants to show that the lordship that is Christ's, his bearing of the name of Lord or *Kyrios*, the exaltation whereby he shares in God's own power over sin and death, is the outcome of the love he showed by his humility and all that this implies.

Quoting this hymn, Paul presents the Christ as one who came into this world having the "form of God" but who took on the "form of a slave."

5

To fill out the implications of this trans-form-ation, the hymn uses the term *kenosis* to show that he willingly laid aside the form of God, taking on existence in human likeness. To this it adds the act of humiliation whereby he became obedient, even to the point of death on a Cross. These four things then belong together to explicate the mystery of Christ: self-emptying, taking on the form of a slave, being in human likeness, and the humiliation of death on a Cross.

A necessary key to the meaning of all these terms lies in the sense given to the term "form of God," and what it meant for Christ to give up this form. Patristic writing usually took the term to mean the divinity of Christ, to affirm his pre-existence as Son of God, so that the song is in effect a song about the mystery of the Incarnation. This however does not appear to be the precise sense of the text, which has more to do with the appearance of Christ as one sent by God, as God's messenger or envoy. As a human, because of his communion with God and his role as God's envoy, Jesus was deserving of honor and glory. This glorification, the glory to which one might accord him a right, he renounced.

The assumption of the form of a slave, *doulos*, is in contrast with this. It is described as a *kenosis*. This word in itself already suggests an abundance of possibilities, since a search on the Internet shows that in English versions of the New Testament it is variously translated as "humbled himself," "stripped himself," "made himself nothing," "set aside his privileges," or "emptied himself." To see, however, in what this consists one must read further down the text.

The word "slave" seems to have a double signification. Taking a first glance at the text, it may seem to be the equivalent of appearing in human likeness, to having a common humanity, to sharing the lot of all for the sake of their redemption. However, there is another meaning that accompanies and qualifies this. The word "slave" or "servant" has in the milieu of the recipients of the letter a social connotation. It says that Christ appeared as one who belonged to the slave class. These are they who must serve others and have no rights of their own. Their very being is defined by the service that they are obliged to render to others. In his flesh, Christ showed himself in the form of the slave, the *doulos*. In human society he is classed among those who belong in the ranks of the civilly unfree, those burdened by slavery, those without rights, those esteemed as nothing.

The second meaning comes from the first. While the text underlines the appearance of Christ among the slave class it also implies that this can be said in its own way to describe the human condition itself, when human beings live subject to a regime of sin and death. They enjoy no true freedom, they become slaves to each other and to all manner of ambitions, be they their own or those of others or of a self-indulgent society as a whole. Most are blind to this; they cannot see below social appearances. It is then fitting that for the Christ to save humankind from its slavery he should have the appearance and undertake actions that they would readily see connote slavery. To save slaves, he assumed the lowliest form of reduction to servitude.

The hymn then goes on to say that coming among us in this form, he humbled himself and became obedient. The term "humbled" again has multiple significance. It may simply mean making oneself lower, doing the will of another as Christ does by obeying the will of God. It may also designate one's behaviour towards others as one who is mild, meek, not lording it over anyone but always ready to be of service, even compassionately so. This is a common understanding in the New Testament when it is said that Jesus was humble, or that Paul or somebody in authority acts in humility, or that all disciples are blessed in their humility. These two meanings are doubtless present in this text, but there seems to be also a third sense, that of being rendered humble through humiliation. This is the estate to which Jesus is reduced, not only by accepting to die, but in the form of death, upon the Cross, he suffered. Crucifixion was for criminals, and at that for those of despised peoples, those who were not ranked among the free citizens of the populace. Not only did Christ take the form of a lowly slave but he appeared as the lowliest and most despised of persons by being put to death on a Cross. It is on this account that God gave him the name and power of Lord, *Kyrios*.

To attain to the lordship exercised in God's mercy, to have power to liberate the slaves of sin from their servitude, the Christ was obedient even to the death on the Cross. The lordship he then received in being raised up is qualified by such an accession. The words, "to become obedient," explain this access to God's right hand because they tell of the relationship between Christ and the Father. In New Testament Greek, "to obey" designates an active state of mind in relation to another. It is to subject oneself to the other, to adhere to the other, to accept, respond, answer the other's call. Used of the relation between Christ and the Father, it tells us of close adherence and communion. In his humble and humiliated state, Christ is closely allied with God, even when he feels abandoned and is handed over to those who persecute him. Passing thus through and beyond death, he is one with God "in obedience," and through this communion has access to God's right hand, is raised up by God and given to share his lordship over sinful humanity.

There is thus a progression in the hymn in showing how Christ saved humankind and how he models the love and service which the Philippians are called to practice among themselves. First, he relinquished all show of power, glory, splendor, he did not impose himself by any display of his role as God's envoy. Second, he took on a common humanity, the human form which all possessed under the reign of sin and death, so as to be like unto those he was to liberate. Third, within this estate he appeared as socially inferior, as one to be ranked among the servant classes. Fourth, he was humiliated before the eyes of all by being subjected to the most despised of deaths, by being shown in the lowliest conceivable condition. Therein lies the full import of the *kenosis* of Christ. It was by such passage that he was given lordship, so that with God he exercised the power of releasing humankind from servitude and from death itself.

All the appeals made to the hymn or to the metaphor of self-emptying in the course of history do not necessarily carry through with the full import of the hymn nor fix its meaning once and for all. Indeed, with its rich potential and interplay of images it can be inserted into a variety of contexts, with variant significance. In fact, over time it has been used in diverse contexts for diverse purposes. To start the investigation into the way that faith has appropriated this hymn and the image of *kenosis* we do well to begin by looking at the place given it in liturgy.

The Anaphora of Basil of Caesarea[2]

Without developing it at great length it is opportune to recall here how celebration of the mystery of Christ's salvation as *kenosis* is found in such an ancient and revered text as the Anaphora of Basil of Caesarea. In his commentary on the Byzantine Liturgy, the ninth-century Bishop Germanus of Constantinople presented the *anaphora* or eucharistic prayer,[3] which Latins often saw as a prayer of consecration, as a contemplation of the mystery of the Divine Trinity in the inner *perichoresis* of their eternity and in their love for creation. The prayer of Basil provides a fine text in which to see this verified and one in which the text from Philippians 2 provides the key to a contemplation of what is revealed through Christ.

This prayer first invites worshippers into the heavenly sanctuary of the quietly flowing wisdom and love of the ineffable Trinity, but where the mystery of divine election in creating the world and saving humanity are already eternally present. Before this mystery, the congregation joins the heavenly choirs in singing out the name of the thrice holy. The prayer then asks that they ponder the wonder of creation and the divine accompaniment of the people of Israel through all the hopes and trials of their faithful response, but also through their infidelities, renewals and prophetic expectations.

The prayer then proclaims that in the fullness of time, there came the Word of God made flesh into the world, and before anything else is said this is looked upon as the mystery of *kenosis*. No doubt following the sense given to this text in his own time Basil thought of the incarnation of the Son in the appeal he made to it. However, what the prayer then does is to fill out the meaning of what occurred in this taking on of mortal flesh. In faithful and loving embrace the text passes through the many episodes of this mystery: the taking on of flesh, the baptism in the Jordan, the teaching, the subjection to death in voluntary submission, the burial in the tomb, the rising from the dead, the ascension to glory, the sending of the Spirit and the final coming. Within the record or memory of these events, Basil notes the Church of the elect already present at the waters of the Jordan, where Jesus is declared beloved of the Father and is anointed with the Spirit. Christ's whole purpose as Word made flesh was to make a people unto himself, to baptize the world in the water of the divine immersion and proclamation of his Sonship and the descent of the Spirit in which he himself was baptized at the onset of his mission. The text from Philippians 2, the image of *kenosis*, by being quoted first, is made key to the memorial of the entire mystery of Christ's days in the flesh, from his incarnation until his coming in glory. To express what is at the heart of this kenotic mystery, Basil incorporates what is already found in an earlier prayer, that which we find in the work entitled *Apostolic Tradition*. Jesus, the one who had come in the fullness of time, the one who came forth from the eternal and ineffable life of the Trinity and brought of this life into the world, stretched forth his arms upon the Cross and by such obedience and exalted suffering put an end to the reign of sin and death. When he reached the summit of his *kenosis*, he set the limits of the powers of evil.

It is not possible to comment upon this presentation and commemoration of the story of the Word without noting that the prayer is, as the liturgists say, through and through epicletic, that is to say an invocation for the sending of the Spirit. No memorial, no remembering, is possible except in the gift of the Spirit, that Spirit which flowing out upon the Church was already present at the taking on of flesh of God's Son. We might add, glossing the texts, that communion with Christ in his *kenosis* is possible only in the Spirit. Being full of the Spirit, the vision put forward by the prayer is necessarily eschatological. The Church that lives and lives communion only through the memorial of Christ is in its mysterious existence the figure of the divine procession through history that continues until all will be accomplished. The prayer's intense concern with travelers, the sick, prisoners, bishops, emperors, widows, virgins, sinners, youth, the aged, those close to death, those already in death, bears out that God's presence can be seen only in the mirror of this motley humanity, and this motley humanity only in the mirror of the ineffable Trinity and its loving and self-giving procession through human history.

Liturgy: Holy Week and Easter[4]

Liturgy shuffles and interconnects texts in ways that project a fuller meaning. Liturgical celebration is dubbed the primary place for the Church's interpretation of the Scriptures and for their appropriation, constituting a basic orthodoxy or theology of what is celebrated. In the annual celebration of Holy Week and Easter, the hymn from Philippians is connected with other texts and rituals in several ways.

While attention focuses on the celebration of Holy Week and Easter in the current liturgies of the Roman Rite, it has to be seen in the longer tradition of Roman Liturgy, which in turn has roots in the Church of Jerusalem. This liturgy proposes in two ways that the *kenosis* or self-emptying of Christ fits into the overall celebration and understanding of his Pasch. The first way is through the use made of the text of the hymn cited by Paul in Philippians 2:6-11. The second way is through four liturgical acts that command the attention of the congregation and that ritually cohere with this text, on Sunday, Thursday, Friday and Saturday night respectfully.

At the beginning of what we know as Holy Week, in the liturgy of Palm Sunday, the Church proclaims the Passion of Christ, but immediately preceding it, the hymn from Philippians 2:6-11. Later in the week, at the office of the days of the Triduum, the antiphon is sung that proclaims the filial obedience of Christ unto death, even unto the death of the Cross, this being the reason why God has given him the name above all names. This provides a key to the unfolding of the drama of Christ's Passion and Resurrection over the course of the week.

On Passion Sunday, or Palm Sunday, by ancient tradition the celebration of Holy Week begins with the solemn procession of the palms, symbolizing Christ's descent from Bethany to Jerusalem. Intense meditation on his sufferings is anticipated by proclaiming him as messianic king, the one who will through his death and resurrection fulfill the promises of the messianic or eschatological kingdom. The reading of the Gospel narration of this episode is at the core of the service. Though the revised liturgy takes the reading from Matthew, Mark and Luke in turn, the text from Matthew's Gospel is the more traditional. The importance of this text (Matt 21:1-11) is that it cites *in extenso* the passage from Zechariah, "your king is coming to you, humble and mounted on a donkey" (Zech 9:9). The passage is from a prophecy told to the "daughter of Zion," announcing the coming of the messianic king to fulfill the promises made to David. The donkey was a royal mount; this ruler will have greater power and glory than David himself. He will, however, be meek and humble in his rule over the people. With Jesus entering the royal city mounted on a donkey, acclaimed by the crowds as the Holy One of God, this Gospel serves very well to pinpoint what the week will celebrate. It is the beginning of Passover, when the rite of the Paschal Lamb is kept. Christ appears as the sheep led to the slaughter, the one whose blood will be shed for the redemption of many. He comes in the name of God, sent by the same God who saved the people from the slavery of Egypt and made covenant with them. In him the eschatological promises are to be fulfilled, and he has all the glory of God's Son. But the reign of God is to be inaugurated through his suffering, in which he will be the picture of meekness and humility, submitting himself to death out of obedience to the Father.

In the Mass that follows, we have the first proclamation for the week of the Passion Narrative, again traditionally from Matthew's Gospel. It is significant that the story begins with the Supper for this gives the paschal note to the liturgical commemoration and also underlines the anxiety of Jesus's anticipation of betrayal and death, as well as the love for his disciples and for sinners that motivates him.

The two readings that precede the Gospel are important in portraying the sense of the Passion. One of these is Phil 2:6-11. The first is one of the Servant Songs, Isaiah 50:4-7. Along with the responsorial psalm, Psalm 21/22, it intensifies the feeling for Christ's sufferings and humiliation, and underlines his attitude of loving service towards sinners. In its own way, however, it anticipates the resurrection, for in the midst of suffering it expresses complete trust in God. Though it precedes it, the psalmodic tract glosses the text from Philippians by illustrating the manner and nature of Christ's suffering and obedience. It gives voice to a feeling of being abandoned by God and abandoned to his enemies. The servant cries out, "Save me from the mouth of the lion, my afflicted soul from the horns of the unicorn." The Mass uses the Latin Psalter, and English translators have special difficulties with one of the phrases. The word that has been given above as "my afflicted soul" in the Latin reads *humilitatem meam*. English translations say variously "afflicted soul," "afflicted spirit," "poor soul," "humbled spirit." The Latin word means all that we have found in the words "humbled himself" of Philippians. It means to be of lowly estate, to be meek, gentle, ready to subject oneself, and this even through the process of being humiliated. Crying out in such a state of lowliness, the Christ, in whose mouth the liturgy places these words, expresses his trust and confidence and calls on his hearers and future generations to fear and praise God. Catching the full meaning of *humilitas* enables us to see the connection between his suffering and his confident praise. In his very humiliation and abandonment he is obedient to God and so ever in union with God.

The Collect of the day in its original Latin tries to express the sense of such *humilitas*, something that English translations hardly capture. I give it this rough rendering, hoping to do some justice to the richness of the prayer: "Almighty and Eternal God, to give the human race an example of humility that it could imitate and make its own, you made our Saviour take on flesh and subject himself to the Cross. Grant in your mercy that we may reproduce in ourselves what he suffered and be companions with him in his resurrection." The themes found in Philippians are here quite faithfully integrated into the Church's prayer.

How the reading from Phil 2:6-11 serves to interpret the Passion is already clear. It is important to give this note of willing *kenosis* and expected victory to the entire annual commemoration. It tells us what the Church is celebrating, living and proclaiming in its detailed journey through the events of Christ's last week on earth in the holy city of Jerusalem. That the liturgy, however, wishes to underscore Christ's obedience, in contrast with the disobedience of sin, is made clear by the verse used as Gospel acclamation: "Christ became obedient for us unto death, even death on a Cross. Therefore God has highly exalted him and bestowed on him the name which is above every name." This is also the antiphon used in the Divine Office during the Triduum. It skips over the image of self-emptying to accentuate obedience and the lordship that is to follow. It still, however, includes the abasement of death on a Cross, and in the words "for us," the notion of service.

When the Roman Church revised the liturgy of the Triduum in the 1950s, one of the primary aims was to restore the role of the Paschal Vigil as the key moment of the entire celebration. There was no desire to undo the importance of Good Friday for the faithful, nor that of Holy Thursday. Early and medieval liturgies, not only of Rome but also of Jerusalem, provided models for the reform.

In effect, what had been in early times concentrated in the liturgy of the Vigil was stretched out over three days. The principal trace of this is found in the placement of the reading of the story of the Paschal Lamb, Exodus 12, on Holy Thursday. This was originally a key text proclaimed at the heart of the Easter Vigil in early Jerusalem. Exodus 12 is the story of the sacrifice of the Lamb, of the redemptive sprinkling of its blood on the doorposts of the Israelites and of its eating in haste, preparatory to leaving the captivity of Egypt. Its reading brought the Church back in remembrance to God's deliverance of the Israelite people from the slavery of Egypt and to the ritual that he gave them for the annual commemoration of the event. Being proclaimed at the Vigil of the Resurrection of Christ, it established the Lamb as a figure of the Christ crucified and risen. Put into the liturgy of Holy Thursday it is intended to offer a symbol of the mystery of the Eucharist, but without losing its original significance of the Paschal Lamb as the symbol of the sacrifice of Christ in the shedding of his blood. Thus the Triduum of Christ's Pasch is launched by harkening to the typology of the Lamb. In its odd history, the text began as a text for the Vigil, then was placed on Good Friday, and finally on Holy Thursday; at every stage of liturgical development, however, it served as a key figure for this annual commemoration.

A number of other readings, both at the Vigil and on the preceding days, fit into the perspective of Philippians 2:6-11. At the Vigil, this appears in the Old Testament types of Christ and his sacrifice that are proposed. On the other days, the texts recall both the image of service or servant and the sufferings endured.

Vigil Readings

In the course of time, Exodus 14 was added to the reading of Exodus 12 at the Paschal Vigil, along with the canticle of Moses in Exodus 15, celebrating the release from Egypt and God's choice of Israel as his own people. To the imagery of the Paschal Lamb it added the symbolism of passage or passing over to express the significance of the Lord's death and resurrection. With the Vigil, however, as the night for the baptism of new Christians, the more immediate reason for its present inclusion is that it has served for centuries as the type or symbol of Christian baptism. Together the reading from Exodus 12 and the reading from Exodus 14 typologically represent the mystery of the Lord's sacrifice and Pasch and the participation of the Church in this mystery through the sacraments of Baptism and Eucharist.

Some of the other passages heard at the Vigil highlight how Christ's sacrifice may be seen as a sacrifice given by God to his people in the abasement of his Son. In other words, we see more readily how they may be read within the horizon of the *kenosis* proclaimed on Palm Sunday and in the liturgical antiphon of the Triduum. Alongside the story of the Lamb, another figurative reading is Genesis 22, the story of the sacrifice of Isaac. This places Isaac among the types or figures of Christ and his sacrifice. Listening to this story today, hearers are bewildered by the order to Abraham to sacrifice his own son, a seemingly cruel act and one that jeopardizes the divine promise made to generations to come. But against this background, the death of Christ is seen as the ultimate act of paternal donation, of God the Father giving his own beloved Son in sacrifice for the sealing of an alliance made at the expulsion of sinful humanity from the Garden. From early on, the text was seen as the identification of the Son with suffering and sacrificed humanity. This is said in the paschal homily of Melito of Sardis, who identifies the Christ and the power of his Pasch as that of one "slain in Abel . . . in Isaac fettered . . . in Jacob a hireling . . . in Joseph sold . . . in Moses exposed to die . . . in David persecuted . . . in the prophets scorned." In proclaiming the Pasch[5] Melito includes in the mystery not only Christ's death but the extent of his identification with mortality; he was "buried in the earth." Unfortunately, there is a strong vein of anti-Semitism in Melito's text; he blames the Jewish people for the death of Christ and excoriates them for this. One has to set this aside to allow the imagery of Christ's identification with those who suffer speak to us.

Typological readings that express the relation of Old Testament readings to the Pasch of Christ or to Baptism are tough nuts to crack. They seem to have gained pacific possession in a rather allegorical fashion as far back as Origen, but today, with more scientific respect for exegesis and more human respect for the Jewish people, they do not go over so well. In recent Vatican documents about typology[6] in scriptural interpretation and about relations between Christianity and Judaism, attempts have been made to get beyond merely paralleling images and symbols, as communities were and are inclined to do. It is only by missing the point of the story and attending simply to the images that it is possible for a congregation on Paschal night to clap its hands over the destruction of the Egyptian army, with its many dead. More attention needs to be paid to the actual struggles and discoveries of the people of Israel in their quest for liberation. Of the Exodus in particular, the Biblical Commission says that it is to be seen in its own right as an experience of salvation and liberation. If that is so, readers have to reckon with all the turmoil that it involved. Only when it is taken seriously may we ask how what the Israelites experienced and were given by God's Covenant finds an accomplishment in Christ or in Christian Sacrament. This is to be interpreted in an eschatological perspective, in which it is seen as an anticipation of the fullness of God's reign in the time to come. Both alliances situate themselves in relation to each other in terms of the desire and struggle to enter into the divine design. Through their empathy with the people of Israel, Christians gain light on how to relate themselves to Christ. In listening to the Paschal narrative of the tribes of Israel, civilly under Pharaoh and spiritually under Moses, we ask ourselves about their experience and how in liberation and covenant they came to know and name God. What we integrate of this into our knowledge of Christ and what we have been given through his Pasch, and thus of own baptismal experience as a sharing in this, is what counts.

While the liturgy no doubt still intends that the story be seen as figurative of Christ and of the Father who gives his son up to death for our sake, the reading of Genesis 22 is enriched for contemporary congregations by the approach suggested by the Commission. The exegesis of the text is quite difficult for scholars when they want to explain why God gave such a command to Abraham. From Jewish and Christian tradition, we know that the story of the binding of Isaac captured the imagination and was given in various versions which heightened the drama, often making Isaac a young adult so that he could play a more active part in the story. Some exegetes content themselves with seeing in the command to Abraham a test of his fidelity and faith, and in the arrest of his hand when he is about to kill Isaac a sign of God's beneficence. Others place the covenant God made with Abraham, the command to sacrifice Isaac and the command of the Decalogue, "Thou shalt not kill," alongside one another. This juxtaposition can illustrate the excess demanded of those who would be faithful to Yahweh: nothing, even the most dear, can hold them back from their obedience and their dedication to God's design of salvation. Other commentators think that Abraham was being tested in his faith, in the sense that even with the son given to him he was to rely on God, never on himself or his progeny. Still others see in the story evidence that at this point Abraham still had to learn more about God and how the religion of the cult of Yahweh was different from other cults: the lesson he was to learn was that no human life is to be destroyed in the service of this God since God is the source of life and holds every life dear and sacred to himself.

There are many questions and issues for Christian communities to ponder in the light of God's gift of his Son and of Christ's own faith in taking on the burden of humanity's suffering and sin. We are to ponder anew how in reflecting on the gift of this most generous excess of love, we still need to learn of God's law and the truth of Christ, how sacred all human life is to be to us—since it is so dearly held by the Father that he gave his own Son to redeem and safeguard it against malice and even against religious zeal.

During earlier days of the Roman Liturgy, two prophetic texts served to give the Pasch of Christ a strong eschatological note. One of these was the song of the vineyard of the Lord (Isa 5), in which Isaiah laments that God's care of his beloved was met by the beloved's rejection, resulting in subsequent misery. Tuned into the Pasch of Christ, the song tells us that God never has and never will abandon his people, for in the gift of his Son, dead and triumphant over sin and death, he has performed an even more extravagant act of loving and tender care. Ezekiel (Ezek 37) invited worshipers to look to the raising of all the dead forecast in the rising of the first-born, the Son made flesh, made sin, made death, made life. This reading from Ezekiel is chanted in the Byzantine Liturgy on Good Friday over the *epitaphion*, or image of Christ laid out in the tomb to proclaim the resurrection of the Lord and the raising up of all the dead with him. This is the ultimate triumph over death announced in John's Gospel when Jesus declares, "I am the Resurrection and the Life," or "in three days he shall be raised up again." It is also the promise given to those to be baptized. For them it speaks of the life they are to receive in baptism and of the final hope of sharing in Christ's total victory over sin and death itself. When we turn from this more or less allegorical liturgical reading to the text itself, we see that it is what can be called an eschatological retrieval of a promise given to the people of Israel in a time of trial. That is to say, the deliverance from exile promised to them is an event whose hope finds a new fulfillment in the coming of Jesus as Messiah and finally in the raising up of all the dead. While they learned to hope for a new life as a people, to be delivered "as though from the grave," this kind of hope contains within itself the seed of hope for liberation from all torment, oppression and death. Looking at the text in its own historical setting, and placing it in the context of the Pasch and of Baptism into Christ, it expresses a hope for the future and for the present. The promise given in the Paschal Lamb, in the new Isaac, in the Second Adam, is not only a promise for some vague time beyond this world. It is a promise that Christ and the Spirit are always with us, always working through us to free human beings and peoples from the living death they endure within the turmoil of human history. Through Ezekiel God was addressing victims, those who had suffered exile and captivity, and were looked down upon by those who had compromised and were able to remain at home. The grace of God is made evident to us through what is made evident in the suffering and abased. We see its import in Christ who is made the victim of human jealousy and opposition but remains faithful to God; it addresses all of those who in suffering are witnesses to the Gospel preached in his word and in his Pasch.

In today's liturgy, the choice of the prophetic readings from Isaiah 55 and Ezekiel 36 appears to have been dictated by the desire to find texts that relate more explicitly to Baptism through references to refreshing and cleansing waters. The latter, however, is a promise of a new covenant written in the heart, a purifying of hearts that make them hearts of flesh rather than hearts of stone. These proclamations retain the eschatological note of prophetic literature. On Easter Night, they are surely to be heard in light of Christ's Pasch. They are baptismal instruction and encouragement for those who know that Christ has passed through the trial of his death, that he has gone down into the netherworld, and that through this giving of himself to the last he has brought new life into the world. The conversion from hearts of stone to hearts of flesh arouses in those baptized into Christ a gift of compassion and love, a readiness to pour themselves out with Christ and in the grace of his Spirit in order to bring life into the world. Those with hearts of flesh can be true witnesses to the compassionate heart of Christ, from which in his death throes there flowed out blood and water.

This eschatological note is in fact sounded in the very first proclamation of the night, the Creation narrative from Genesis with which the Vigil service begins. While the idea of renewal of God's creation may on one level be heard to mean spiritual regeneration as a spiritual creation, its more forceful meaning is that in the Pasch of Christ the entire creation is saved and renewed. It is an act of genius to begin the Vigil with the story of creation; it provokes awe, wonder, and silent reverence. In the context of the Pasch of Christ, it serves to allow congregations to see the creative and transforming love of God at work in the death and resurrection of the Saviour. More than that, it brings us back to the origins of the world, and of the human story as an act of divine gift, a giving that continues and reaches its climax in the gift of Christ as Mediator.

Readings for Thursday and Friday

The hymn from Philippians as key to the reading of the Passion Narrative and the Triduum antiphon based on it are not the only ways in which liturgical readings present the Passion of Christ as an abasement or self-emptying. On Friday, the reading of the Gospel is complemented by texts that underline the suffering and obedience of Christ and the humility embodied in his self-giving. Good Friday joins one of the Servant Songs to the reading of the Passion from John's Gospel, namely, Isaiah 52:13-53:12. Good Friday also appeals to Hebrews 4:14-16; 5:7-9 to bring out some aspects of Christ's mediation. He is a mediator who was tempted or tried in every way, who offered prayers to God with a loud cry and tears, who even learned obedience through suffering. While Philippians describes Jesus's self-emptying even unto death as an act of obedience, Hebrews adds the notion that in this very act he *learned* obedience. In being obedient he gained full knowledge of what it was to hand himself over in this way.

Another way in which the liturgy of the week brings out the nature of Christ's mediation as humble service is the reading of John 13:1-15 on Holy Thursday, after the evocation of the figure of the Paschal Lamb. In this Gospel, we hear Christ pronounce himself servant or *doulos* and we see him acting as such in washing the feet of his disciples. Jesus himself wished this act to interpret what he was about to do for the world in giving himself over to death, to the subjection he suffered in being condemned and crucified. The liturgy is not content to proclaim the Gospel, but has the celebrant act it out in washing the feet of members of the congregation. A rubric in the present Missal rather mishandles this text by reading it as the institution of the priesthood in the person of the twelve, who are to be servants as the friends of Christ. The meaning, however, is deeper, and serves to give a sense of Christ's own passion and of his relation to sinful humanity. It is on this day that the story of the Paschal Lamb is read, being presented as a divine act of liberation and as a remembrance to be kept. The Gospel shows who the Paschal Lamb is for us and how his memory should be kept: certainly in the Eucharist but also in the testament of service like his own.

Ritual Acts

Besides the proclamation of the Word, liturgy is served by ritual actions that focus faith on its object. On Thursday, Friday and at the Vigil there are three symbolic rituals, one for each of the three days, that together invite faith in Christ's Pasch as an act in which, by entering into death and darkness, he redeemed humankind from enslavement to them. The historical background and present adaptation of these rites are worth pondering as dramatic ways of expressing the meaning of the death and resurrection of Jesus. They may be more fully appreciated when the hymn of Palm Sunday is kept in mind.

The first, the washing of the feet, dramatizes the Gospel story that is proclaimed. It graphically portrays Christ as the humble servant, ready to give his life for his disciples but ready also to care for them as a servant would care for members of the household or visitors. The ritual had its origin in monasteries where on Holy Thursday, as on other days but with more solemnity, the monks received the poor as guests and rendered them this service before giving them to eat. It was then incorporated into monastic and episcopal liturgies of the day. Knowing its origins and its inspiration in Christ's love command, we can more readily appreciate what it was that Jesus did for his disciples and how he wished this to be a way of interpreting the meaning of his death, fulfilling the figure of suffering servant proclaimed by Isaiah.

The second, the veneration of the Cross, originated in Jerusalem after Helena dug up the beams of Christ's Cross on Golgotha. It became customary for the faithful and for pilgrims to venerate this holy wood on

Good Friday as they kept the memorial of his death. Pilgrims were wont to steal splinters of this Cross to carry back to their home countries, where they were then exposed for veneration on Good Friday. In time this was incorporated into the liturgy and eventually any wood in the shape of the Cross could be honoured as the symbol of Christ's death and triumph over death. The acclamation used during this rite proclaims him as the one who saves from sin and death, as the one who triumphs, through the obedience to a cruel and humiliating death. The wood as instrument of this death keeps people mindful of the way in which he died and becomes the object of the people's love and faith. It is through such a death, such a price paid, that he who was obedient unto death was victorious over the enemies of sin and death and merited the name of Lord.

The blessing of the Paschal Candle at the Vigil, the third ritual, is the culmination of what the first two rituals show and achieve. The candle itself is a symbol of light in darkness and of passage, a recall of how the pillar of fire led the people of Israel from Egypt. Made from the wax of bees, it is also a symbol of how the earth itself shares in Christ's mystery, how all of creation is made to sing out in thanksgiving. The hymn of praise sings of Christ whom the Candle represents as the dawn of the light of salvation, the one in whom all the dead are raised, because through love and the Father's will he dared to risk the darkness of night and the shadows of death. His resurrection marks the eighth day of God's repose when in the firstborn creation is made new. The hymn to the Candle gathers in the images and themes of the earlier Vigil: the wondrous work of creation, light and darkness, the Lamb and the crossing of the Red Sea, the covenant love of God for his creation, setting the stage for the baptismal liturgy and the invitation to the paschal table of the Eucharist.

The annual commemoration of the mystery of Easter is introduced by the proclamation of the Son's *kenosis* and is sustained in various ways throughout the week. When considered in the light of divine *kenosis,* the whole liturgy proclaims and celebrates a God whose love is shown through weakness. He made covenant with a people who were small and weak, and in the face of other powers or stronger nations, kept faith with them. He is a God who by ordinance and invitation sets up among this people an ideal order of justice in which the weak, even the weak foreigner, is privileged. The people themselves can remain faithful to such a Lord only if they keep memorial, keep in mind their previous condition of slavery, giving up ambitions to become powerful through powerful alliances. Their Lord and God made his presence manifest in prophets who knew weakness, such as Jeremiah and the ideal Suffering Servant spoken of in Isaiah's servant songs. As much as Abraham renounced earthly hopes when he obeyed God's command, God himself gave over his Son to death and is known for his love and his holiness precisely in this surrender of his Son. The Son himself, ironically called the image and splendour of the Father, is known and hymned in the shedding of his blood, in the renunciation of a majestic name, in images of such as Abel and Isaac and the Suffering Servant. The saving blood of the Lamb is the blood of one who places himself in the company of such as these.

The Christ of Common Devotion

The Church's public prayer cannot be too narrowly defined. While liturgy is essential, the faithful often express and appropriate their faith in Christ through what are called devotions or popular piety. The focus on Holy Week is retained to see how many persons and communities in their own practices find the significance of Christ's Passion and Death. As remarked, the devotion of the people has in the course of time had an impact on official liturgies. It was especially important in developing the veneration of the Cross on Good Friday and in the worship associated with the sepulchre or altar of repose on Holy Thursday. But it is of the devotions of more recent times that I am now thinking.

The aging among us recall the practices of a time before the Vatican Council. For a while the old and the new were mingled. Those who as seminarians studied in Rome in the early years of the fifties remember how we celebrated a double tradition, the revised Paschal ritual, with its key moment the laud of the Candle towards midnight, and the older custom of more readily marking Thursday and Friday, followed by the maimed rites of Holy Saturday morning. In 1951, Pius XII had allowed a restricted celebration of the revised Paschal Vigil but did not suppress the older tradition of rites early on Saturday morning. So on Thursday we still walked the churches to see their competing decoration of the Altar of Repose, and on Friday did the Stations of the Cross at the Colosseum and climbed the *Scala Sancta*, opposite the Basilica of Saint John Lateran, on our knees. On Saturday morning we listened to the twelve medieval readings and saw the candle lit and the water blessed in almost empty churches, to gather again more joyously after nightfall for the solemn Vigil. Whether Lent ended with the bells at noon on Saturday or with the singing of the *Exsultet* at the Pascal Vigil we were not sure. In the merging of the two traditions, we gathered in the memories of the childhood of our Catholic past, and opened our imaginations to the splendour of the new liturgy, which we learned to be ever ancient ever new.

The recall of childhood that this prompts is the recall that for centuries Good Friday was the focal remembrance, with the Stations of the Cross, the observance of the three o'clock hour and in some countries the procession and dirge for the dead Christ, accompanied to the tomb by his sorrowing mother and the several women who bore the name of Mary (the holy women bearing other names being for some reason left out of Passion plays and lamentations).

Though it is a trick of the imagination, Maundy Thursday seems always to have been a day of bright sunshine, the gay crowds walking from

convent to convent, flowers smelling sweetly, bright lights and white
clothes adorning the Altar of Repose. All was light and spring, and Christ
was adored in his splendrous courts, even as in their devotions people
anticipated his Passion. Friday on the other hand was thought of as wet,
dark grey, yet church-thronged. Cinemas closed, shopping had to be done
in advance, since in those religious times before we became post-Christian
the city of Dublin silenced itself to show its values. In early morning dark-
robed figures chanted their dirge-like lament in dark churches, something
that I was only later to learn was the chanting of the Passion. To stand
throughout was to prove oneself a Christian soldier, to be merry when the
Saviour dies was to sin. The three o'clock hour must not be missed, with
its awesome and inspiring mourning when the world stopped spinning.

Saturday was child's day, beginning with the agonizing wait through a
long morning, listening for the noon-day bells to chime. It was then that
the Resurrection was announced to the world due to the odd practice of
blessing paschal fire, candle and font in the early hours of Saturday. The
people knew little of such clerical ritual but they heard the good news from
the church towers at mid-day. For children, darkness was lifted from the
earth and all the penances of forty days earned recompense in the savoured
taste of noon-day chocolate. The breakfast on Galilee's shore repeated itself
in the happy gluttony of small children. The Lord had gone once more
through his earthly ordeal of betrayal and suffering: the sun shone now
more brightly, outdoing even Maundy Thursday, telling all of God's bright
countenance.

Whatever the historians of liturgy may say about the role of the
Paschal Vigil, it is true that common piety has shown a special tenderness
towards the death of Christ which it remembers on Good Friday with far
more exuberance than is shown at the Vigil. The devotions of Holy Week
that I have recalled were anchored in the keeping of that day which is called
"Good" because on that died Christ died for our sins. Whether in the Stations of the Cross in Irish Catholicism or in the procession with the effigy
of the Dead Christ in Latin piety, it was by considering his death that people knew his love and what he had done for us in the weakness of his
human flesh.

As far back as the travels of the Spanish nun Egeria,[7] we see this devotion emerging in ways already mentioned. Egeria recounts how the people
gathered on Friday to venerate the wood of the Cross that the mother of
Constantine, Helena, had dug out on Golgotha. Bringing it splinter by
splinter to Europe for pious veneration lead to much fabrication, but the
efforts eventually allowed people to see in any piece of wood properly displayed the holy rood on which Christ had given up the ghost, giving wood
so venerated its iconic status. The clergy in time appropriated this veneration into liturgical action and as happens when this is done, the people lost
their hold on it. So other devotions arose as their very own way of showing piety, such as following the way of the Cross around the town or

church compound or filing along in procession and lamentation, carrying the effigy of the dead Christ to the sepulchre where the body would await resurrection.

When I think back to the Stations of the Cross I am struck by one note that gave the practice its leitmotif, namely, the inclusion among the fourteen stations of three that mark the times when Jesus fell. This may now be blurred when congregations make the way of the Cross more biblical, reading passages from the scriptures at each station. The falls, of course, have no historical or Gospel basis, but the fall of Jesus on the ground as he carried his burden gave the whole story a symbol of what took place. It is a symbol readily accessible to the imagination. One could follow through the episodes of his condemnation, his scourging, the consolation he offered the women and his own mother, the nailing to the Cross and the dying with a loud cry, but what this meant had to be pinpointed.

This was done by the recital of "Jesus falls a first time," "Jesus falls a second time," "Jesus falls a third time." There is no other line that recurs like this in the course of this sorrowful journey. It tells participants that Jesus the Son of God, the Saviour, falls in human weakness, falls down before the beholders, that he is scarce able to carry through his destiny, which he has been given out of love for sinners, but that he rises up and goes willingly to his death "for our sake." The face of Christ on Veronica's towel served as a kind of consolation, a popular rendering of the figure of Isaiah's man of sorrows.

People are quite adept at retaining such a devotion, even as they accept the new. For Holy Week and Easter of 2003, I celebrated the services for a small community on the small island of Fakarava, in Polynesia. It is an atoll with little vegetation, a strip of land bound on either side by water, where pearl farming is the main occupation. There are about five hundred inhabitants, about half of them Catholics. The highlight of the week was certainly the way of the Cross from one end to the other of the unpaved village, the Catholic Church being in the center. Along with Catholics, a number of Protestants took part in the procession, the entire island community being united in the memory of Christ's Passion. It was quite a traditional Stations of the Cross, with the prayers of Alphonsus Liguori translated into Puamotu by one of the old French missionaries. What was special about this celebration was that the people carried a heavy cross on their shoulders from one station to the next, taking it in turns family by family. The priest had nothing to do except follow the cross, the *katakita* of the island being the one who led the prayers. At the end of the stations, the cross, now bearing all the love and penitence of the island community, was received at the door of the Church. The liturgical rite was then celebrated, this cross being used for the common veneration.

For Holy Week 2001 I had presided at the services in the township of Pamatai on the main island of Tahiti. There the official liturgy was also preceded by an outdoors Way of the Cross. This was more biblical, with readings from the Passion of John, parishioners again taking turns to carry a heavy Cross. The three falls were, however, marked by readings from the Servant Songs of Isaiah, to describe the pitiful state of the Lord, who took on the appearance of a worm, no man. The role of the priest on this occasion was to sit aside in an accessible place where people could leave the procession to confess their sins and leave them behind. As the procession neared the door of the Church he had to leave the place where sin was left and receive the Cross, which was then used for the liturgical veneration.

I know that if one could make a tour of the world, imaginatively taking the wings of an angel, it would be possible to record various ways in which popular devotion still mingles with liturgy, with Good Friday often the high point of the week. While there is outlet for sorrow and repentance, and Christ's sufferings are brought to the fore, it is the Cross as instrument of salvation that takes centre stage and is honoured. In its symbolic veneration it assumes a double role: on the one hand it recalls the suffering of the Lord and his display of weakness for our sake, but on the other it has been taken over by the people and made to carry their sins and their love. The self-emptying of Christ and the repentant but loving response of the community are made to meet and converge in the one symbol and in the symbolic acts of procession and veneration.

I do not think that such memorial was or is untrue to the spirit of the Three Days or to the memory of the Saviour. The going up to Calvary and the going down under to the place of the dead is central, not to be forgotten, to be ever respected and prayed. Thursday and Saturday with their joy make sense only in coming before and after Friday. People do not think much, I believe, of compensation for sin but are rather drawn by the sorrow of such suffering, by human betrayal, and by the love that Jesus showed. The three falls or the carrying of the Cross by the faithful tell clearly what is happening. There are some who now add a fifteenth station, one that recalls the raising of Christ from the dead. This captures what was missing from the original devotion. Reflection on the sufferings of Christ and on his death, even when practiced with great compassion and gratitude, can be a comfort in pain and encourage endurance. Without belief in the reality and the symbol of the Resurrection it misses the hope placed in the transforming power of God's love working through Christ. Hope for the future beyond this world needs to be accompanied by hope for the present, hope that the energy of divine love remembered in the death and resurrection of Christ transforms even our present, our life here on earth.

In its own way this devotion captures much of what the liturgy had sung for centuries. The entire Holy Week from Sunday to Sunday may be seen through the prism of *kenosis*, of Christ's making himself a slave and abandoning himself to death, even to the death of the Cross. With the words of the Scriptures given back to congregations, and the purity of the rituals restored, let us hope that the mystery may be more wittingly contemplated and the power of the risen Christ affirmed, even as some inventive communities quite properly combine the old devotions with the revised liturgies.

Conclusion

Within the liturgical settings reviewed, the proclamation of the *kenosis* of Jesus Christ gives much food for thought and praise, and has a richness of meaning. He comes in the name of the Lord, the God of Israel who made covenant with the whole human race through this people. To them and through them, God promised liberation from the reign of sin and death and the powers of evil. From the time of creation he made known his love and compassion, a love crystallized in such figures as Isaac, the Passover Lamb, the suffering servant, the dry bones raised from their graves and given flesh and life. In the midst of their quest for freedom, their search for justice, their tribulations, in the times of their fidelity and their infidelity, God remained with Israel, renewing and reviving his promises. To fulfill the expectations that arise from such divine fidelity, Christ was sent as a Saviour who is meek and compassionate, who claims no earthly or divine glory, but on whom God's Spirit rests. He comes as one who is willing to sacrifice his own life for the life of the world, subjected in obedience to God to the grossest humiliations. But in the moment of his expoliation on the Cross and in the tomb, God's love and Spirit do not leave him. In his earthly abandonment, which seems to be even divine abandonment, he remains in deep communion with the One who sent him. There is already a fullness of life in this communion that is made manifest in the glory and the power given to him when he is raised up, owning now a Name before which all bend the knee, recognizing in him who was emptied out the great gift bestowed upon them. Whether the faithful give their feet to be washed by him who makes himself servant, whether they stand in the shadow of the glory of the barren cross, whether they listen to the consolation spoken by the one who falls down in weakness before their eyes, whether they let themselves be bathed in the glow of the Passover Candle, they know themselves truly blessed in and through the *kenosis* of the servant who is both God's and theirs.

2

Divine Self-Emptying in Christ: Scriptural Conjunctions

--- ✠ ---

My reflections in this chapter are derived from a reading of the scriptures prompted by seeing the revelation given in Christ as *kenosis*. Since they do not represent an exegetical commentary, or even a logical pattern of development, I call what is offered "scriptural conjunctions," or the putting alongside one another a series of biblical texts and images. This is consonant with what we have seen done with the biblical word in the Church's liturgy. When the faithful of different communities appropriate the scriptures in faith they shuffle the texts, believing that God has this way of addressing them through the Word and through the Spirit that opens the Book in an apparently random fashion, where they are gathered together in faith and hope.

The metaphor of the *kenosis* of Christ, as it is proclaimed in the hymn cited by Paul in the Letter to the Philippians 2:6-11, is taken here as key to this scriptural presentation of the mystery of Christ. The word suggests an abundance of possibilities. Other texts are here built around it, to tease out its significance, its plenitude of meaning, through joining it as a metaphor with other passages. While to be true to their biblical origins one needs to look carefully at the images in their textual setting, they may be related to other texts and passages, such as the Pauline texts on the wisdom of the Cross or the Johannine texts that present Jesus as the servant or slave. The texts are stretched in this way beyond their original context and meaning, as is often the case with root metaphors and with liturgical proclamation of the scriptures.

The insight into the mystery of Christ as *kenosis* depends on narrative recall as well as on hymnodic acclamation. It is in the dramatic enactment of his mission that Jesus lives out the obedience that leads him to take on lowly form and even to death on the Cross. I thus begin with a recall of narrative elements, first from the Gospel of Mark and then from John.

24

Against this background, the meaning of the images of abasement, of descent and of wisdom stand out more clearly.

Mark's Gospel:
Story of the Son of Man

In looking at the narrative basis for our knowledge of Christ, it is possible to undertake a reading of the Gospels challenged by the Pauline proclamation of *kenosis*. A reader is struck by the fact that Jesus put the question, "Who do you say that I am," when he was on the point of making the first of his predictions of his betrayal, suffering and death (Mark 8:29). This is one entry to a reading of the story as one of self-emptying: there can be no response to the question unless in faith one is ready to encounter a Saviour who hands himself over to this humiliation. To answer the question ourselves, now that we have the complete Gospels in hand, and the evidence of lives lived over generations in faith, we do indeed see in Jesus himself and in the mystery of his Pasch an embodiment of the reign of God, centering on Jesus, the Servant, the Christ, the Son. The three titles it may be noted however are self-effacing: they point back to the One whom he serves, the One by whom he has been anointed, the One of whom he is all together and totally Son.

To see how the remembrance of the mission and death of Christ is grounded in narrative, it has been suggested that the Gospel according to Mark could be looked upon as a typical early Christian *anamnesis*, showing a relation between a present of affliction, a past that keeps promise alive and a future when this promise will be realized. Mark has in mind Christian communities that are anxious and perturbed about persecution and the failure to see the promises of the kingdom realized. Without betraying the tragic element in the mission of Christ, Mark wants to assure them of hope, a hope expressed especially in the vision of the Son of Man who is to come in judgment and glory. He also wants to encourage them to do the one thing expected of them, to testify to Christ and to the advent of the reign of God in him, and to hold in mind that in service of the kingdom he had to suffer and to die. There is much about the anticipation of Jesus's passion and about the tragedy of his betrayal, but there is little about the resurrection. It is the anticipation of the eschatological judgment that Mark offers as consolation or strengthening. The Gospel could be organized around the threefold use of the title for Jesus of Son of Man,[1] relating to past, present and future, even though exegetes argue still about the provenance of that title and about the extent of its usage by Jesus himself.

It is made clear that the title Son of Man is used of one who has from the start been offered to the world as God's "beloved Son" (Mark 1:11). If he has a mission it is because he has been sent by God and because he has been endowed with the Spirit. It is in the power of the Spirit that he has been driven into the wilderness (Mark 1:12) and that he embarks on his mission, to begin which he must first be confronted by Satan, the one whom through his suffering he is to overcome. Whatever the dark side of Mark's story, it is a story of divine love and divine initiative, in bringing to humanity the gift of forgiveness of sin.

A first set of texts using the title of Son of Man present Jesus's prophetic and eschatological mission. He came preaching the forgiveness of sins and healing the sick. The first use of the title in Mark 2:10 is connected with this. The title probably underlines that Jesus is one with his people in being one of the children of Adam, but it also underscores the newness of his teaching. Not only does he preach and offer the forgiveness of sins that marks the advent of the messianic kingdom, but as Son of Man he is lord of the Sabbath (Mark 2:28). Precisely by his authority to forgive sins he brings his hearers back to the true meaning of the Sabbath, the remembrance of Israel's liberation from slavery and captivity, her call to be God's chosen people.

A second group of verses fixes on the suffering he is to endure: Mark 8:31; 10:45; 14:21, 41. This carries the story a step, a very large step. The Son of Man who preaches forgiveness of sins and has his preaching confirmed by God through his works of mercy is destined to be betrayed, to suffer and to die. This is required by the advent of the long-awaited reign of God, under the guise which it takes on in the person and work of Jesus. There is a strong tragic note in the Passion Narrative of this Gospel. Even the account of the Last Supper is offered as a tale of betrayal, desertion and anguish of heart. Jesus is truly cast low, left alone by his disciples and by his Father, subjected by the prevailing powers to humiliation and death.

The third set of verses retrieves from the past of Israel the image of the awaited eschatological judge and the judgment he will pronounce: Mark 8:38; 13:26; 14:62. This is how the future is envisaged, a practical as well as a hopeful one. The disciples are to expect trial and tribulation and all manner of disaster, but they are also to be assured of the gift of persevering in their testimony. All is under the judgment of the Son of Man, whose day and hour are not to be predicted or guessed, and the ultimate hope is expressed in the ecstatic and eschatological vision that the reign of God is already at work in the world, that the Gospel will touch all peoples, and that the world—because of the preaching and the suffering of the Son of Man—may live in hope. Of this, those who keep memorial are to be witnesses, even and most especially under persecution and amid tribulations.

Within this framework we can attend especially to the Passion Narrative. To put flesh on the bones of the hymn of his death, to see just how cruel and humiliating it was, we get an inkling of a darker tale from Mark's account of the supper in the upper room (Mark 14:12-31). There Jesus is with "his own" on the night he was to be caught in the garden, saying his prayers while his friends dozed, and another who was more wakeful, and awake to opportunities, found his way there with an armed cohort. At the table, he is sorrowful. He has travelled the roads, preached, instructed, healed, rescued from stressful demons—and always with these twelve by his side, witnessing what he was about, and being solaced by him with a tender and special care. He has even said to them while explaining the parable of the sower, "To you it is given to know the mystery of the kingdom" (Matt 13:11). And now he reads it in their eyes and the gestures of their hands, which Rainer Maria Rilke describes as scattered like birds at bird-shot from the dish at the sound of his voice: they are frightened and even resentful.[2] Whatever their protests, they will not withstand the trials of this night to come and of its dreadful morrow. He has failed to strengthen them, to give them a faith even as strong as a grain of mustard seed.

The wakeful one is going to try to turn things around by betraying Jesus's whereabouts to those who would make him captive, far away from the throngs that would make his arrest well nigh unthinkable. This is one who, not for the first time, dips his hand with him into the dish, the common platter of food in the middle of the table, like the herbs and spiced vegetables and meats of a Middle-Eastern or Chinese dinner. Trying to "make some sense of this betrayal," John the Evangelist would have Judas a thief, but he may have been moved by darker motives, hoping to get his teacher to react out of character. As for all that happened the next day, the Letter to the Hebrews seems to strike the right note when it says, he was crucified "outside the camp" (Heb 13:13), where the entrails of beasts were incinerated, the smell quite different from the odor of incense within the temple.

We can see this Gospel story as a willing abasement, joining it with the image of *kenosis* as it has been examined. The assumption of the form of a slave is the condition of the mission of the Son of Man and it is allied with his self-emptying. This conjunction of passages expresses where he stood in the social and civil order: he is somebody who had no rank and no rights, and no business except to serve. This emptying of the divine image and the divine name before the world, in order to testify to the true name of God, is done in witness before the powers of the world. Jesus was arraigned before the Sanhedrin, before the high-priests, before King Herod, before Pilate, the Roman governor, and even before his own people, and before each and all he refused to compromise with whatever power was invoked. Powerless before the powers, he continued to testify to the God who revealed himself as Father, loving, pardoning, merciful, despite what humankind might want to make of him, for its own interests or its own consolation.

Christ the Slave

When we listen together to the scriptures we do so in response to Jesus Christ's invitation, of which we can find a biblical example in the words of the Gospel according to John (John 6:60-69). While the text is first and foremost about accepting Christ in faith, it has eucharistic implications that have been developed over time. Jesus invites us to eat of his flesh and drink of his blood and thus to share his own eternal communion with the Father. Offering bread, he offers that flesh in which the Word entered the story of the human race (John 1:9), that flesh by which God's Wisdom is truly one with humanity in all its aspirations, in all its distress, in all its anguish of sin, trial, conflict. It is the flesh in which the Word took on the sins of the world, to deliver humanity from sin and release it from the hold of death, so as to enjoy, even now, eternal life, a life that knows no end. In offering wine to drink, Jesus offers the blood shed on the Cross, the price of redemption, the blood in which humanity is washed clean of sin. This being so, nobody can receive this gift without entering into the drama of Christ, the drama of the Pasch, of which in eating and drinking the Church keeps memorial. It is in living the Pasch in communion with the Son that Christians find their place in human history, as they look forward in hope to eternal life.

Tradition has given two meanings to the word Pasch and both are valid. The one sees in the word an expression of passion, the suffering to which the Saviour was subjected and in which he revealed the fullness of divine love. The second takes it to mean passage, a passing through, the way along that road the Son followed in order to bring humanity out of death into the glory of the Father.

Whichever of these two meanings prevails, the Pasch of the disciples is to be a communion with Christ in his condition as servant, *doulos* or slave in the Greek of John's Gospel. In the chapters of this Gospel having to do with the evening Jesus spent with his followers and companions before his betrayal, there is striking play with this word. In John 15:15 Jesus tells his disciples that he does not consider them servants but friends. In their relation to him they are not defined by the tasks they have to do, but by the condition of being nothing in themselves, nothing but what they do in his service. No, they are friends and companions, those who share his life, his love, his very being as children of the Father. Yet in the washing of their feet Jesus has presented himself as their servant, as servant before the world (John 13:14-17). Thus as his friends they share his identity, his very being, as servant or slave. This was brought to Peter's attention at his first stubborn refusal to have his feet washed by Jesus: if he were not to accept this gesture of service, this self-revelation of Jesus, he could have no part with him (John 13:8).

The Johannine text recalls the image of the Suffering Servant of Yahweh in the songs of the prophet Isaiah (Isaiah 49-53). Jesus appears to retrieve this imagery in order to depict his relation to the Father and to the world. He is the one who in obedience to God has taken on the burden of the world's sins, and is ready even to hand over his life as a price for the reconciliation of humankind with God. Even if this is a primary meaning, we should not neglect looking at the form that the servant of these songs takes on before the world. The dramatic character of these texts from Isaiah is pointed out by commentators. They start by hailing God as the Holy One of Israel who has chosen this people as his own, who rules over them, who is worshipped by them with solemnity. But from this sublime beginning they turn to how the divine mercy and favour show themselves in a figure who appears before others as slave and worm. Do the songs speak only of divine condescension or do they show something about how God is to be seen? Not only has the Holy One chosen to appear before the nations as the God of lowly Israel, but he also appears under the form of this suffering messenger who has no status.

In subsuming such drama into a reading of John, it appears that it is not only to God that Jesus hands over his being, his freedom, his life itself—but to the world. Indeed he hands himself over to God in handing himself over to those who would mock him and hound him to destruction. It is in that act that he reveals God. Jesus and the Father are one: only through being one with Jesus as slave are his friends one with the Father. Only by attending to the way in which the Son shows his love can they know God's love. Only through what he reveals of his own image as God's Son, in his service and through his Cross, do they have an icon, a perfect image, of the Father.

Descent

A theology of *kenosis* may also turn to other biblical images or metaphors besides the narrative. Christ's descent is one of them. To the common Christian this image is best known from the article in the Apostles' Creed, "he descended into hell." He or she may also be familiar with the explanation that this means that Christ entered the place of the dead after the crucifixion and that the reference is to 1 Peter 3:19 and 1 Peter 4:5. The term as it stands in the Creed,[3] though, is not found in the New Testament, though the image of descent is used frequently, as are different ways of telling how Christ shared the lot of all the dead.

The two verses from 1 Peter say that Christ preached the Gospel after his death to the "spirits who were in prison" and that the Gospel was preached "even to the dead." The author of the letter is concerned with those who lived under God's covenants, beginning with Noah, but who died before Christ. For them, too, who lived in obedience to God's law under a former dispensation, Christ's death in the flesh and his new life in the Spirit mean ransom from sin and death. In these particular verses the writer is not talking about Christ's association of himself with the human lot of death but about the abundant effects of his own death through the shedding of his blood (see 1 Peter 1:17-19). On the other hand, the image has often been transposed to read "descended into hell or *hades*" and is aptly used to express the full weight of Christ's assumption of sin and death for the redemption of humanity. Does this have any biblical foundation?

In the Old Testament the image of descent is often associated with the cloud of Yahweh, with that visible manifestation of his presence among the people, whether on the mountain, in the Ark, in the Temple or in the city, which conveys the idea of divine generosity and condescension, where the majesty of the divinity remains clear. The rites of descent and ascent are, on the other hand, quite commonly used to express the back and forth between heaven and earth, just as descent into the lower parts of the earth or *Sheol* speaks of the finality of human death and its darkness. In the Gospel of John, the descent of the Son simply indicates his provenance and his mission (e.g., John 3:13, 31), though, oddly, when he ascends or is lifted up it is on the Cross. There his glory and the full nature of his communion with the Father are made evident.

The common appeal to the imagery of descent and ascent is known to us from Eph 4:8-10, which for all its apparent clarity is difficult to interpret. The author proclaims Christ's victory over death and his raising up of those who are his followers and the members of his Church. Ascending on high after his resurrection he rules and guides his Church from there; he has given gifts to those who preach the Gospel here on earth. Furthermore he has put an end to death and sin, making that which held humanity captive itself captive. The crux of interpreters is in an expression that Paul uses to suggest even more strongly what it means for Christ to have ascended: he says that he who ascended is the one who descended even into "the lower parts of the earth." This could be no more than a telling contrast between heaven and earth, an expression of Christ's place among those who are earthbound. In this case there would be a suggestion of Christ taking on human flesh and thus of condescension in his subjecting himself to a sojourn on earth and even to death. But it could also be a reference akin to 1 Peter's image of the abode of the dead as a prison and so of Christ's lowering himself even to the extent of going among them. This provides Christian faith with the ground for seeing the descent into hell as a way of affirming the extent of the Saviour's association with the lot of those whom he came to redeem from both sin and death, from all that held them captive. In this case, the convergence of the image of descent with that of emptying himself, of making himself nothing, of laying aside all his privileges as the Son of God, need hardly be argued. It is the solidarity of Christ with humankind in its captivity, his own ineluctable combat with death, that gives him the right to be proclaimed Lord, the living one who holds the keys of death and of the abode of the dead (Rev 1:18).

Wisdom of the Cross

In complement to talk of self-emptying, the discourse on wisdom in 1 Cor 1:18-25; 2:1-5 teaches us that there is a subversive kind of plenty in divine weakness as this is shown to us in the cross of Christ. In 1 Cor 1:25 we read that God's weakness is more powerful than what humanity offers as power and wisdom. Paul recognizes that the Gospel that locates salvation on the Cross, and the way to salvation in the way of the Cross, is seen by many as folly. For the believer, however, it is the power of God. Paul wants to undo the wisdom of the world, all philosophies and systems of thought and life that look to humanity itself as source of power and wisdom. God has already put on show this "unwisdom" of the human mind by making manifest the divine wisdom in the folly of the one who opened the way to his condemnation by his word and action, who gave himself to suffering and death, in the process of testifying to the divine truth and the divine wisdom, to the love of God who gave his Son and his Spirit.

When Paul says that God has chosen those who were nothing, in strict exegesis he does not seem to refer in particular to the socially poor. What he means is that all those, whatever their walk of life, who were nothing in terms of realising a genuine human existence, have in Christ been given a divine power and wisdom. By the Cross which is folly or scandal to the world, they have been released from sin and even from the clutches of death itself.

The choice of the translation in the Bible of Jerusalem, "who count for nothing," has given some theologians occasion to think further on the manner of God's revelation and Christ's presence, and of course to relate this translation to that of *kenosis*, which says that "he made himself nothing." They emphasise that it is by appearing as without power before earthly powers, and by choosing the little of this world to be witnesses to the Pasch and the Spirit, that God reveals his own truth and his own self. It is among those who lack human prestige, who are counted as socially nothing, that the wisdom of God is to be found. It is among those who are accounted as "no-thing" that God dwells, and it is from these that the Gospel is to be heard.

What Paul has in mind first and foremost is the salvation that the Corinthians have found in the Cross of Christ and in the Body of Christ. If they live by the Cross and its promise, they will have found true wisdom. It is in the configuration to the Cross of Christ, with its promise of resurrection in Christ, that believers find their true identity in God's sight. They must dare live by this identity before the world. Paul himself draws no economic and political conclusions, though he is writing for a community that builds up its own life within itself, trying by Paul's counsel to overcome social and economic divisions and rivalries so as to live a full communion together. It is not, however, hard to see the implications of this wisdom of the Cross for believers of another place or generation who are engaged more fully in constructing the *res publica*. If one believes that God esteems the "no-things" of this world, if one is persuaded of renouncing one's own advantage so as to serve the least of society, if one introduces the ethic of divine justice into human affairs, then the stance towards the common good is greatly affected. It is in particular situations and societies that the implications find concrete forms, and it is not easy to convince others of the same vision. A Christian community does not give up on the hope to inject society with this wisdom and outlook. It is for this reason, for example, that John Paul II invited the Italian parliament to incorporate an ethic of forgiveness into its penal code.

The Powers Held Captive

Alongside the hymn used in the Letter to the Philippians, in Christian repertory there is the hymn invoked in the Letter to the Colossians,[4] which celebrates how Christ through his Cross is established as the Lord of Creation, holding in check all heavenly and earthly powers that bind human freedom and seek to hold sway over the world. To the power that subjects and dominates, in Christ the Father opposes the power of the Cross and transfers humanity from its slavery under the powers of darkness to the kingdom of his Son (Col 1:13).

The contrast between powers that dominate and divide and the power of the Cross that frees and reconciles blends with the imagery of Christ's self-emptying in taking on the form of a slave. Paul has two things in mind. First, he wants to bring peace and unity to peoples who are at enmity, showing that the one way to reconciliation is through the blood of the Son sent into the world, and who was from all time with the Father. Second, he wants to show how faith in the power of the one who is both Lord and Crucified releases the community to which he writes from its domination by spiritual powers that are demonic. There is a connection between the two things, for it is submission to warring powers from above that is at the root of divisions between peoples.

It would seem that the people of Colossus conceived of powers in the heavens, or of spiritual beings, who ruled peoples' lives and to whom the people were beholden for all their earthly needs. These spirits needed to be worshipped and honoured, and there was a host of laws and rites that determined how they were to be served. In contrast, Paul proclaims the power of Christ, the power he has in creation and which is confirmed and once and for all established in his death, where all false decrees and laws are nailed to the Cross (Col 2:14).

People today do not have ideas about intermediary powers between heaven and earth in the same way as peoples of New Testament times. In various cultures and countries, however, including Europe and North America, there are a variety of idols to which people do either religious or practical honour. These may go by the name of spirits, gods, ancestors, religions, or they may go by the name of ethnicity, race, culture, family, history, heritage, from which it is impossible for people to break free and which cause opposition and enmity because they elicit division and separation. People are subservient to what is uniquely their own; they look to these things as a way of trying to dominate others. In Christ, diversity is not overlooked or suppressed but is made non-divisive, the source, rather, of rich communion. His way was to give himself as gift to all. For the sake of those held captive, he gave himself over on the Cross to the power of what divides and subjects in order to render it null, to release people by his own emptying of earthly power from the principalities and powers of their closed and confined worlds.

Paul, being united with Christ as his servant, his minister, and one with him in his Body, talks of filling up in his own flesh what is lacking in the afflictions of Christ, for the sake of building up the Church, which is his Body (Col 1:24). This is a christological declaration. Jesus Christ who gave himself for all through his suffering, continues to give himself for all through the sufferings of his Body. This Body is to be present in the world as reconciler, as a people that continues to stand free of false powers and that offers reconciliation and peace to all who are divided by a diversity of allegiances. The witness of the Body is the witness of Christ himself. The power of Christ in the Spirit to be free by giving glory to God alone, whatever the affliction, is at work in the Church. Paul thus begs the people of Colossus not to fall prey to "any philosophy or false deceit" (Col 2:8) and asks of them that they live by the virtues of compassion, lowliness, meekness, kindness and patience (Col 3:12)—those attitudes that are the spirit of the Beatitudes of the kingdom established by the Father in Christ.

God's Wisdom and Power

We know that in the sapiential literature of the Bible, Wisdom is associated with the creation and provident ordering of the universe. This is the background to the identification of Christ as the creative word as well as the redeemer and head of the Church in the hymn from Colossians. While the Book of Wisdom and Ecclesiasticus (e.g., Eccles 43) are richly eloquent on the wisdom shown in the harmonious workings of all created beings, great and small, the same literature reveals the just who suffer and are persecuted as those who know wisdom and are God's special servants. This tension between two perspectives on wisdom is found in Colossians, but in

Corinthians it is tilted towards the wisdom of the suffering, especially the wisdom shown in the one who suffered for all on the Cross. We may find divine wisdom in the ordering of the universe but its ultimate revelation is in the folly of the Cross.

Similar tensions in the imagery of power are carried over into the New Testament from the Old. In Egypt, Yahweh contests the power of the Pharaoh by all manner of signs and wonders, but the real demonstration of his peculiar power among the gods of peoples is that he chooses as his own a slave people, one with no earthly status. When this people began to think of itself as one among the nations, competing with them for land and honour, they asked for a king. Samuel gave them dire warnings about the consequences of having a king rule over them (1 Samuel 8:10-18), that is, of subjecting themselves to the kind of rule associated with kingdoms, but they persisted. Ever after, the role of king in Israel is a highly ambiguous one, both an ideal and a plague on the house of Israel. David is lauded as a great king and as a father to his people, but the stories of his weakness and domination of the people are many. To look forward to an ideal age, to a messianic king, the ideal of kingship itself had to be transformed by the prophets. Not even they, however, could quite foresee the kind of kingdom that Jesus preached and the kind of king that he was. Yet it is only by the power shown in his shedding of his blood, in his self-emptying in death, that God can be said to reign. When Colossians says that the powers are held captive, we have the stories and the images that help us to glimpse by what kind of power Christ holds power over the powers in the name of the Father.

In the Spirit

By the gift of the Spirit, the disciples of the Lamb are given the "power and dominion" which is the gift of God's outpouring. No one can say "Lord Jesus," except in the Spirit. To be able to see in the *kenosis* of the Son an act of divine lordship, believers need the gift of the Spirit. To be one with Jesus in his self-gift, his followers need the travail of the Spirit which makes them groan for redemption with the whole of creation. To know the divine name revealed in the death unto the Cross, they need the Spirit that engenders trust in God the Father of compassion and mercy, even in the midst of sufferings and in the eye of death. Even to be able to think back on what Jesus said and did, they need the breath of love that casts light on the complete communion of the Son with the Father, when he is lifted up on his strange wooden throne.

On the day that those in the upper room received the gifts of fire and tongues, when Peter addressed the crowds at Jerusalem about Jesus as Saviour, he told them that the prophetic and eschatological Spirit, about which

Joel had spoken, was being poured out (Acts 2:16-21). The Spirit had been at work in the world since creation, along with the Word, and it was in the bestowal of the Spirit that Jesus himself was baptized and entered into conflict with the reign of Satan, and gave himself over in the Spirit on the Cross. Now this Spirit was with the disciples, in their very hearts, to ready them to keep memorial of Christ, to remember all that he had said and done, to live in communion with him and the Father, in the service of a reign which was for all, and for the poor by preference, without any power structures that belonged to this world.

It is in this Spirit that the Body of Christ is formed and communes. Unable to show the fullness of the stretch of God's love in his Nazarene flesh, the Son takes to himself the diversity and the plenty of all who profess faith in him in the Spirit. All of them can say with Paul, I live now not I but the Crucified Christ lives in me (Gal 2:20), and Christ can say, I live now in the world and in the hope of the world by the Spirit of the Father in the flesh of those who have believed. Here indeed in Christ is the love of the infinite God at the heart of history and the hope of finite humanity. Here, too, in the bodying forth of the Son by the Spirit in the weak flesh of the faithful is the love and power of the Father from whom all have origin and in whom all have their destiny.

Maranatha[5]

The last words in the Bible, the conclusion of the Book of Revelation, are the great cry for the Lord to come, a cry put up by those who suffer trial. People and peoples need imaginative depictions of ideal worlds, worlds that they might aspire to inhabit even while caught up in the struggles of the present. These are often presented in narrative or epic form, but visual representation is always powerful. We have seen the appeal of films like *Lord of the Rings, Two Towers* and the *Harry Potter* series, which draw adults as well as children. In an ideal way, they are shown the forces of good and evil, the powers of light and darkness in contest, and are perhaps able to see their own world, their own lives, from another perspective.

The most imaginative book of the New Testament, which lends itself readily to visual representations, is this Book of Revelation, which in my childhood we called the Apocalypse. Along with 1 Thessalonians, it is a book to which many appeal in making apocalyptic predictions about the end of time or the millennium of the messianic era. When read carefully, however, its prophecies, visual images, and stories concern the lives of disciples of Christ in their own towns, cities and civilizations. By describing the end times it describes a transcendent world into which the readers/seers are invited to enter so that from there they may see their own surrounds and struggles differently. They may look upon the trials of the just from the perspective of the Holy One, of the Lamb slain on the altar, of the white-robed martyrs beneath the altar. The seven churches are called upon to be faithful because they may "foresee" this end to their tribulations and persecution, to their inner turmoil as well as to their external trials. In other words, they may see what happens from above, a depiction of a world and a city bathed in the light of the Lamb. They can even attribute all that shatters the earth and wars among peoples to God's design, knowing that they can have confidence in what he promises and assures through the Christ, so magnificently described in many passages of the book. They are to endure a struggle between what God decrees and the efforts of the tribes of the archenemy, but they will be upheld and given eventual victory. If the book is not about the conflict of powers, powerfully portrayed, it is about nothing at all. But being about conflict, it is also about the wonderful love of God that consumes all reality and brings about the triumph of life over death, good over evil, the glorious communion of Jerusalem over the Babel and disunity of the city of Babylon.

Whatever about the when, as to whence the triumph comes there is no doubt. At the centre of the city is the altar with the Lamb as though slain. If the Christ has freed his followers, if the Lamb unlocks the seals, if around him the heavenly dominions gather, if from him a light shines forth brighter than the sun at mid-day and the moon and stars at night, it is because he gave himself in sacrifice, because he spilt his blood for the peace of the world. It is this and not some mighty exercise of power that explains that world into which readers are invited and that gives them the ultimate assurance of the truth of their hope. Privileged among the elect are the white-robed martyrs, those who gave testimony to the Lamb and were his most faithful followers. If Christ has disempowered the powers, if his witnesses overcome the dragon, it is because he has given himself in the shedding of his blood and thus given witness to the true Lordship of the Triune God that is made manifest in his sacrifice.

Conclusion

These scriptural conjunctions show how the mystery of Christ's *kenosis* resonates with other biblical texts and in this way takes on fresh resonance. The narrative of the Gospel of Mark illustrates some of the implications of his renunciation of glory in face of the powers of this world so that this has not only an abstract but a concrete significance. Connected with the title Son of Man and Mark's emphasis on his being sent to suffer and die, reviled by the leaders of the people and by the gentiles, the eschatological promises associated with the Saviour are dependent on this willing self-emptying. The passages in John's Gospel in turn fill out the figure of Jesus as one who is servant in the midst of his disciples, as well as the embodiment of the image of the Servant Songs of Isaiah, as it also brings attention to his abiding communion with the Father, finding glory not in marvels but in being lifted up on the Cross. Turning to the imagery of Wisdom, of the Cross as Wisdom and of the powers held captive, we see further what is implied by Christ's humiliation and self-emptying in obedience, and how it is revelatory of God's own love. Recall of the Gospel of the Spirit within the Gospel of Christ, we are introduced by *kenosis* into the economy of the Blessed Trinity. The final reference to the Book of Revelation displays the hope that is born of this mystery.

3

Relating to Theological Interpretations

---------------------------------- ✠ ----------------------------------

On the foregoing liturgical and scriptural basis, let us think further about *kenosis*, starting with the varied appeals made in writings on the mystery of Christ, both past and present. There are many issues discussed in current theology about Jesus Christ that affect belief in him and our recourse to God in his name and in his memory and that are here by-passed. Such are the debates about the retrieval of the Jesus of history, about fidelity to the Chalcedonian christological formula of one person in two natures, or about the historical path taken by the Church through the Nicene Creed's proclamation of the divinity of the Word made flesh. Considered as parts of a theological opus, all these issues give important guidelines, but they are not adequate to express the fullness of the divine revelation given in Christ and they leave much room for further theological exploration. Within the one faith there is room for a diversity of expressions of belief.[1]

The mystery is about God, about the name of God, about what God gives to the world in the person of Jesus, called the Christ, who lived among his own and who is proclaimed to the world as Saviour and Lord. The search for the Jesus of time and place, for his forebears, for his life among his people, for his manner of being prophet, for an accurate account of his passion and death has its point since it convinces us of God's presence and action within human time and human place. Elaborate research, however, yields much insight but little enough by way of factual detail. What is involved, after all, is an effort to retrieve a story which from the very beginning was interpretation and the work of the Spirit. What we know of the story of Jesus of Nazareth, done to death for his claims and teaching about God, we know from what was proclaimed of him and is found in the scriptures. In other words, we know something of the facts of Jesus's life and preaching from what has become history in the form of the salvific proclamation that comes to us through the scriptures, the liturgy and the preaching of generations of believers.

It is the telling, we need to remind ourselves, its poetic form, which fits

Jesus as the Christ, as the Son of God in the flesh, into human history. This is what allows the events recalled and proclaimed to shape human destiny. Of the identity that prophetic proclamation gave him we learn from the Gospel and from Paul. They tell us of an intimate communion with God, told now in the light of the Law and the Prophets, a communion of Son with the Father, a fatherhood which is gift not only to him but to those who have faith in him. In him, in his story, in his history, we have witness of God's forgiving love for the world, of the divine gift of Spirit, of the divine desire to bring humankind into communion with the Godself in all its richness. Dogmatic and doctrinal questions are not unimportant, but it is this knowledge of Jesus as God's Christ, Son and Word, expressed through the appeal to a creative and poetic use of the image of *kenosis*, already enriched through liturgical interpretation, that captures the attention of many today.

No reading of scripture or tradition is possible unless Christians begin with something of the sense of wonderment evoked by the words "I Am" at the moment of Jesus's Passion, or to which Paul often invites his readers and listeners (e.g., Eph 1:3-23). It is a truly stupendous thing that God has revealed himself at all, that he has in the wonder of his eternity turned toward humanity and the world, this truly generous and free turning being part of the hidden mystery of his life, love and being. This is what Paul celebrates in benediction and song at the opening of his letter to the Church at Ephesus,[2] inviting praise from believers among a people quite used to the splendours of the gods and the profligacy of the many-breasted Diana. If one is not struck with amazement along with Paul, then one has understood nothing at all. And of course in other letters, Paul has made it even more astounding by shouting out (as written words may indeed shout out) that it is on the Cross that such wisdom is revealed (1 Cor 1:22-25). It is in becoming sin for the sinful that the author of life manages to share his life with sinners, in truly spendthrift fashion.

Walking in Faith: Traditions on *Kenosis*

There are many ways today of approaching this mystery, of asking the question "who is Jesus Christ." Since this reflection takes its point of departure in the proclamation of *kenosis,* it is only right to ask what theological traditions past and present offer about this metaphor.[3] It has not always been at the heart of the Christian story. Its prevalence is not self-evident. Nor has it always been given the same reading by authors. But the very diversity of these interpretations is a challenge to think further of what is opened up to our imagination and understanding by this poetic word.

Many of us were bred on a theology of sacrifice and satisfaction, and though theology may have begun to change, this has a habit of hanging on. Even as I think of older generations, experience tells me that the catechesis of the young, from generation unto generation, is often still at that point. Jesus is thus imaged as paying a debt to a God offended, of paying with the price of his blood in an orgy of suffering so that God may turn his eyes from our sins. We can both profit from such a reading and integrate elements of it into a larger context. For example, Thomas Aquinas (*Summa Theologiae* III, Q. 48) may be quoted on the theory of sacrifice and satisfaction, in the language borrowed from his predecessor, Anselm of Canterbury, but one needs to read on down the page, continue to where he speaks of the excess of Christ's love, rendered tangible in the excess of his suffering. This is no compensation to God but an act of God through his Word and Son in the flesh to augur in an order of justice which is an order of mercy, not ruled by human standards, of each "having his ought," but by the abandon of divine mercy. It is the superabundance, the excess of the grace of Christ, that captures the imagination of medievals, of Reformers and of our contemporaries, as it first captured the imagination of Paul, right at the point where he contrasts the sin of Adam and the grace of Christ, which saved us from it (Rom 5:12ff.).

Looking Backwards in Christian Doctrines

The path learned in earlier theological training was to go back to the Fathers from the medievals, and with caution it is possible to stick to this route, going from the familiar to the less familiar. However it might be criticized, this way has the advantage of making us rethink what we thought to hold in possession. Oddly, it is the study of the origins of ideas of priesthood that reveals new insights for us into the meaning of Christ's self-emptying, when he took on the sin of the world. Priesthood, that of Christ and that of the Church, seemed well-defined in scholastic theology, but it looks different when traced back to early Christian literature.[4]

One finds that quite often early Christian writers take the *kenosis* of the hymn in the Letter to the Philippians to refer to the mystery of the Incarnation, to the taking on of flesh by the Son. Nonetheless, even within such a hypothesis, they have much to say about the conditions under which this took place, They had to sustain the turbulence of sustaining faith in Christ in the midst of struggles with those who seemed to make not quite enough of him. To bring together the fact of his divine provenance and the truth of the salvation that he brought to the humanity that he assumed, what they say gravitates around notions of mediation, priesthood, kingship and sacrifice. To read Athanasius or Cyril of Alexandria from this perspective draws attention to how they portray the drama of the Word made flesh who makes himself sin, as Paul says, thus engaging in combat with sin, with the powers that reign and with death itself.

For the Alexandrians, giving sense to Christ's priesthood, kingship and sacrifice can be understood only within the broader descriptions of his work of mediation. It is because Christ, the Word of God in his divine nature, took on human nature and human flesh that he is mediator between God and a fallen humanity. The imagery used to describe this is quite diverse. It is not simply incarnation, the taking-on of human flesh, which is the willing abasement of the Son and Word. The core insight in this metaphor is the notion that the Word took on human nature in the weakness of the state to which sin had reduced it. He did this in order to lift it up out of this state and bear it with him to the right hand of the Father. He chose to pass himself through death, his death being portrayed as a conflict with death itself and with sinful flesh. He, holy and innocent, encountered sin and death on the earth, entered into conflict with them and won a victory for all those for whom he chose to live, suffer and die. Without willing abasement, this would not have been possible.

Athanasius, Cyril and others used various biblical metaphors to describe this mediation. Enlarging upon the language of painful but victorious conflict, they use the language of paying a debt, occasionally of paying a debt to the devil but most of all to death itself. The language of sacrifice, taken primarily from Paul in all the harshness of the victim's identification with sin is also employed. They call the Mediator King because he was victorious over sin and death and now reigns over the faithful who have been redeemed and who dominate these enemies in their own flesh, in the hope of being with Christ in eternity. Drawing especially on the Letter to the Hebrews, they call him Priest because he offered himself as sacrifice in his death and his entry into the heavenly sanctuary.

There are some strong images of this combat and also strong implications. The images are the shedding of blood, the cross as divine abandonment, sacrifice as identification with sin, and redemption as paying a price. In a way comparable to what we have seen Basil do in his anaphora, all these metaphors can be gathered under that of Christ's emptying himself, not only of his divine glory but even of any human beauty. Redemption and humankind's deification are won through the combat with sin and death undertaken by the Word made flesh, the abasement and suffering that this implies and that is the mediation of the power of divine love which conquers sin and death.

The understanding of *kenosis* as a way of explaining the mystery of the Incarnation is also present in the tradition of the Latin West. There, too, it is not simply a matter of the Word's assuming human nature but of the weakness that he thereby embraced—what it truly meant to take on the form of a servant or slave. It is quite clear that for Leo the Great, the self-emptying of Christ and the assumption of the form of a servant occur in the Incarnation of the Word. He saw this as a kind of veiling of the divinity, an act of pity rather than "a failure of power." However, in his letters on the Incarnation, Leo pointed to the extent of Christ's human appearance in the form of a servant or slave (*servus*). Signs of this human weakness appear already in his public life. "Taking food," he wrote, "resting in sleep, being troubled by grief, and weeping out of love, are the marks of the form of the servant." It was, however, in the Sermons on the Passion that Leo pressed the full implications of appearing in this form, for Word of God though he was Christ was subject to the torments imposed on him by his persecutors. This does not mean that the Word made flesh lost anything of his divine nature or power but rather that for humanity's sake he chose to live and suffer in the form of a slave.[5]

In similar vein, Fulgentius of Ruspe (fifth century) took the *kenosis* of the Son and the taking on of the form of a slave to mean the Incarnation (Letter 14). [6] This consists not simply in the fact that the Son took on a human nature, certainly inferior to the divine, but that he became human in a way that enabled him to be priest and victim, that is, to embrace human suffering, to pass through death, to give his life for the life of the world. Following his own reading of the Letter to the Hebrews, he wrote of Jesus the Mediator of the covenant as a true priest in the sense that he saw all mortals as his brothers and sisters, that he showed compassion in his own suffering, that he gave up his life with a loud cry and tears. He is that extraordinary thing, a priest who is likewise victim. To be a true priest who would pass into the heavenly sanctuary, he needed to be victim, to suffer with humanity, to take on death itself, to shed his blood.

God's Suffering

Even when Christian writers, East and West, applied what is said of the self-emptying of the Son and of his adoption of the form of a slave to the mystery of the Incarnation, they were at pains to explain that this enabled him to suffer travail, torment and death in his combat against sin and against death itself. The Word or Son did not simply become man but did so under a dispensation of sin and death in order to make of it a dispensation of redemption. In writing thus, one thing that these early writers faced was the dilemma of how the faith could speak of God's own suffering. Indeed, they often pointed to the Word's adoption of human flesh or of the form of a slave as something that made it possible for God to suffer, since he could not do so in his immortal and impassible divine nature. They wrestled with the dilemma of how God both cannot and yet does suffer out of his love for sinful humanity.

Two who may be quoted to show how complex the question was in patristic times are Cyril of Alexandria and Gregory of Nyssa, both of them anxious to exclude suffering from the divine nature. Cyril had got himself into a quarrel with Nestorius over the right way to speak of the reality of Christ. Gregory writes more placidly, even if still aware of threats to truth from heresy. Both of them seem to have been very sensitive to Christ's suffering and indeed to his cries of abandonment, yet both wanted to keep far away from any kind of gnosticism that would place necessity in God and see God evolving in his being through suffering. What then is to be made of the divine sonship of Jesus? Nestorius thought it best to emphasise that it was a man, Jesus of Nazareth, who experienced this sonship to an utmost, but mortal, degree. The sufferings were then those of a mortal who in the midst of the world's sin and tragedy looked to God as Father and remained faithful even in suffering to this Father, knowing the Father faithful to him. You cannot really know what it means to say that God is Father unless you pass through the way of suffering, or without knowing the Son who in his mortal flesh suffers. We know now that for Nestorius this did not mean denial of the kernel of the mystery of the Incarnation but was a way of explaining it that would revolve around the humanity of Jesus.

For Cyril, however, Nestorius's thought threatened the fullness of redemption. Cyril's ire was provoked by what seemed to him too great a distance in the Christ of Nestorius between the human and the divine. Are we only to say that it is a man who knew sonship as no other who suffered and died? Or did God suffer and die himself? If not, how are we saved? Neither did Cyril want to say that God suffered in his divinity for this seemed to give ground to those who thought that God could not be God without creatures and without suffering his way to full divinity through a created being. Cyril's own way of speaking was to say that the Word, truly a divine person, suffered in the humanity which he had taken on to himself. God is implicated because he sent the Word, the Son, but he does not have to endure earthly suffering in order to be God.

Gregory of Nyssa for his part considered suffering and mortality alien to the Godhead as such, but he also believed that through the Son God is implicated in human suffering. Gregory, like the other Cappadocians and many contemporary Orthodox writers, made a clear distinction between contemplating the Trinity at action in the world and contemplating the Trinity in its own eternal mystery. Before the latter we follow the way of the silencing of the mind, but in the former we note how revelation follows the way of opposites. What we call the power and the election of God, God's generous and free desire to create and save humankind, is revealed in its opposite, in weakness and suffering. It is because God's love and power show themselves in the self-emptying of the Son, both in taking on flesh and in suffering in the flesh, that we know the extent, the power, and the utter freedom of this love.[7]

Another tension that arises in the work of these writers, besides that of the relation between God and suffering, is how to reconcile the power of the Word in creation and the power that comes from Christ's willing subjection to the powers of the world. Athanasius, for example, writes quite poetically of the role of the Word who is God's Wisdom in the creation of the universe.[8] If there is order, harmony, beauty, in the workings of creation it is because it comes from the Divine Word. Without the ongoing protection of the Word, its provident guidance, the world would simply slip back into non-existence. To see this action of the Word from eternity is, for Athanasius, necessary to understanding the Incarnation and the work of redemption. If the Word were not the creative principle of all things, the sufferings of the flesh of Christ would be useless to us. Humanity would not be divinised, the world would not be transformed. Maybe it is the word "transformed" that raised questions. How can something wonderful be made more wonderful? Only by a fresh exercise of Wisdom and Power, which is put on display in the Word Incarnate's combat with evil, in the Saviour's subjection of himself to the powers of sin, death and Satan. Athanasius does not resolve this dilemma. But it remains that in *kenosis* there is a different and greater power on the part of the one who created. The God made manifest in the splendour of the universe is known more splendidly and even more otherly through obedience unto death, death on the Cross.

Reflecting on Contemporary Theologies

These patristic debates are remarkably convergent with the issues and questions of our own time. In the midst of horror and suffering, of the denials of God provoked by suffering, it is inadequate to postulate a permissive divine will. Rather do we see a divine love that takes on suffering. This arouses both theological and philosophical problems, but the issues have to be dared, in the very memory of the Cross of Christ.

Though efforts at historical reconstruction of the figure of Jesus are limited in their achievement, theologians have learned from this that they need to do two things. First, they need to place him and the beginnings of the Church within the thought and practice of Judaism. It was within the religious and cultural limits of this time that God showed his face to the world in the image of his Son made flesh. Second, and this has been more fully developed, they need to ask how is it that in a wholly human way God is revealed. In other words, it is only by taking Jesus's humanity seriously that we can attend to divine revelation. Even if the word *kenosis* is not used, it is this mystery that theologians reflect on when they look at the religious, cultural and human conditions of what is given to us in Jesus Christ.

It is thus, for example, that one can connect the play of the metaphor of *kenosis* with the thought of Karl Rahner, though he does not appeal to it himself. Rahner's thought invites his readers to take a look at the one who here below walked some rather dusty roads and entered some rather grubby homes, while not being slow to accept a meal in a rich Pharisee's dwelling, though the man in question may have had occasion to doubt the wisdom of entertaining a rather inconvenient and outspoken guest. To make up for going to the rich Pharisee, Jesus also went to the rich publicans, Zacchaeus and Levi, and took time out for enjoying friendship with Mary, Martha and their rather taciturn brother, from whom the ages have ne'er a word.

For Rahner, by making the transcendent show forth through the concreteness of human being, Christ is the one in whom God's grace and gratuitous love is shown to the world and is present to the world. In order to show God's gracious self-communication, Christ showed us what could be wrought through a human nature graced by God, totally open to the Fatherhood of God, and feeling in himself the yearnings and the unbearable sufferings at the heart of humanity's walk through time. In the flesh, Christ walked with suffering humanity along unexplored paths, a way of discovery and of obedience, as the author of Hebrews makes us note. Walking the earth, Jesus was finely attuned to the reign of God, to the grace that was all around, to the spirit of divine generosity that had brought creation into being and clothed it in glory. One could easily imagine him singing the psalms of creation, or, if one tolerates anachronism, the Canticle of the Sun of Francis of Assisi, in whom some of his followers thought to find Christ again, even to the marks of the stigmata, ushering in the end of the ages. But walking the earth, among the poor, humble and suffering of Judea, Galilee and Samaria, Jesus also knew the anguish of the human heart and the excesses of discrimination that outdid, time and time again, the excess of divine bounty.

As is well known, a political twist was given to Rahnerian theology by Johann Baptist Metz,[9] who wanted to place Jesus and his following, the dangerous memory of his Passover, firmly in history, and in history "after Auschwitz," a time of remembering lest we forget. Keeping memory of Jesus, Jew, enables Christians with their brothers and sisters to keep alive the memory of those whose names as well as existences the furnaces of Auschwitz tried to send up in flames and smoke.

What we need to retain from such Christologies, learning something from the efforts at the retrieval of the historical Jesus, is the appreciation of what he prayed, sought and suffered in his human spirit and in his human flesh. Jesus in his life was "on the way." Though living in an increased communion with God, calling him Father, he endured separation, puzzlement, the need to grasp the full meaning of the Law and the Prophets, the dread of facing his inevitable destiny, and, in the hour of death, even his sense of abandonment by disciples and by God. Scholastic theology has unfortunately clouded the human story of Jesus by too much talk about his knowledge, beatific, infused and acquired. This risked obscuring the extraordinary "exchange" of divine and human that marked the mystery of Jesus of Nazareth, an exchange taking place in time and place, in the history of the Israelite people and a fulfilment, as Jesus called it, of the Law and the Prophets.

Some authors have made more explicit appeal to the metaphor of *kenosis* in order to take account of the issue of divine suffering. The two names that stand out in this regard are Jürgen Moltmann and Hans Urs von Balthasar. In the mystery of Christ's *kenosis* in the flesh they see the expression of the eternal relation between Son and Father, the one who in the Spirit witnessed unto death and the one who in the bestowal of the Spirit crowned that witness by giving him a name above all names. The theology of hope and of the Crucified God elaborated by Jürgen Moltmann incorporates this imagery as a sign of the relation between Christ and the Father and of the Father's own engagement in the suffering of the world. Moltmann began with the quest for the living signs of hope in a desolate world, and in the steps of Luther found the reality of salvation on the Cross, in what Christ suffered. From there he moved on to the involvement of God in the suffering of the world, within his own divine mystery, walking through the circles of hell. There is a strong Lutheran accent in the account of Christ's death. Moltmann places the origins of this mystery within the Trinity, no less. Grasping the mystery of divine circumincession, *perichoresis*, dance, means looking to his combatful and distressing involvement with the children of the earth in their turbulent writhing, in the flesh, in history.

Though reluctant to predicate suffering of the divinity, Balthasar does find in the eternal relation of mutual gift between Son and Father the ground for the Son's earthly self-emptying and abandonment. His cogitations are quite dramatic and deeply based in a meditation on the three days of death, entombment, and resurrection.

These theologies influence my reflections, which look at Christ's *kenosis* as divine involvement in humanity's story, a mystery of salvation that is both paradox and drama, and bears the mark of the liturgical and the scriptural conjunctions earlier invoked.

Christ as Paradox

God is belittled in his Son. It is in the abasement of Christ that the justice of God reveals itself; it is in the reversal of values and perceptions that this folly of the Cross speaks as wisdom. When God enters the world and becomes engaged in how humans set about arranging their world and exercising authority or imposing order, the divine way of acting is paradoxical since in abasement it shows its own power at work with a different wisdom. If one employs social or political categories to designate God's action and presence, one has to resort to the image of slave. In the worldly order this stands in sharp contrast to the enjoyment of privilege and social freedom, as well as to the exercise of power and domination. Echoing Karl Barth, a number of writers note that the *kenosis* and the exaltation proclaimed in the hymn of the Letter to the Philippians are not to be thought of as a sequence of events. The two together—reduction to the form of a slave and exaltation as Lord—constitute a tensive symbol. It is in the taking on of the form of slave, in the abasement of death on a Cross, that the lordship of Jesus, Son of God, is revealed. In this act of generous mercy and love, giving himself over for others, the power of Christ to free from sin and death and to give life is made manifest. The paradox is that in submitting before the powers of the world in an act of free self-gift, Jesus shows the true power of God at work.

The paradox of Christ lies in the fact that the true lordship of God is made known in his abasement. In fact, it is possible to talk of a threefold aspect of *kenosis* when this is seen to designate the entire mystery of the Son's salvific mission. First there is the presence in the finitude of human existence, in all its limitations and travail, but also in its joys, companionship and hope. The limitations of God's revelation through Christ include those of time, place, culture, religion; it is among the people of Israel, in giving fulfilment to the early Covenant in terms of that Covenant, in speaking the language of a people and of a geographical area, that Jesus speaks of God. In his ministry, we see how Jesus bore the sins of humanity by bearing the sins of those around him, whether in the weakness of the flesh of those he healed or in the hardness of heart of those who chided him or in "weeping out of love" for his friends.

The second aspect of *kenosis* is in his witness before the powers of the world, especially in his trial, passion and death. There he was reduced to humiliating forms, that of the slave, of the criminal, of the body metaphorically "burned outside the camp."

The third aspect is death itself, knowing death to its fullness in order to show God's revelation of love and mercy in this death. It is in dying, not in avoiding death to show himself superior to Hades, that Jesus, the Son and the Christ of God, overcame death. This is death among others, with others, for others. It is passing through death in order to enter life and to open the way for others to make the same passage. To have some grasp of this, we need to think about what it means to say that he abandoned himself to death and that he felt abandoned by the Father. Jesus looked at the world and at his own mission in terms of his Jewish heritage and his desire to renew the Covenant, with its twin precept of the love of God above all and the love of neighbour, be this even an enemy or a stranger. The world he knew was the world around him: his companions and friends, the sick, the poor and the haughty. He thought of his prophetic mission in terms of these people, though his mind and heart were ever expanding the more he knew the Fatherhood of God and his own communion with the Father. To abandon himself to death was to submit to severe limitations and restrictions. It was to abandon the people and his friends. It was to accept the term to his work, the term to a life that he might well have imagined coming to greater fulfilment. In all of this, he felt himself abandoned by God. That for which he had been sent, he could not accomplish. The communion of the kingdom's blessed that he wanted to form would be no more. If ever we want to think of how death imposes its limits, or what it means to abandon oneself to death and to abandon others in dying, we could do well to think of what Jesus, prophetic witness to God's kingdom, suffered in giving himself over to death.

This final abasement in death, abandoned by God, is hardest to penetrate and yet vital to faith in the mystery of the Son. The abandonment by the Father which Jesus suffered in his death was brought about by his love for sinful humanity, by his desire to save all from being overcome by death, his wish to bring God to all and all to God. One with them, even those sinners to whom he offered God's forgiveness, he saw some rejecting this love, excluded from the life that he had come to bring. This was to feel himself abandoned by the Father, abandoned in his solidarity with sinners, since God's love had not conquered them all, since the Spirit had not raised all from sin and death, had not softened the hearts of those who refused to forgive their enemies. This is indeed the pain of hell, to see persons refusing love, to see the love of God missing its mark, that love out of which he abandoned his own self to death and the abyss.

Nor can we think of this only in the abstract, as though Jesus had some vague and general place in his heart for "all humankind." The pain of this abandonment was very concrete. It was to see Judas deflected from the way he had been taught. It was to see scribes and Pharisees and practitioners of the Law turning from the invitation to see how fundamental and thorough was the demand to love one's neighbour as oneself, to care for the sick and the suffering and those outside the Law. It was to see his own companions and friends at risk, denying his name or standing far off, outside the circle beneath the Cross, hesitant, doubtful, unable to accept the way of the Cross for him and for themselves. The abandonment by the Father was his vision, his heartbreak, over love failing. Yet he still gave himself over to death so that all these might live. Paradoxically, it was by carrying the abandonment of sinners and dying, of their failure to enter the circle of the Mount or the circle of the Cross, and so seeing them and himself with them outside God's love, that Jesus in the obedience of his suffering overcame sin and the hold of death on humanity. It is only with the cry "into your hands I commend my spirit" that this was possible. The extreme act of death was to abandon himself into the hands of the one by whom he felt abandoned, accepting that finally all is in God's hands and that God's power is best shown in an abased servant, who learns how to die, "learning obedience by his suffering."

Implications of Kenosis

In various ways theologians are trying to incorporate this imagery of *kenosis* into the theologies of salvation through Christ. Latin American Liberation Theology wished from the beginning to bring to mind the demand for justice within social structures that exudes from the figure of

Jesus Christ. It is perhaps in the reflections of this theology that the imagery of the redeemer's slavery can take on most poignancy and power. In the social order, he is classed among those who suffer oppression and persecution, who have no rights, who are made to serve in economic and political subordination.

Some, for example Juan Sobrino,[10] keep both the divinity and the humanity well in focus but underline the paradox of the revelation of the divine in the weakness and abasement of Jesus. In this there is the challenge to the structures and exercise of power in human institutions, which stands out even more strongly if we keep in mind the association between his ranking among slaves and his self-emptying. Against Gnostic strains, it was necessary for the Church in the early centuries to stress that in Jesus Christ true divinity and true divine salvific action are revealed. However, despite the quite poignant words of Leo the Great in his intervention in Christological debates, in a document referred to as the *Tomus*,[11] about the fatigue and the distress of Jesus in his flesh, attention turned gradually to evolving concepts of the divinity as prelude to considerations of the mystery of salvation. In his human suffering he was seen to act for human salvation, but the connection between the revelation of the divine pity and love and the weakness of his humanity was obscured, often in favour of theologies of lordship. Liberation theology reverses this procedure.

To see how Jesus in his mission as Word and Son restored justice and the horizons of just systems of human community and interaction, and in this revealed the divine, one may profitably follow the interplay between Jesus and his accusers in John's Gospel. The text at first appears to exude such calm and peace that one can miss the violence. Jesus is in quiet possession of his relation to the Father and always turned with compassion and goodness, and indeed pardon, towards those who suffer or are alienated. In the meantime, his accusers take up stones to throw at him, push him to the abyss, launch blasphemies against him, seek in many ways to do away with him. His unstressed replies only seem to exasperate and inflame them the more. Yet he claims no power, appeals to no legions, shows no violence, and classes himself with the Samaritan woman, the adulteress, the blind man, the paralytic, the bereaved Martha and Mary. None of these matter in the long run for others, except to the extent that they provide the opportunity to entrap Jesus, to get him into trouble, to offer reasons to make charges against him, "worthy of death." And when he is before Pilate, the one who rules, who has all the might of Caesar behind him, Jesus remains silent, apart from a brief question about the source of Pilate's own power.

At the beginning of the Passion story, other evangelists are pleased to play the paradox of the ass and her foal to the full (Matt 21:2-7; Luke 19:30-38). They know that this is the mount of a king, one that the great David rode. They let the children and the crowds cry out Hosanna to this king, who enters the city of Jerusalem in a royal cortege. But this procession and acclamation is prelude to the voices that shout for Barabbas, not

Jesus. On another note, therefore, the writers tell the reader that it is a humble mount, that the rider is humble, that he is making no claims to power or lordship. He is not going to be received as royal legate, whether by Herod or by the chief priests or by the Roman governor. These other powers have no place for his power, which is that of truth, and of truth alone. Yet he holds sway. He has the force to make the stones cry out. He makes truth stronger than lies, goodness more than invocations of law and rite or government. His last words are the words of an abandoned Son, crying out to the Father, but the tombs open, the veil of the temple is rent, the sun is darkened, the earth trembles.

In those who have the freedom of the Spirit, the Christ in his body is there where there are those who suffer from violence. He is there in truth and love, speaking the name of the Father. If we ask today where the presence of Christ and of the Spirit, as envoys of the Father, are to be found, we would say where there is violence, in their identification with those who suffer and in those who retain a freedom of spirit in the face of injustice and violence.

Divine Drama

In order to see the glory of Christ as Word and Son, in communion with the Father, revealed in his suffering flesh, one may consider the Cross and its humiliation as a form given from above to divine revelation and as a response to human yearning, as does Hans Urs von Balthasar.[12] There is, he opines, nothing in humanity that can make one expect anything like the condescension and drama of the divine gift of life. There are no anticipations in human sentiment or reason that God might so have acted, only stunning surprise. The believer, and the theologian finding form for his beliefs in the dust of library tomes long perused, can only take a position at the foot of the Cross and open the heart to the glory so strangely revealed. From that spot that is the bolt of the universe, they perceive the harmony of the divine-human drama that is enacted.

Balthasar's is not a philosophical Christology, for all its philosophising, but one that places confidence in the disturbing aesthetic of the divine artist. From this point, Balthasar goes on to develop a divine drama of the conflict between divine freedom and human freedom, lived out by Christ himself in his ministry, passion and descent into hell. Of the continued drama ample and terrifying evidence is found in the Book of Revelation, as this tragedy goes on in the fiendish pursuit of the woman and her child by the dragon, but breathes its last in the call on the Son to come, Maranatha, Lord Jesus.

The drama involved is a drama of freedoms and a drama of power. It is above all the drama of a love that claims only the power of love, seeking no domination other than that gained by the power of love and the power of self-emptying, of stripping oneself of claims, of placing oneself naked in face of the other, open to its claims, its demands for love, and even its assaults. The freedom of God is simply to have loved, indeed to have created. If there is any sense to the definition that the world was created for the glory of God but that it adds nothing to the divine self-contentment, to the divine beatitude of Trinitarian *perichoresis,* it is that to have created is a free act of pure outgoing, of self-giving. We may be in doubt as to the implications of this for the divine life in itself, but we see its operations in the world in Jesus Christ. There we learn the extent of self-gift and what this means in the face of the power that humans, in multiple forms, claim for themselves, with a terrible and dreadful penchant to claim power over others. Following the drama of Jesus—at his baptism (Mark), in the 40 days, in his interaction with the chiefs, even with his own disciples, with the demon, in his betrayal by Judas—one finds constantly the consequences of loving too much, of compassion, of being with the one who suffers, even with the sinner who suffers reprobation.

What are the implications? I think here of a poem of Rilke.[13] The powers, the "gods" as Rilke puts it, are in conflict over the very name of God. They might also be in conflict over the name of Christ whom the Church unveils to the world and who is in conflict with the powers. Some of these gods incline their heads, give up their power, and make way for the wisdom of the God who is crucified outside the camp. There is the Cross and the blood. One may not stray far from the impact of these images in telling the drama of the "conflict of powers" and in naming the God who is the Father of Jesus Christ.

No doubt, in all of these ruminations there is a contrast with yesteryear in its confident predication of Christ's divinity, and therefore of his authority and his teaching about God, and with the assurance of the divine order of justice represented in the paying of the debt of sin in humanity's name in the sacrifice of Christ's death. The road to follow in rethinking this is precisely that of the drama of divine self-emptying. One does not have to take sides between von Balthasar and Rahner, though at times it is good to give thanks for belligerent theologians, for they keep us restless. What is retained is that *kenosis* is the very condition and substance of divine revelation and of a divine invitation into the communion of divine love. The liturgical chant rings throughout: Christ emptied himself, obedient unto death, even death on a Cross. On this account, God has given him a Name which is above all names.

Christ, Peoples, *Kenosis*

Attention to the *kenosis* of Christ as key to the mystery of the divine Trinity and the eternal design for human salvation is not confined to European or North American theologians. If it is through drama and paradox that Christ brings the love of God for the world into the world, it has to be true for all peoples. On more than one continent, the *kenosis* of Christ provides a key to his embodiment among peoples and cultures of various kinds. The relation between the self-emptying of Christ and the evangelical poverty of his disciples is transparent, for the Church is his living Body. If the Gospel is to take root in non-Western cultures this means that because of its history the Church too must empty itself to be present among the poor and present to peoples whose culture it has often disregarded in its missionary activities.

Along these lines, there is a remarkable take on the relation between the *kenosis* of the Church to that of Christ in some African theologies.[14] Since the days of the Council, African bishops and theologians have been among the first to stress the need for inculturation in evangelisation. They have latched on to the comparison that the Decree on the Missionary Activity of the Church makes between the incarnation and inculturation: as Christ took on flesh within a particular culture and lived by that culture, so the Church his Body must find roots and life in each and every culture. In a way that is different from Latin America's interest in a liberation from the injustices of political and economic structures, in Africa attention was first given to how the Gospel relates and sows its seed in the African cosmic, organic and religious vision of all reality. It is respect for the religious vision of the peoples of Africa that matters in their evangelisation, lest inculturation rest at the stage of assimilating traditional modes of expression into catechesis and liturgy. In relating faith in Christ to an African vision of the universe some spoke of him as Protoancestor, a title that relates him to both the people in their cultural heritage and to the Church as God's family. Other writers preferred the title of First Born, while in some cases his mission of healing was brought to the fore. In all of this they operated within a perspective that allowed them to find seeds of the Word and the breath of the Spirit in the religiously minded cultures of the African continent and so to fit the advent of Christ into this cultural world, not as something totally new but as a fulfilment of God's action throughout the continent's history. These theologies may help those of the West to fill out their own thought on the *kenosis* as a key to responding to the mystery of the triune God revealed in Christ.

Looking more sharply and anxiously at the division, turmoil and suffering in African countries today, some have given a new twist to their understanding of the incarnation of the Son in highlighting the image of *kenosis*. As in his earthly being the Son emptied himself out before the world and among his people, so today he empties himself out in his identification with a people that is abased and deprived of so much: justice, peace, wealth, culture, life itself. But he does this in and through the Churches of Africa, because they are his Body, assuming into his being the memories, the traditions, the suffering and the hopes of the peoples. It is through his Body that the compassion of Christ takes flesh and it is among the people that he empties himself out for their salvation.

Asian theologians on their part have assimilated various titles for Christ as Mediator that ally Christian faith with the religious insights of Eastern religions, as recalled in the exhortation *Ecclesia in Asia*. Some of them too make a distinctive appeal to the imagery of *kenosis*. For the Church in parts of Asia, especially where Hindus, Buddhists or Muslims are the majority of the population, Jesus Christ cannot be proclaimed as Saviour without taking into account the life and the salvation that is given to people through these immense religious traditions. Hence while looking to Jesus Christ as the Saviour sent by God, they see him as One who empties himself out, who is at work but often remains hidden along with the Spirit, in creation itself, and in what God works in and through other religions. Christians hold to their faith in Christ only when they see him and the Spirit at the service of God's Kingdom, in which all peoples are united in divinely given freedom, fellowship, love, justice and eternal hope for a life that overcomes death itself. To be witness to such a work of Christ and Spirit in the world of religions, Christians need to take a humble role of service and dialogue, not being quiet about Christ but working with others in service of this Kingdom where God is not present in glory and power but in service among the poor and suffering. This is a compassionate and healing presence for those who suffer and are the least of people in the eyes of those who hold worldly power.[15]

For the Sri Lankan Jesuit Aloysius Pieris, the *kenosis* of Christ is vital to the dialogue with Buddhism, inasmuch as this term articulates the mission of the Son who comes forth from the Father and returns to the fullness of the Father.[16] The encounter of Christians with Buddhism hinges on this imagery of *kenosis,* for it relates to the Buddhist practice of complete forgetfulness of self on the way to the fullness of the state of "no-thingness," which at the same time exacts regard and respect for all forms of life. In Christ, the process of self-emptying meant giving himself over completely to the service of others, becoming as sin itself, or as nothing, in order to enter with the whole of creation into the fullness of communion with the Father. Associating the mission of the Spirit with that of the Son, one finds the inner force that enlivens the hope of eschatological achievement residing in the communion of Christ and his Body with the One who is Source and Destiny. By naming this destiny the Father, Pieris believes that he can invite Buddhists to see that as well as a destiny to the process of self-emptying there is a Source who is the origin of the gift of life, wisdom and love.

Nor indeed can I forget the peculiar disregard for power and survival that marks the story of the coming of Christ to Polynesia. It was the members of the London Missionary Society who brought the Gospel to these peoples of oral tradition, so that he arrived under the guise of a Living Word. It was not, however, until Christ was revealed through a king who does not take hostages nor claim victims that people were won over in large numbers. The Gospel had arrived in 1797, winning over the sovereign of the island but not many subjects. In 1815 an insurrection of those who resisted Christianity as a foreign imposition sought to put down this ruler. When Pomaré emerged victorious, he did not follow the custom of taking human sacrifice from among the defeated, but sent the conquered home to their dwellings and families, with the explanation that the Son of God whom he worshipped, though he was not yet baptized, had abolished all need for sacrifice by his own willing death for the world's victims. It was thus in the renunciation of the spoils of power and in the guise of being a victim who spent his life for others to effect reconciliation that Christ came to be accepted. As long as the ruler was thought to enhance a hold over subjects by a compromise with the powerful God of the foreigners, there was no faith in the living Word that the missionaries brought. When it was seen that Jehovah had given his Son in the form of abject victim to undo victimhood, leading captivity captive, then faith could blossom. This was at the same time the inauguration of a new kind of warrant for authority among the people themselves and the end to the need to sacrifice the life of some to stabilize the life of others.

The proclamation of Christ as saviour could thus in Polynesia be related to the traditions of the people that speak of salvation and that establish modes of reconciliation when peace is broken by violence. In their creation myths, the peoples of the islands related the Creator both to the appearance of the cosmos in all its parts, from plants and streams to oceans and firmament, and to the suffering of the world. One of their common images is that of the Creator God bringing forth the world in pain, with a great cry, and this is extended into quite a number of stories. If humanity suffers, if the earth itself suffers, it is the Creator who suffers in it through the act of bringing it forth. The Christian missionaries in proclaiming Christ as Living Word, in whom the Father creates the world, wished to dissociate themselves from emanation myths, from the idea of a God who needs the world, and from images of divine suffering within the Godhead. On the other hand, they could show that God does take on the pain of the world through his Son, the Living Word incarnate. God creates through the Word, sends the Word as Son into the world, and through the sacrifice of this Son reconciles those who oppose each other, bringing an end to wars and to rituals of violence as a means of establishing rule and harmony. Thus the Son of God, who is one with the Father and his Living Word, enters the world to take on suffering and bring about reconciliation, but does so by identifying himself with victims, with those in Polynesian society whose only worth was to be offered in sacrifice, and who otherwise had no place in the life and future of their peoples.

Whether it be Latin America, Asia, Africa or Polynesia, there are economic, social and political consequences of this vision of a divine love incarnate in the *kenosis* of Christ and his relations to both the powerful and the weak of the earth. In the endeavour to restore their dignity, their culture, their land and their true being to peoples, the wisdom of the Cross and Christ's total self-gift dictate a stance on human affairs that works itself into the vision of the fabric of society. Believing in the import of this witness and trusting in the grace of God from which alone comes life, Christians do not withdraw from the world but partake in it and in its "otherliness," with passion for the vision of true justice which they bring with them. It is through those who are grafted into him that Christ continues to bear the gift of a loving and total gift of self, even through self-emptying.

Not dismissing the poignancy that this imagery has for Africa, nor the respect for other religions that it demands in Asia, nor the link with the removal of rites of human sacrifice in Polynesia with its new grasp of true power, all Christians would benefit from thinking about this kenotic model of incarnation and Church. Everywhere when Christ embodies himself in a church he does so in line with his own, and his people's, preferential option for the poor and the espousal of evangelical poverty. A community of faith will realize that, as Christ's Body, it, too, must in self-emptying find its identity in and with those who are nothing—with the suffering, the oppressed, the depressed, the divided, the culturally and socially torn.

To be genuine bearers of witness to Christ's lordship won through *kenosis*, and so to the divine Name revealed, we are to know from the willed weakness of Christ what it is to be a weak Church. In the form of evangelical poverty that conforms to culture and to whatever the moment or the hour of the drama of salvation, the Body of Christ lives the strength of God through its very weakness, not up to the measure of its calling yet with an opening heart to the breath of the Spirit, wherever and howsoever it blows.

Christ and Time

In light of Christ's self-emptying, do human events and the flux of time have any significance within the drama of God's creative and saving love? The question has been mulled over for centuries. When early Christian communities were converted to Christ they were filled with the awareness of God's mercy and the gift of the Spirit. They were able to express their hope in terms of the resurrection of all the dead, brought to birth in the raising up of the First Born from the dead. Whether actively persecuted or considered a nuisance in societies organized around other religious beliefs, they remained convinced of Christ's communion with them and firm in their hope. Temporal orders and historical events had no particular significance. There was no need to look for another Cyrus through whom God would establish a benevolent temporal kingdom since such figures had been fulfilled in Christ, who was to reign until the end of days. Reading Augustine on human events, who gave focus to this faith, some have expressed his vision as one of the world as the stage on which human salvation is worked out by God's grace, and in which believers could be schooled to live only by the desire for God, awaiting Christ's return in judgment and the resurrection of all the dead.

Indeed, Augustine gave classical expression to Christian hope when he recounted his meditation with his mother, Monica, on eternal life.[17] In the course of this meditation they found that in a moment of "total concentration of the heart" they had entered into eternal life, fully consumed by the desire for God. While this gave them hope it was only passing: normally the mind had to suffer the indignities of trying to focus, trying to remember, trying to gather all its forces together while subject to the scattering of thoughts and desires, yearning for many things and hardly able to tell the difference between past, present and future. As he showed elsewhere in his writings, events that occurred around them were of no significance in themselves for Christians. In their liturgies and in their common life they could but model for themselves and for others what it means to live totally by the desire for God and in the hope of the life promised in Christ, incarnate mediator, priest and victim, in whom all could ascend to the Father.

This vision of an order restored, lived now precariously but lived nonetheless, remained dominant for centuries and has its advocates in the Church today.[18] Though before and after Augustine some sought the meaning of events and persons, this was in light of the peace they might afford the Church or the peril to which they subjected it. Constantine gave some brief hope to those who thought in terms of an era of divinely restored peace, but he himself meddled too much in spiritual and ecclesiastical affairs to guarantee it, to say nothing of emperors and princes who came after him. The Church was always caught up in some kind of struggle for freedom and power, as emperors, popes, kings and bishops contended with each other for dominion over people and over land.

The Church needs peace to worship in spirit and in truth, but who or what can guarantee that? Hence from time to time, in varying intensity, apocalyptic expectations emerged with the reading of the signs of the times that indicated the advent of the end of the world or of the millennium of Christ's reign that would precede it. People, the common folk as well as monks and scholars, were ready to see these signs in various catastrophes or to see Antichrists in kings, popes and heretics, or even in spiritual and philosophical movements that banished the wisdom of Christ in favour of human wisdom. Like Bonaventure in his reading of the life of Francis of Assisi, they could also see in prophetic and saintly persons the figure whose presence among them meant the imminent advent of Christ in his second coming.

When we think of such matters nowadays we are less inclined to look to the Book of Daniel or to the Book of Revelation to find the signs or configurations of eras of history. We wonder nonetheless about the presence of Christ and Spirit in human events other than what takes place within the narrow boundaries of Church communities. We are caught between the consolation of seeing them at work in all movements towards human community, justice and peace, and the desolation of seeing the divine life extinguished by repeated human atrocities. Vision of Christogenesis through anthropogenesis and even cosmogenesis for a time inspired some with hope. People even found confirmation of this in scientific hypotheses about matter, time and space as the world was seen to move towards its fullness in the resurrection of Christ and the advent of a new heaven and a new earth. Time could be seen as broadly linear, the evolutionary force of grace at work through the lordship of Christ.

The sheer viciousness of human action, its capacity to destroy not only human life but the cosmic environment, quickly destroys such optimism. It is in the midst of the antithesis of love that Christian hope has to survive. Is it possible to live in the hope of a future, not only at the end of history but within history itself, when it is so marked by demonic forces? In such a context, eschatology becomes the "mother of theology," as was said by the exegete Ernst Käsemann. The light from the future is the only thing to dispel the darkness, but where and how is it to be found? Is it possible to place the symbol of divine *kenosis* alongside that of the coming in judgment of the Son of Man to express the place of Christ in history?

What prevails is the draw of the future promised in the resurrection of Christ, but this is not an evolutionary force, a pasch or passage that works itself out over time in the lives of the faithful or in works inspired by Word and Spirit. The meaning of such hope is better expressed when it is said that the resurrection of Christ is the anticipation of how all things will be caught up and given new life in the love and glory of God. Such hope remains always alive and operative, infusing a broad range of human action with the meaning of being drawn towards a divine plenty. Thus the resurrection of the dead and the new heaven and new earth remain living and vibrant symbols.

Possibly, however, such vision is still too weak to express the how and the where of Christ's presence in human events, both good and bad. To fill it out we need to look to the *kenosis* whereby he earned lordship and still is lord. We can glimpse there what and whom he enfolds into his loving embrace. At times the efforts made to establish the common good of the diverse, to restore peace and justice, seem to work. At times they simply fall apart, and one thinks wryly of the caption for a cartoon in the *New Yorker*, "things were better back then when they were worse." Whether the times are good or bad, they are under God's judgment and can be enlivened only by a gratuitous divine irruption. This advent is signalled in witnesses, in those who continue to testify to a divine revelation through *kenosis* and to the blessings of the reign of forgiveness and reconciliation proclaimed by Jesus Christ. This is a power at work in history and event, but it is neither evolutionary force nor a simple draw towards the future. It disrupts and challenges. If it contains a seed, the difference between seed and fruit is as great as that between the grain and the ear of wheat. In the seed itself there is no clear evidence of what is to come. Trusting in love, knowing that God works through an emptying out of claims to glory and through unexpected gift, Christians are invited to live by promise. The promise anticipates only insofar as it is remembered in all its ungainliness and its power to deconstruct human desire. Although the hope is given form in a variety of images, and, although one can be sure of God's future and the world's future in God, one trespasses when trying to spell out what this future will be. It is to be left in God's hands.

Yet this is not a hope without action. On the contrary, it commands interruptive action, an effort to insert Christ's kind of love into human affairs. It bears the burden of witness to the love, forgiveness, peace and justice that are of God's bounty, against the powers and forces that subjugate and victimize. It even dares to ask that this order of mercy intrude into the orderings of justice in society and between peoples. In that regard, John Paul II's plea to the Italian parliament to insert clauses of mercy into penal codes has the symbolic quality of auguring the impossible in virtue of the hope to which Jesus Christ's kenotic "power play" gives rise.

My Father and Your Father

This reflection on the mystery of Jesus as the one sent by God leads into further reflection on the mystery of God. In particular, it allows us to know what it is to speak of God the Father, who created heaven and earth, or to seek the presence of the Spirit in the world. It is in the story of Jesus that we see the implications of calling him Son, Lord and Word. We need to consider this before we look for dogmatic definitions or theological theories about divine and human nature, or about the divine personhood of Jesus. In his teaching and in his mission, ending in his condemnation and his Cross, the justice and the holiness of God are revealed. The justice and righteousness of God long spoken of within Israel and in the Covenant are sharply focused here. It is in his powerlessness that he lives the Sonship that says much about his relationship to God-Father, and it is in this that we see the eternal Word of God take form, in a harmony sensed in the descent of the Spirit of the prophets upon him.

He addresses God as Father in a unique way, though it was already presaged in the Hebrew scriptures. These were at first careful to avoid calling Yahweh Father, since this only confused him with Babylonian and Canaanite genealogies and emanations, where generation was crass and worldly, as the Israelite prophets saw it. In Yahweh's relation to Israel, the reality of free choice prevails, not a generation or emanation that bespeaks a necessity in God himself. It is with prophetic critique, and mostly in connection with the ideal King David, that the imagery of God as Father began to make a return. It then became connected with the ideal of being pastor, of being protector of the poor, of settling Israel with a justice of divine, not human, origin. This is the necessary background to Jesus's addressing God as Abba, and to the way in which he is Son.

Matt 11:22f. shows how God's election works and where it resides. The text affirms first that it is only the meek and little of the earth who will know God, who are the chosen ones. It then talks about the relation between Jesus and this Father; Jesus is the chosen one, the beloved one of all eternity, but he is so joined to the Father that he shares totally in the compassion and mercy that flows from the Father. He is chosen from among sinners, but is the one in whom—primordially and then as go-between—the Fatherhood of God is made known. This is an election that has eternal roots in a perfect Father-Son relationship. Jesus himself enters completely into this relationship in the face of his passion and in his death. The figure of David as son plays a part, and is evoked in Psalm 21/22. God does not abandon him whom he has chosen, even in his miseries. This is another kind of "kingship."

The Three Levels of Discourse

As noted earlier (pp. 3-4), Christians may testify to Christ on three levels of discourse that fit the paradox and the drama of the Lord's *kenosis*. It is by living on this triple level with openness of heart, with the desire to meet and truly live with others and yet also to speak a powerful message, that the participation of Christians in a quest for justice is possible.

On the first level of discourse, we encounter one who confronted the sin, the suffering and the violence around him in the firm persuasion that love prevails over evil in the heart, that life is stronger than death. To show the power of love, he endured the hatred of those who sought to prevail in other ways, always speaking of the forgiveness, mercy, and reconciliation that comes from a fatherly God. When faced with judgment and condemnation, he testified to a judgment of mercy and love. His own power to overcome evil and to bring life was strongest in the abasement he endured in his death. When feeling deserted by God in the failure of his mission to renew the religious sensibility of those around him, he gave his most forceful witness to the God who prevails over death.

On the second level of discourse, Christians dare to say that in Christ's self-gift and his self-emptying in fidelity to God, they have found the road to follow. It is only through compassion that suffering is made endurable. It is only by facing hatred with forgiveness and the desire for reconciliation that violence may be eradicated. It is only in living by faith in divine mercy and in the transformation of hearts that justice and the good of order may be established. It is only by passing through death in the hope of a gift of life from God that death itself can be seen as a fulfillment. For some, who have lived justly, this brings what has been lived in trust to its climax, in the hope that the redress of fault and failure is assured by no other than God.

On the third level of discourse, which integrates the first two into a fuller vision, Christians proclaim Christ as God's Son, the one on whom God's Spirit reposes, God truly among us in the flesh. They witness to him as God's greatest self-gift, God's compassion for humanity in its suffering and conflict and his presence among us. It is because God so loved the world that he gave his own Son that we are sure of mercy and that we live in hope. We might have expected God to have shown his power in mightier ways. We might have found our ideas of God verified in law enforcement, in harsh judgment on the evil of the world, in all kinds of miraculous interventions. But God in sending Christ has renounced such actions. God in his Son who was among us as one of our race, learning obedience through suffering, has lowered himself, has totally changed the ideas we have of divinity. It is when we accept *kenosis* as God's chosen way of revealing and giving himself that we begin to know God. It is in the Son who makes nothing of himself that we begin to know the Father. It is in living with the Son, according to his example, one with him on his way, that we feel and are moved by the power of the Spirit.

This is a God for all peoples. This is a God for all races and all nations. This is a God for all times. This is the God who will continue to take many forms though always bearing the name of Love. This is God through whose power in self-gift all things are transformed. This is God for the world and for a new creation.

Conclusion

There is no discussion here of debates about the recovery of the historical Jesus or fidelity to the definition of the Council of Chalcedon on the two natures in Christ, the Son of God. Rather than repeat such matters, what has been mined here is an expression of faith grounded in liturgical, patristic and theological traditions. How God is revealed, through the proclamation of Jesus as Saviour and Lord, in his fatherhood and in his gift of self to the world, is unveiled through the links offered by the imagery of the *kenosis* of Jesus, of whom the Gospels speak as Son and Word of God. To know God we look to Jesus. There is no more potent name whereby to know and construe how God advented, advents and will advent through time, for those who keep memorial of Christ.

PART TWO

THE KENOSIS OF THE CHURCH
AND ITS MISSION

Paradox is the language of the incalculable. We are doomed to live by paradox, by the hope that rises from the tomb of Christ. On Easter morn, the women at the sepulchre were half overcome with joy, half afraid. Never more to be afraid of death makes one afraid. Never to hold on to life makes one greedy for life. Never to be tied down by love makes one love beyond limits. Never to want anything fills one with an insatiable desire for everything. The women were afraid beyond belief at what they heard and saw, as they went forth to announce to the disciples the Gospel of an obedience unto death that was a transition to the fullness of life.

As the disciples searched in their heritage for words that fit in preaching Christ dead and risen, they often lit upon terms like ransom, price and sacrifice. Sacrifice is well calculated, as it is measured out by what the Law prescribes; a sacrifice that is incalculable disrupts the economy. When there is no economy to live by, one is hard put to find the measure of an economy of the incommensurable. Being simply not up to it, believers have to get down to it. Remembering and weighing the words of him who had proved Redeemer, they tried to capture the excess of his prescripts of love and forgiveness. At the tomb and in the Supper Room while they were still afraid, they learned that the way to live life is to lose it.

The Church through the event of the Second Vatican Council had perhaps begun anew to catch this sense of paradox, though how well it holds up in ensuing years is yet to be proven. At any rate, Pope John XXIII and the Second Vatican Council called for an end to shows of triumph and worldly power in the Catholic Church. Paul VI followed this up by doing such things as suppressing the Nobel Guard and cutting the trains of the eminent Cardinals. Nobody could have imagined how much the Church would be humbled beyond its own intentions fifty years on. In Europe, the Church still has to account for its actions during the Nazi and Fascist regimes. In Africa, Asia, Latin America, Oceania, the Church in bringing the Gospel was often complicit in aborting local culture and the Gospel's own inculturation. In North America, bishops, clergy and religious are publicly humiliated by revelations of sexual and financial misdeeds.

Reflection on the call, life and mission of the Church, as an extension of the kenotic mystery of Christ viewed as *kenosis* takes place in this context. The key to the theology of the Church that does justice to the mystery of being followers of Christ on the way of self-emptying is the call to evangelical poverty.

4

The Church: Witnessing to Christ
in Evangelical Poverty

———————————— ✠ ————————————

The paradox of the *kenosis* of Jesus Christ is given form in the life of the Church by the excess of the evangelical poverty to which the Beatitudes and his example call it. Birthed by Christ the slave through his self-emptying is the Church of the Poor, a body made up of the poor in its midst and serving the poor of the world. The postsynodal exhortation on the ministry of bishops,[1] quoting *Lumen gentium* no. 8, remarks on the almost tangible presence of Christ himself among the bishops during the Synod, as one "who carried out the work of redemption in poverty and under oppression."[2] It then goes on to say that the bishop, to be an authentic witness to the Christ who was poor, a witness who can exercise an apostolic ministry, must be a *vir pauper*, a poor man. Not only is this an ascetic imposition that would free him of self-interest, but it is "demanded by the Church's concern for the poor." It makes of the bishop one among the poor in a Church that is the home of the poor. While the exhortation is addressed to bishops, the call to poverty in communion with Christ may be addressed to the Church and all its members, according to their respective places in it, and applies in a particular way to those who profess the way of consecrated life according to the evangelical counsels.

Mission and Evangelical Poverty

When Churches, Eastern and Western, consider the urgent call to bring a liberating and healing Gospel and a promise of God's reign to the poor of the world, they are aware that to accomplish this they must identify with the Christ who became poor so that humankind might become rich. By the gift of the Spirit, the call to be a Church of the Poor and a Church that is "poorly" is given to those who profess themselves to be disciples of the one whose name is revealed in *kenosis*. In its mission for humanity, living by the grace of Word and Spirit, the Church today might do well to take more stock of that current at the Vatican Council that espoused evangelical poverty as key to the witness of the Church and to its mission, with its special predilection for the poor and the oppressed of the world.

To those who have lived long enough, personal memories may call them back to those moments when the life of evangelical poverty, lived in new ways, seemed the road to travel into the future. Hence I dare to intrude some recollections from my own life as a member of a body of professed religious. Responding to the mandate of the Second Vatican Council, religious communities were called upon to undertake a renewal of life and mission in the light of their charism and in response to the call to live publicly the evangelical counsels of poverty, virginity, and obedience. In 1966, at its General Chapter, the Congregation of the Missionary Oblates of Mary Immaculate was among the first to embark on this course. The agenda was large, but to get to the heart of renewal, the capitulants needed to ask how the evangelical counsel of poverty related to the evangelization of the poor and to action on their behalf.

In the months preceding the event, the superior general, Father Leo Deschatelêts, sometimes walked the gardens of the General House, or OMI headquarters, chatting with a few of the student priests then in residence in Rome. One of his concerns was precisely this liaison between espousing poverty and living for the poor. As I walked with him one day we spoke about the role during the Council of the group of bishops that called itself "The Church of the Poor." This group of bishops held its own regular meetings to probe the implications of what Pope John XXIII had called the preferential option for the poor. For them, it meant locating the voice of the poor and the service of the poor at the heart of the mystery of the reign of God, and attending particularly to them in the work of evangelization. They heard an invitation to the Church to be poor in its own way of life. The connection between a personal option for evangelical poverty and the option for the poor needed to be articulated.

In our conversations, we wondered whether it had been a good idea in the conciliar pronouncements on religious life to list the evangelical counsels in the order of chastity, poverty and obedience, reversing the more standard listing of poverty, chastity and obedience. Was it not true that poverty, personal and communal, is the foundation of the evangelical life, both as it is presented in the New Testament as an ideal of discipleship and as it has been lived down through the ages in religious communities? Being poor expresses the Church's most intimate union with Christ in his incarnate mystery of "being poor so that we might become rich" (2 Cor 8:9). It is on this basis that we bring the good news to the poor.

Fifty years later some may still sense in their bones that if a religious community does not recover the charism of poverty, according to its own tradition, it shall not undergo a serious renewal in its life and mission, and that if the Church itself as a Body does not confess its own poverty before God and the world, it is hard put to preach Christ.

Many religious orders and congregations now interpret their mission, in light of their founding charism, as mission to the poor or mission in their service. They appeal to such statements as those of Paul VI in his letter *Evangelii Nuntiandi*, which presents human development and a concern with justice as an integral part of evangelization. The mission to the poor has taken a large place in the mission statements of many Churches and in statements of mission and evangelism of the World Council of Churches. In ecumenical dialogues on mission and witness, this issue plays a considerable part. What is put forward is rather different from the disinterest in things terrestrial in personal life and in pastoral work, to which religious used to be exhorted, and is an aspect of Gospel teaching which we have yet to fully assimilate.

It is not always clear how mission relates to the counsel of poverty. The counsel has been given new interpretations, ones that focus more on the common life and sharing goods together than on corporate renunciation. Communities spell out their mission as the call to be with the poor in their struggle and to be present in those places where the future of the poor is decided. What happens then is that they give corporate efficiency in their mission a clearer place than the renewal of the witness and way of life of the community's own corporate poverty. The latter, however, might well be the priority for renewal and for a veritable proclamation of the Gospel of Jesus Christ, in being and act as well as word. Perhaps the Church can evangelize the poor and work with them for justice only if it is internally poor itself. In order to be present among the poor as Christ was present, it needs to witness in poverty rather than aid through a generous exercise of the power of wealth. *Lumen gentium* (and then *Pastores gregis*) reminds us that we are to be one with Christ "poor and oppressed." This puts the Church, its pastors and those bodies that avow to live the life of evangelical poverty among those who are without power, who are the victims of history and of development. It identifies the Church with Christ, the *doulos,* the slave, the one who is as nothing before the powers of the world, without portfolio or status.

The Appeal to Biblical Foundations

At moments of foundation, and later at moments of crisis and refounding, religious communities read their past, present and future in the light of two sets of texts from the New Testament. The first is the combination of texts that describe the life of the apostolic community in the days after Pentecost. Principal is the passage from Acts 2:42ff., describing the life of the first community of disciples in Jerusalem, including the placing of possessions in common, with the needs of the "widow and the orphan" particularly in mind: a common life with no claims to individual personal property rights and a community service to the poor. The life of the hermit Anthony, to whom we can attribute the beginning of religious life, says that he was prompted by this text to renounce all he had so that it be given to the poor.

The second set of texts gives the instruction of Jesus to his disciples as he sent them forth to preach the kingdom of God. Among them, Luke 9 takes pride of place. These admonitions prescribe the way of a radical poverty, making the apostle a person of no substance and dependent on the hospitality of others. That is the way of being poor among the poor, after the manner of Jesus who ended his mission naked on the Cross, deprived of all possessions and of all human rights, left with a few courageous women to anoint and bury his body.

Though the Book of Acts had a great influence on monastic traditions, in the course of history it is the inspiration of apostolic mission that has characterized important moments of evangelical renewal and evangelization, such as the Franciscan way in the thirteenth century. The Oblate Founder, Eugene de Mazenod, presented such a model and such a set of texts after the French Revolution to the group that he founded as missionaries of Provence. They were in no way to rely on the power of money or property in preaching the good news of divine love and election to the poor of Provence.[3] Their riches lay in the word they proclaimed. When some of this group went abroad to "mission fields," it was de Mazenod's and their desire to be poor among the poor, to represent (even in their habit, to say nothing of their habits) the poor and crucified Christ in the radical poverty of his complete despoliation of possession, power and glory.

In the postsynodal exhortation on *Consecrated Life*, John Paul II, encouraged by synodal deliberations, took the practice of evangelical poverty as witness to the kingdom of God to be the foundation of mission. As he says, evangelical poverty embraced by communities is an embodiment of the First Beatitude found in Matthew and a witness to God's reign and its values. It has to be given modes of realization suited to the contemporary world. He sees this as a challenge to many prevailing ways of life that exploit the earth's resources.

It is sometimes said of nineteenth-century founders, and perhaps rightly, that despite their great devotion to the poor they did not have good insight into social issues and were perhaps too inclined to separate earthly happiness and eternal beatitude. However, we may now be moving in another direction, prompted by too much learning about today's and yesterday's social issues. Without quite forgetting the radical espousal of poverty, we think mainly of promoting the rights of the poor, and do this quite often by dint of our power of corporate possession, which gives us entry to those places where the future of the poor is decided. One would indeed hope to be heard in such places, but is it to be by virtue of monetary and business competence or by dint of preaching Christ, foolish upon the Cross, and by offering a testimony of true poverty of body and spirit?

Church of the Poor

To consider the Church's call to evangelical poverty, one has to ask in what sense the Church may be called the Church of the Poor? It is true that the vow of poverty in religious communities has sometimes in the past been explained purely and simply as a renunciation, as the removal of an impediment to the focus of mind and heart on God. The Constitution on the Church and the Decree on Religious of the Second Vatican Council gave a new twist to this renunciation when they called religious or consecrated life an evangelical sign and spoke of religious communities as signs of the kingdom of God or of the ethic and blessings of the Beatitudes, reminding them that they are followers of the Christ who became poor for others. Of priests too and of bishops the Council asked a life of evangelical poverty. This belongs in God's design so that the Church may be the Church of the Poor.

What was said in the clearest way by John XXIII is that the Church in its ministry must allow for a preferential option for the poor. This is inherent in God's salvific love and plan for the world, starting with his choice of Israel and with the position the poor were to have under the Mosaic Covenant. Jesus, especially in his discourse at Nazareth (Luke 4), and in his works, gave a key place in the work of redemption to the poor, the destitute, the sick, the troubled. This is how he fulfilled the messianic expectation of a ruler sent by God who would truly be father of the poor. Amongst these, the Council could place all those who are victimized by others, all who suffer from the injustice and discrimination of the social order.

Following up on this, the Popes, bishops and religious have devoted more effort in the last fifty years to "promoting the kingdom," to struggling for peace and justice, to serving not only the physical needs but the rights of the poor of this world, and that on an international level. The charity of all the faithful has likewise taken on new dimensions in this direction, with the formation of lay communities devoted to this purpose.

The Church of Christ ought to be a communion and a community in which the poor "feel at home." The poor are not to be simply objects of charity of ministers and faithful; they are one with all in being members of Christ; they are to be respected in their human and Christian dignity, and have as loud a voice in the life and work of the Church as anybody. The First Letter to the Corinthians gives inspiration in this regard, with Paul's attack on the practice of discrimination symbolized in eating and drinking at separate tables according to social status, even while daring to share together the Body and Blood of their communion in Christ.

It is most of all the Liberation Theology of Latin America that added another aspect to the nature of the Church as Church of the Poor.[4] It calls on all Christians everywhere to see that the community of disciples in the teaching of Christ is a place where the poor have a privileged voice. The Church is the Church of the Poor because they are its primary and most powerful members. The insight they have into the kingdom of the Beatitudes is found to be at the heart of giving flesh to the reign of God proclaimed by and in Christ. All those who wish to be one with them, even to serve them, have to learn from them the meaning of Christ and of the God of salvation. Liberation Theology itself is not the work of writers, professional theologians or bishops: it is the work of communities of poor Christians, discriminated against not just by individual persons but by the economic, social and political structures of society. The writers are the servants of these communities, those who have the ministry of articulating the biblical, liturgical, social and theological insights of the Church of the Poor.

This is hard for all of us to understand and to live. How some protest against such a vision of salvation and Church was illustrated for me by three incidents. At a meeting of theologians where the topic was the ministry of the Church to the poor, one participant demanded quite vehemently that this talk should stop. He deemed it impossible to "define poverty" so that we knew not of what we were talking. Someone responded, equally vehemently, that definitions aside, he knew very well who the poor were when he met them. On another occasion, when we were talking about poverty in class a student threw down his pen, exclaiming that the poor were no better than anyone else and had no special claims on God or on us. A third example of the difficulty of this way was given me one Christmas night after Midnight Mass. I was accosted by a member of the congregation who wished to teach me that Jesus had never been poor, either in his birth or in his life, since he was an artisan and son of an artisan. While refraining at the time from comment, I was reminded of how the medieval Franciscans were split over the dispute about whether Jesus and the twelve ever possessed anything or had only the usufruct of what the holy women and others gave them.

It is indeed a hard saying that the poor have a privileged and primary place in the Church and in the kingdom of God. What some suggest is that all Christians, beginning with those who profess "consecrated" life, need to learn the meaning of the Beatitudes by seeing how the poor live them out among themselves, since these are the ones for whom Jesus intended them in the first place. Much critical attention has been given to what Liberation theologians say about the poor organizing themselves in the effort to claim justice and change sinful structures. What can be missed is that this is the second step, for such work can be done only by those who live the life of God's kingdom among themselves. Living together in communion, those especially subject to life's difficulties show great respect for the personal dignity of each member and find concrete ways to support and love one another. They aid and assist as needed, in their own way living out the communion of goods and the care for "the widow and the orphan." They exemplify the manner of living and working together, practicing the virtues of meekness, patience, mercy, joy over life's blessings, consolation in life's sorrows, such as they are listed in Gal 5:22-23. They know what it is to be despised and persecuted and yet to keep hope in God alive, as well as hope in the life of Christ's grace given superabundantly (Rom 5:20) and transforming human conduct. They also know what it is to keep alive the hope of eternal life, that begins now but awaits completion. On the ground of this life of Gospel Beatitudes, which they know in a special way, they band together in action to change society. To live evangelical poverty, the Church must learn what this means from the poor, and thus what it is to be "where the future of the poor is decided."

This understanding of the Church as the Church of the Poor offers a different way of perceiving the presence of Christ through his Body across history and in civilizations. In the postsynodal exhortation on the Church in Europe, John Paul II is at pains to highlight the role that, through the Church (and, indeed, Churches, through a new emphasis on ecumenism), Christ has played in the history of Europe and its various peoples. Much that is positive in appreciation of the person, in efforts at reconciliation, in movements towards the bonding of peoples, is attributed to the work of Christ and to his presence. Whatever his intention, some discomfort with this optimistic view of the place of the Church and Gospel in history and culture is expressed by the Pope himself, when on other occasions he calls for the purification of memories, for the recognition of how the Church has camouflaged or dimmed the presence of Christ and the power of the Gospel. When it is put in writing, the history of the Church and its influence in society is all too often the history of popes, bishops and Christian princes. Some have called for a history that attends more to "ordinary folk," to the lives, devotions and communities of the baptized as they relate to a larger society. That may be the place to look to grasp how, and to what effect, faith and hope in Christ have remained alive, despite sin. The more authentic fidelity to the reign of God, to the beatitudes of this reign, to being the family of God, is perhaps to be found on the margins of history books. The mission of the Church as community of believers is to retrieve for Europe and other continents the story of the action of the Trinity through Word and Spirit in the lives of the poor of the ages. The attitudes, values and orientations to which they give evidence are what the new Europe and the new global community need in order to be authentic bearers of God's loving creation.

Bishops need to stand back; neither now nor in the past have they been the most faithful bearers of the Gospel but have to a great extent failed in their mission. From the long list of apologies which John Paul has issued over some years, we see where and in face of whom this Church has failed. If Christian faith, hope and love are to be inherent to human development, their history and present vitality must be found elsewhere. History is the making of memories, the rewriting of what is stored in mind from new perspectives, the inclusion in memory of those who were forgotten. The Gospel proclamation of the kingdom bids us attend more closely to how the poor have lived it. Bishops and priests have to lead by learning and by making room for other voices, all the way from religious education, through devotion and liturgy, to social involvement. Otherwise, to speak of the Church of the Poor is but to pin another label on the merchandise.

There have been several efforts at remembering what is necessary for a different history and a different hope. With the catastrophes of World War I showing how base was Enlightenment ambition, several Jewish thinkers recaptured their own Jewish heritage and the sufferings of their own people as a foundation for a new way of considering life and culture and a new way of looking towards the future. With the appalling events of Fascist persecution, this was taken up and carried on by others. They looked to the time of the common era to see how the messianic hopes of the Abrahamic and Davidic dynasties have continued to be lived out in times of peril and destruction.

It is almost trivializing to write of this in so few lines but the point is that Christian peoples may learn from this in retrieving their own heritage from within as it were, by looking to those whom they themselves have systemically forgotten. We have many examples of how feminist and womanist theologians have recaptured the stories of women and the origins of the Christian reality in the Jesus movement and the hope of the advent of the reign of God. This was a movement not only for the poor but of the poor. In renewing ourselves as Churches, we have to unearth the memories of two thousand years of how the poor have lived this hope, even when Churchmen had other ambitions. If God wishes to reveal the divine glory, if God wishes the divine Name to be unveiled, if God wishes to give hope to the world, the Church of the Poor is the preferential option of a *kenosis* that is completed in the glory of the freedom given by the risen Lord and the hovering Spirit.

As it so happens, the hope placed in the Church of the Poor coincides with the self-realization of the Churches of Africa, Asia, Latin America and Oceania, as well as those of minority groups in North America and Europe. These are Churches that have been poor from the beginning. This is so not only in the obvious sense that many of the people live through an inhuman material poverty but in the deeper sense that they have been dominated by external powers. Mission-sending Churches of Europe and North America played their part in a European neglect of human and cultural resources of peoples, for themselves and for their incarnation of the Gospel. Now that they are finding their own voice and their own way of living the discipleship of Christ, quite often embodied in base Christian communities, it is time for those of the North to listen and learn and let the center of communion shift to new places.

All the prophecies and all the imagery of messianic advent, and indeed of the *parousia*, link remembering and rewriting with preceding catastrophes, human and cosmic. In a fundamentalist interpretation, this can surely lead to compiling a Rapture Index and an effort to calculate the end of time by reading the signs. Ironically, alongside this there is talk of the end of history, when the American dream of worldwide democracy is realized and we can all live in an ideal state of things. This too can be ascribed to God by those who indulge in God-talk while harbouring such ambitions.

Over against such tendencies, it is possible to live by the hope of the advent of God's reign, of the way of justice and peace as preached by the Prophets or by Jesus Christ, by seeing that catastrophe and its resolution by divine intrusion are linked together over the whole course of human days. While we are heartened by the imagery and poetry of an ideal time when tears are wiped away, faith and hope in Jesus Christ and the Spirit are to be lived in what is present.

We are all too aware of catastrophe though many of us can be blind to the worst, such as the AIDS pandemic. What messianic judgment tells us is that failures in enlightened thinking have been mixed up in the causes of these disasters and that it has proved impossible, as Kofe Annan has pointed out, to bring nations together in an enlightened way to overcome them. There must, we say in Christian hope, be an advent of God that enables us to live through catastrophe in the desire to live by what the Gospel tells us of the blessings of the kingdom. This is not an easy formula. It is not easy even to discern the signs of such advent so as to plan accordingly. What is asked of us is to keep open the hope that God gives us a new vision, and that what is already taking place is a transformation of human community and of humanity's commerce with all the things of creation. We can hope for some more wondrous future on condition that we live now by the apocalyptic sting that injects our present.

When the focus is on institutions, the history of the Church has to be rewritten as a history of a constant struggle in the course of which the Gospel was not always best served or passed on. Theologically, we cannot avoid the question whether or not there was systemic failure in the ways in which church ministry was organized, so that failure may not be explained simply as the failure of certain persons. Failures and catastrophes have their human reasons and these are not to be neglected, but at bottom we are left with the question of the reasons and signs of our perversity. The advent of divine grace, the in-breaking of transience, can come only when we let the victims be our judges, the judges named by God. Philosophers and theologians, as well as artists, dramatists and poets, have to render their service in communion with the poor and the victims who suffer. While our focus is necessarily on the present, looking to the past forces us to include those whose memories have been erased. From that vantage point, some will point to moral breakdown, some will look to self-preference incarnate in discrimination, some will describe the betrayal of earth and its resources, some will meditate on the loss of the sense of beauty. All of this contributes to a new sense of history and a new hope. We are now, however, in a time under judgment. We do not know where the "original sin" resides. We must suffer awhile the coming judgment to let the Word speak and the Spirit breathe.

This is not to ennoble material destitution. It is quite un-Christian to decry action in behalf of justice or the effort to influence the processes of globalization in such a way as to affect the lives of the poor. Never may Christ's own Church renounce working with the poor as they work for their own economic and social liberation. Never may it cease to be a prophetic voice. The more disciples of Christ become present to the life of the poor in its worst forms, the more they remain at all times conscious of the terrible straits of poverty in which billions live, and the more they feel called to be where Christ would wish us to be. But will we be present according to the presence of Christ and his Spirit, in the ways of divine love, by assimilating the ways of power, the wealth of money, of investment, of the influence of a claim within power structures, or by being poor, in possessions and in economic or political influence, and also knowing ourselves poor in knowledge and in the power of speech?

This is the cutting edge of the vocation to be the Church of the Poor. It relates both to what is called the eschatological sign value of religious communities and to the mission of the Church to preach eternal life, already begun but to be perfected at the *parousia* by a gracious and consuming divine action. While Church and communities are by no means to ignore the lot of the poor nor to neglect action for justice, they are held in the long run to vision, to anticipation of the eternal life that Christ has promised and that only God can give, to the truth that in the present time we already live by that eternal life, but in hope.

This does not mean giving up on involvement with how the reign of God is among us nor on how to serve its advent. But it does mean living with the vision that life is totally a divine gift and that the future must come from God's bounty and irruption into our history. To live by and for eternal life does not mean possessing a clear view of paradise, or of the condition of individual persons after death and in the resurrection of the dead. But it does imply professing and acting out, embodying the belief that the life promised by God in the future, in what is after this life, is the ultimate conquest of death, the ultimate reality of creation and grace, and the ultimate gift that God gives—and that such a destiny leaves its mark and judgment on history. The more obscure and naked such faith, the more poor are we to be in its expression. We have nothing, not even our imagination, to tell us what God is to give or to help make it anything other than what God gives. Some victims of injustice and poverty, even when they strain to change life here on earth, show us what it means to see life lived now by the blessings of the kingdom as "eternal life," straining ultimately towards receiving the gift of communion in God forever.

To live evangelical poverty is to live by hope that rests in God alone. It means knowing that truth rests in sharing the eternal life of the Triune God in which living and dead already commune. It means testifying to what Johann Baptist Metz dubbed the "apocalyptic sting" of history. All human action is subject to divine judgment, a judgment represented in the vision of the coming of Christ. All human action, lived even by the commandment of love of God and neighbour, is insufficient, but a paltry thing: it is only but entirely by the gift of God, given in ways unexpected, that evil and death are overcome, that life prevails and prevails abundantly. Witnessing to the presence of the reign of God that is among us through the gift of the Word made flesh and the Spirit, witnessing to the quest for God's justice that commands our actions, and witnessing to the truth that only by God will the heavens and the earth be transformed, creates a tension in life and ministry. But one may say that it is a "creative tension."

Not only religious families but the Church itself are reminded that the call to witness in poverty is addressed to all who proclaim the Gospel and to all communities. Luke 9 is a missionary text, not one addressed to religious but to all who bring the good news of the kingdom to others. They are not to rely on human or material resources but on the power of the Word itself. They are to be able to recognize peace where it is to be found and to accept hospitality: it is in this manner that they can take up their presence among others. Alongside this, 2 Cor 8:9 asks all who witness to Christ to be poor as he was poor: to give of one's all, just as "he who was rich became poor" for humanity's salvation. In persecution too, as we find in several texts, it is in the weakness of the witness that the Spirit is strong. The words addressed to the rich man in Matthew 19 calling him to renounce all in order to follow Christ posit a condition of discipleship, the only way of knowing the hundredfold of belonging to the community of the kingdom.

A consultation on mission promoted by the Secretariat for Christian Unity on the occasion of the Sixth Assembly of the World Council of Churches in 1983 notes that actual poverty, and not simply poverty of spirit, needs to be one of the characteristics of a missionary Church. Both actual poverty and poverty of spirit, it notes, go together in the design of Jesus. Those who can enter into the task of witnessing to Jesus must be people who have nothing to hope for from the world and look to God for everything. Much may be done to them by the world, but despite this they bear no rancour and are wholly open to God. They are sent to bear witness to the way of acceptance and loving service of Jesus himself.[5]

Mission statements are not always as forthright as this on the call to poverty. Much is said about serving the poor and about solidarity with the poor. The insights of those who suffer poverty and of those who practice voluntary poverty are recognized. It is often acknowledged that the Churches have to give up much of their power and much of their wealth in the service of the poor and of God's reign. Churches, however, do not always go as far as affirming that their own corporate poverty is of the very essence of discipleship and a condition of mission.[6]

Poverty is often imposed by cultural and social situations and comes in many forms. In its present poverty, the Church now finds that it is deprived even of the power of language, as well as of a position in society. It seems to have no place of discourse. It no longer has the firm footing of the respect of the public and the strength of its manifold institutions. It finds itself where what is spoken is not germane and fears that what is said by appeal to the past may be untrue to the vibrancy of the Gospel. It ought to be fearful of misrepresenting the claims of the Gospel by hanging on to the prestige of position and the power of possessions. It risks accepting too easily what has been woven into systems of thought or into systems of Church organization, or working with assumptions about the exercise of power that relate more to a fabricated ideal of Christ's lordship than to the reality of his poverty.

A Special Invitation: Consenting to Be Poor

Those who are called by religious profession or by ministry to live evangelical poverty have to learn what it means by the testimony of the Church of the Poor. In their own weakened state and in confessing the failure to testify, the ordained can start to attend more fully to where true witness is given. This is possible by consenting to live in a new place, rather than to stress a new priestly dignity and power. Evangelical poverty in each age has taken on a configuration marked by the events and realities of a particular epoch, as with the foundation of monastic communities, mendicant orders and more recently founded missionary bodies. Today there is a new set of conditions imposing new kinds of demands. Awareness of failure, external circumstances and inner scandals make Churches weak before God and the world, with their reputation in tatters, yet called to live out their testimony and mission in faith.

Often enough we think of the commitment to live a life of poverty, whether on the part of bishop, religious or new lay communities, as something chosen. There are those who remind us of how much commitment of any sort is a matter of consenting to live under conditions not of one's own choosing. This is true of both persons and corporate beings. One has freedom to refuse these conditions or to accept to live openly and hopefully in the place in the world that is inevitable, and find there that the inspirations of the Spirit are to be lived. Like Christ himself, the Churches are invited today by the Spirit to testify to the God of love out of a position of powerlessness, not chosen but forced upon them. Are they truly able to consent to this and find the freedom of the Gospel there, or will they resort to various forms of compensation?

For the Church in this age, all across the world and most particularly where it has been long in existence, a key factor to its evangelical witness is the consent to the poverty which is not of its choice, a readiness to live through the *kenosis* to which it is subjected. In the social conditions of our era, hounded with accusations in plenty, with fewer in Sunday congregations, Churches are left in many respects quite powerless. The Catholic Church in some of our English-speaking countries is particularly weak, by reasons both of neglect and of sharp criticism, with little voice it would seem in shaping the future. In Ireland, where my roots remain despite long exile, this is quite striking and makes one wonder about the role of Christians in a country once poor and powerless, which is now a prosperous nation enjoying its role on the world stage of economic and political power, but with its many poor, and its new poor, still within its shores. Do we find our presence and our mission, and the power of Christ, in being weak? There is a ring of truth in a saying among the Irish that happiness is not terribly important and that what matters is to live by the truth, for all that it might be discomfiting. Is this the kingdom that the simple and the little ones of the earth, once pretensions are shed and the eye sharpened and set on edge, see beneath the aura? Is life then lived in the search to live more honestly in a realm where there is no adequate saying and where one falls back on unarticulated desire and "despairing" hope?

The Poverty of Discourse

This calls for consent to another factor in the life of the Church in our time: It shares the broader cultural reality of weakening discourse. Owning to solidarity with human debility, the poverty of discourse may become a prophetic voice about humanity's condition and God's love. This was brought home to me in a peculiar way through reading material given to me for a long transoceanic journey. What people bring aboard flights is always interesting and often seems to have a touch of the random about it, which might say something about our constant mobility. In any case, I was given a couple of small books that deal with the non-said and the non-written of human discourse and point to religion as a place where this needs to be taken seriously by those who navigate the seas of our contemporary world. They were quite short volumes intended to be popular, and both works were written by contemporary philosophers, both of whom have Catholic roots. Though quite different in tone, they have in common a desire to give witness in face of the apparent decline of religious systems. The authors are the American, John Caputo, and the Italian, Gianni Vattimo.

The work of Vattimo, entitled *Belief*,[7] is testimony to the foolishness of believing in Christ "despite everything," foolish, that is, in the sense of Paul writing of the Cross. The text of Caputo, entitled *On Religion*,[8] is the word of a philosopher whose métier is bound up with words, and who trembles in face of linguistic turns that call meaning into question and, in a particular way, the meaning of religion. Can a thinker even speak of God? Vattimo's call is for the Church to be true to the sign of the Cross, to the self-emptying of Christ, disabusing itself of illusions of grandeur and power, and learning anew what it is to embody love. Caputo wants the struggle of speaking to be respected, and posits a willingness to live with the slipperiness of saying and knowing the non-saying between the cracks without resorting to systems and firm foundations, whoever purports to provide them. But can one somehow live this poverty and slip into the cracks of language, and remain a bishop who is supposed to teach, or a professional theologian, or a philosopher, ironically with multiple publications (and royalties) to one's name?

Both works call for simplicity but leave to readers to spell out what that means in a complicated world where people simply cannot be expected to survive and live their lives without complexity. In any case, the issue is there for the Church and, in its particular way, for the theologian. Catholicism on the whole, at different levels, was too sure of possessing the truth, of knowing the right and the wrong, and ready to claim its rights, even in opposition to others. Nowadays, weak in the face of society, it is coming to know its internal weaknesses. There are moral faults and uncritical uses of power and money to be confessed. These point even more deeply to fragility in face of the divine. The Church has to live from its own incapacities to express the truth, either by doctrine or by comportment. In some kind of divine irony, does this make it and its members more fitting instruments of divine revelation and presence, given how God chose to make his presence evident?

What's the Difference?

The link between the poverty to which the Church is called as Body of Christ and the metaphor of *kenosis* lies in the way it expresses what the power of God at work through divine self-emptying through Word and Spirit, and how this fits the mission of the Church in our time.

We are used to hearing of sacrifice and pasch or passage. It may be useful to compare this with other ways of speaking. Of late, there is a recurring mention of divine *koinonia*, or communion, and of salvation as the gift that offers a share in this communion of persons. This gives strength to the image of *kenosis* and allows us to see the poverty of the Church as a way of living in communion with Christ in his self-gift for the world. As believers we are called to participate in the self-emptying of Christ and of God in order to have a part in their abundant riches. Does it make a difference whether one chooses to privilege the language of sacrifice, the language of Pasch or that of *kenosis* to sing the symphony of our communion in being?

The interplay between language and action offers some insights. How we speak makes a difference to what we do and what we do makes a difference to how we speak. Humans look for meaningful action and for meaning in their action. They look to poetry, painting, music and the like to express their insights, that is, to a heritage of language and cultural expression that has been passed on to them and in which they find the impulse to act. Most of all, they search for stories that underpin their own personal and common stories. These stories have a plot and employ images and types of linguistic expression that uncover the meaning of the plot. In times of change our manner of speech finds new power in old tales. Even the story of what we call history undergoes change when in times of disruption we look to a common past in search of ways to face the future. It is usually the need for action that throws out a challenge to the adequacy of the prevailing language.

In Oceania, it seems that the first settlers on the atolls and volcanic isles in the South Pacific arrived in pirogues, whose shape and sail allowed them to be carried along by wind and wave. Following the current, they mapped their progress by marking stellar constellations that they could find again. The ships went where led until by chance some island was discovered. The constellation of stars, however, made retracing the voyage possible but also allowed the navigators to situate themselves in making other journeys. Moving out on new ventures, they could allow themselves to be borne by a different wave or wind, but they could take their bearings by looking to the stars.

We are like that with the use of language. We follow movements and know that chance carries whole communities along through time. But in language and especially in story we trace a path that can be refollowed, retraced and retrieved. At times this does not work very effectively, so we do things to the stories, we work our collective memories to meet what is new in our existence. Polynesia provided an example of how peoples coming together learn to speak of themselves as a people. An oral tradition grew up among islanders, who had little contact with any other part of the world, in which they entertained memories of navigation from some faraway land mass. There was a harmony of ethnicity and culture whose origins could be recovered from their mythic history but whose living form they retained in the power of their boats to sail the seas. Considering this past, historians can speak of a "people" that shared past, vision, rites, practices and values. But the harmony of common life was disrupted by the arrival of outsiders, the meeting of variant cultures and the subsequent infractions of ethnicity. Does tradition with its capacity to innovate allow room to welcome this diversity? People there now add adjectives to the word "people" and speak of multicultural and interracial communities and more poetically may even talk of orchestrating or choreographing unity. Creative use of language allows those who live it both to find threads from the past and to map a vision that embodies the values that will hold communities together in search of a future.

In terms of seeing their place in the world and of being faithful to their mission Christians look to their inheritance of faith when they wish to discern the appropriate action and way of life that the time demands. They often gather the challenges facing them in the world of today into two categories. One covers what we see as the vast and terrible injustice and violence that holds the human race in thrall. Is their any inspiration in our God-talk to harmonize an effective action? The second refers to the vaguely dubbed process of secularisation, which speaks to both the elimination of certain ways of talking about God that in effect failed, and an increasing reliance on human ingenuity with its potential to build a future. When this was first noted in theology in the sixties it was seen as a liberation, for it rid us of the God of the gaps, of notions of a rather whimsically interventionist God. It may, however, be necessary to attend even more to the need to purify speech, since those who think and act as though might were right do a lot of God-talk, at times quite fundamentalist in character. Nothing seems to prevent some American leaders from invoking God even while claiming the right to dominate the future of global reality by virtue of military and economic power. They are quite adept at adapting Bible stories to this vision of their chosen people. When, however, we let ourselves be truly inspired by the law and the prophets and by the New Testament teachings of Jesus, we find that God-talk embodies another way of talking about power, justice and human community. We have to look for a language that inspires another vision, an alternate globalization, where ideals of service, peace and justice may prevail and where divine power features as quite OTHER.

Parsing the Language of God's Power

When Jesus sent forth his disciples, he gave them the *exousia* (translated as authority or power), which he himself had received from the Father. This was to preach the forgiveness of sins, to exercise the compassion of God in exorcism and healing, and to testify to the advent of God's reign. Ever since then, Church communities have tried their hand at defining this authority and power in ways suited to their mission.

While theories are always put forward, it is the liturgy which most often gives us living ways of talking and singing of God's power as it is revealed in Christ and in the Church. Liturgy has always attempted to be a proclamation of divine power and a stripping of self in order to receive God's Word and Spirit in love and in truth. With the weakness of discourse acting upon it, at liturgy today the Church needs to be aware of the poverty of language itself. It is ironically in the poverty of language that communal worship across the centuries has looked for words and images that express the truth of the manner in which God remakes the world by divine power, and by divine power alone.

The literary and popular heritage of faith expression includes a multitude of stories and a variety of ways of presenting what is key, that is, the story of Jesus, his ministry, his life, his death, and his resurrection, as this provides insight into the mystery the Church lives and its own self-understanding. Diverse images offer the possibility of being open to the gift that God gives and to the way in which the gift is given. Thus we hear speak of Pasch, sacrifice and divine abasement, all of these with profound implications for the life of the Church and its mission. These, however, are "showings." They are not theories, though they have often being theorized, which makes them problematic.

It is always a mistake to view any liturgy, any liturgical tradition, any set of stories and metaphors as self-contained and complete, adequate on their own to express the mystery of the divine condescension. An Irish poet has called language "a habitable grief."[9] It aspires to wholeness, it wishes to express the deep down truth of things, to take in all reality, yet always fails. But it brings a passion born of the effort, a yearning, whatever partial vision of the whole it gives, into the everyday and ordinary. It is enough to hold us together however tenuously and to heal wounds, but it leaves scars that may at any time tear open. Liturgical language is like that: it keeps wonder, trust, a sense of communion alive but it leaves us in grief, wounded, scarred, at risk of tearing apart. Heeding it, using it as best or as badly as we can, we are godlike indeed but not quite God-centred, not fully possessed by Word and Spirit, not fully obedient to their vitality.

Whatever tradition we worship in, there is always another tongue, another set of stories, another galaxy of metaphors, another image of the divine, that we do not command or even understand, outside of which we dwell. In some attempt to overcome this grief we inhabit, we try to attend to a number of ways of imaging God's power, try to see what best expresses for us and for our age a sense of being possessed by this power, wondering what language can offer us tenuous dwelling and hold us together.

It is as to a habitable grief that we turn to the images of sacrifice, of Pasch, of *kenosis*. The language of sacrifice has ever been given a place in religious traditions, as it still is. It has, however, been used differently from one age to another. Used in Paul and in early Christian literature to express the obedience and homage of the Son and the spilling of his blood to free humankind from the dominion of sin and death, it was later absorbed into a thinking too closely based on ideals of human justice. On the other hand, this sacrificial language was quite successful at suggesting an alternate way to an emerging system of justice when it was encompassed within the language of mercy. Thomas Aquinas could speak of an order of mercy, established in Christ's name that supplied an alternate to the developing ideals of human justice in his time, based on distribution and keeping order through meting out.[10]

Rather unhappily, however, the word was associated with notions of making compensation for sin and reordering a justice in which God receives the honor and glory that sin took away. There has been some evolution in this thinking today. Even with the insistence that the sacrifice of Christ and of the Church is a sacrifice in the proper sense of the word, the image is now related to an appreciation of the gift given and of the exchange effected. The sacrifice of Christ, of which the Church keeps eucharistic memorial, is the obedience unto death which is the Son's gift to the Father and their common gift to humanity.[11]

The language of Pasch has a very long Christian history and has been given a more recent coinage in a Christian liturgy more attentive to early spiritual and liturgical history. It has a double importance. One is to accentuate the suffering of Christ and the redemption given through his blood, typified in the Paschal Lamb. The other lies in the power of the image of passage or crossing over to express the extent of the change effected. Through the sacraments, believers pass through the gift of the Spirit into a new life, which can be likened to the passage of Jesus Christ himself through death to life. Against the background of the Exodus, it is also used, as in the theology of liberation, to arouse hope for a liberation from slavery in whatever form it is suffered.

Picking up on the language of *kenosis* and calling for a renewal of the ways of following Christ in evangelical poverty, we have a set of images that addresses more directly the notion and operation of power, at least in the face of the ways in which society conceives of power. To what kind of power, quite distinct from common human ideals, may we look to give direction to how the Church lives and evangelizes in this age of vast human suffering and in response to the human aspiration to live as a community of peoples? From the strength and hope of faith we are looking for more just ways whereby human peoples may live together in creative peace. Christ's self-emptying is the way chosen by God to reveal his love and his promise and it is the way the Church is invited to follow in communion with him.

Some members of our Christian Churches are persuaded that good liturgical renewal is at the foundation of all renewal in life and mission. This does not mean simply greater devotion and piety, though I trust it would mean that too, but the retrieval of a story that speaks to us of God and humanity, and of a language that leads to and climaxes in doxology. In taking liturgy as memorial, they look at the components of ritual, narrative and doxology and find that these constitute a fundamental response to the challenges of injustice and secularism. It is how we talk of God, Christ and Spirit that is at stake, and the presence of this triunity in history. It is then within that constellation that an empowerment of the language of divine self-disempowering may be the star that guides us as a Christian people as we speak not only to ourselves but to all. It is to listen in poverty for the impact of the liturgical key of divine *kenosis* that gives the Church its own being in the world.

Conclusion: Witness to the Truth of a Poor and Unworldly God

When Jesus prayed for his own before he went about his death, he prayed that they might be one, as he and the Father are one (John 17): One in communion, in the world and before the world, though not of the world. When the communion of Father, Word and Spirit took on visible forms, it was done in a worldly powerlessness and self-denial, an abjuration of power. The Church is sacrament of this communion; its communion is its part in the divine communion. The Church is called to be Christ's Body, to be, as contemporary theology has it, a living sacrament of Christ, a sign thus of the living and loving presence of God. If it is to be the manifestation and servant of such a Master, if it is to live by the alliance that God has made and remade with humanity, the Church has three options in this age of the declining power of the Gospel.

One is to try to be a strong Church again, reinforcing the sacred, making authoritative declarations on theological, liturgical and moral questions, defying the "culture of death" with the "culture of life"—always of course defined through authoritative statements! The claim to power in this is clear.

A second option is to serve the poor above all, to be with the poor in their struggle for justice and the basics of life, to be prophetic in declarations on war and peace, on immigration, on the rights of peoples to freedom. As the OMI Constitutions have it, to be "where the future of the poor is decided," which means using our not inconsiderable portfolio with discretion and finding a place in boardrooms and international organizations around the world to serve the interests of those who suffer discrimination, perhaps even of the earth itself when it is subjected in slavery to the one who sins.

The third option for the Church, the harder road to travel, is to be poor itself. This last option means first of all to recognize something that is too often avoided, namely, the Church's weakness. The Church today is weak, at least in part from its not inconsiderable failures of the past, and also from the lack of credibility given to its ministers and the word that it has to proclaim. Christians have to appear before the world as beggars, as people who claim no worldly authority, who recognize their weakness, their sins and their poverty, and are even ready to carry the opprobrium and the sins of others, as Jesus did. It also means to be poor in literal ways—"possessing nothing." We, for we are all Church, ought claim no other power than love and service. This means a discreet presence and careful listening to God's presence among the poor, the destitute, the alienated, the illegal alien, the refugee, the unhoused, the lines outside the dole office. It is a presence better expressed by the quiet of an unassuming neighbourhood, with people meeting around kitchen tables, not in board rooms. Which is, of course, what base Christian communities often do, with or without the succour of the ordained, whom they are glad to have but do not necessarily find necessary.

Most radically, this means living for eternal life, the life that God alone gives. Whatever efforts we make in the name of the Gospel to live in justice, with concern for the poor, with love and respect for the ground on which we dwell and the rivers and oceans in which the earth bathes, in the end life and a life with God is totally gratuitous. The truly poor live in the expectation of God's advent and God's time, in the expectation of an everlasting life that we cannot even imagine, of which only the love of God is the measure beyond measure. It is of this expectation that the Church must preach and itself be a sign and a witness. It is the vocation of religious communities, whether contemplative or active, to be living reminders of this nature of the Body of Christ.

It is within living by this third option, being present as poor before the world, that the truth of the first and second options may be retrieved. If the Church speaks with authority, this can only be the authority of Christ, the insight derived from knowing Christ in his *kenosis*. If it is to be where the future of the poor is worked out, this will be by being poor itself alongside them, or more truly in recognizing the privileged way in which they themselves embody the Church and humanity's aspirations. It is among them that the communion of the Son with the Father, and in turn with the world, is richly revealed.

Which means that the active have to learn to be at root contemplative.

The Church of Christ Sent Forth and Emptied Out in Spirit

The theology of the Church is a continuation of a Christology that weaves together the sending of the Son and the sending of the Spirit, through whom God is made known as Saviour, Creator, Love itself. Indeed, without a theology of Church there is no complete Christology and no adequate theology of the divine missions. It is in the Church, Christ's Body in the Spirit, in its life and its mission, that the triune and creator God makes tangible a divine presence, so that a reflection on the Church leads us to contemplate the mystery of God. If it is in the *kenosis* of the Son that the mystery of the Trinity is made manifest, so, too, the Church, his Body, must live by this divine self-emptying. It is in this context that we see the implications of communion with Jesus Christ through evangelical poverty and the forms that this may take.

In Phil 3:10-11, Paul, who has proclaimed the self-emptying of Christ and his death through obedience, calls on the members of the Church to become like Christ in his death, so that they may attain the resurrection of the dead. Taking the *kenosis* of Christ as the mystery to be shared by faith and as exemplary for his Body, the Church must be configured to his three-fold self-abasement in order to be a sign of unity and instrument of salvation, showing forth the love and the mercy of God for the world. The Church is to take on the finitude of human existence in the embrace of its own weakness, but with and for suffering humanity, especially its weakest members, being itself weak and sinful. It is to empty itself of claims to power and glory before the powers of the world in order to show the face of the Son and of the Father, and the true power of the Spirit. It is to enter death for others, to die to what is limited in its own being in order to embrace reality more fully. This applies especially to structure and forms of power that have to be renounced in order to let God's power show forth. It is odd that Church authority and Church faithful want to see Christ represented in a show of a power analogous to worldly power, instead of in lowliness like unto his.

Further reflection on this ecclesial mystery leads one along several paths. First, it may be said that the Jubilee Year challenge to purify memories is an invitation to self-emptying, to laying aside claims we once thought justified. Second, much of what we sensately think about the Church is conjured up in key figures, persons who in different ways embody an answer to the call to follow the wisdom of the Cross. Third, in the call to this kind of poverty we gain insight into what it is for the Church to live the beatitudes of the kingdom of God by the life of the Spirit and to more fully recognize the place of its weaker members.

Purifying Memories

Since Christian Churches claim to live from the Gospel and to speak God's name to the world, when their witness is flawed they betray and even falsify this name. Today Christian communities have no way of seeing themselves as God's People or as the Body of Christ and the Church of the Poor if they do not partake of the purification of memories that John Paul II associated with the Jubilee Year of 2000 C.E. [1] It is possible to talk in the glorified terms of a text like Col 1:15ff. and to see the Church as the embodiment of God's holiness and the immaculate Bride of Christ. As a body, however, and even as Christ's Body, in which he shows himself forth as mercy-laden Saviour, this corporate reality is sinful and ever in need of conversion. The exercise of the purification of memories may help it to understand better why it can be called, even in its sinfulness, the sacrament of salvation.

A Conciliar Key

The term has a nice ring in theology books and papal documents, but it is hard to digest, and tastes sour in the belly even if it is sweet on the tongue. We are, however, given a key to the process of reviewing memories in some lines of the Second Vatican Council. There are two vitally important texts among its documents, which represent the underpinning of much else that is good and opportune in its teaching. One is the document on revelation, which invites us to see revelation not as a series of truths spoken by hierarchy but as a living encounter and communion with the God revealed in the Word made flesh and in the gift of the Spirit. To have persisted for so long in making truth a matter of a submissive intellect has done harm to the Church, to its faithful, to other Christians. The Council's teaching on revelation shows up ideologies of the past, which were all too often an abuse of authority, sins of thought that need purification.

The other vital text is chapter two of the Constitution on the Church,[2] which lays out a vision of the Church as the people of God, all the baptized faithful called to be the living presence and living sign of God's vitality, for all nations to see. There are tensions within the Constitution as a whole but this chapter, the truly inspired chapter of conciliar deliberations, is quite clear on the fact that the hierarchical organization of the Church is servant of the reality of the people of the baptised, of the royal priesthood of God's holy people. In the face of this liberating news, many of us will well remember learning in theology lectures that the Church is a hierarchical society and that bishops and priests are given apostolic powers over the laity. This was not only a definition; it was what the Church actually lived. There was no harm meant, but much harm done. Are we yet in quiet possession of the truth of the vision proposed by the Council? Maybe that is not possible without the corporate confession of bad thoughts of the past. From such points, faith in the Church as body of Christ emerges.

The Catechism of Memories

Today one sometimes hears regrets that the Catholic people have lost much of their institutional memory, as though that explained things like not going to confession, not saying the Rosary, not getting married in Church, and the like. What is really needed is due confession of sin and request for forgiveness by all, particularly on the part of bishops and clergy. In a proper practice of solidarity in sin and repentance, we carry the sins of those who went before us and the sins of others, and for that we join in faith with Christ and ask him to take us on his shoulders. That is what Christ's redemption is all about. We also have to get beyond the point of blaming individuals who sinned and recognize the corporate and institutional character of the sin. The Church was badly organized, its canons and approved practices were sometimes harmful instead of salutary. Understanding that is the true sense of practicing the purification of memories.

Naturally, the memories evoked when reading these texts are great memories, large events, and deeds that moved history to dastardly actions, or on southern continents were an obstacle to evangelisation. But for little people, to grasp the significance of recalling the past with penitence do we not begin somewhere else, with smaller memories that need purification, of things done to us or of things that we did? Things that in their great smallness bring home to us how much in its day-to-day doings the Church needs purifying. These are memories that would not have existed were it not for what the larger memories evoke, but which give them concrete form.

I can think of a number of things that touched the lives of Catholics very closely and that require the purification of memories, but will give just one example. It has to do with how social division and discrimination were built into the way in which the Church was administered and organized. When I was a boy in a Dublin suburb, the parish Church opened two doors to its parishioners on Sunday morning, one at the main entrance and one halfway up the side of the building. Entering by the main door, the congregant paid two pennies to the usher but could not go beyond the locked railing halfway up the Church. Entering by the side door, where one found oneself ahead of these midway railings, the congregant paid sixpence and thus knelt closer to the altar and came to the mouth of the sanctuary for communion. Families, if they came as a body, got entrance into the sixpenny lot for one shilling, a reduced rate for praying as a family. People were seated by social distinction in a parody of the heavenly banquet, except that there was no inviting those who took the lower places to come up higher. For communion in the Lord's body (the blood being reserved to priests), the priest came down the Church, never the tuppenny congregant up. Those who did not want to be associated with the lower classes chose to enter by the narrow gate, joining the social elite of the parish. Has any bishop or parish priest ever thought about purifying the memories of those who as children were initiated as Catholics through such social distinctions or apologizing to the parishioners banished with their tuppence to the back of the Church?

From such realities as this, we may be able to get a feel for the extensive catalogue of requests for pardon made by Pope John Paul II, before, during and after the Jubilee Year of 2000. There is no need to revisit each item here. Suffice to say that the list shows a clear acceptance of the weakness and wrong-headedness of the Church on many past occasions, as well as a sense of whom and what the Church offended against. Some redress is needed for the Church truly to renew itself and become the sign for the world it is intended to be. The fact that there is no clear acknowledgment of how much the ecclesiastical structures need to change to serve God and Church may cause us to wonder how incomplete the confession has hitherto been, despite its undoubted magnificence.

The people of Israel, we recall, recognized often that they had not lived by Yahweh's covenant with them, that the order of things, with peace as its first sacrifice, fell asunder when they lived by another justice, and in such circumstances they repented. They looked into their memories and saw the past anew, and even recast their stories of Yahweh under a new light. The Church called of Christ seems so assured of its place in the divine scheme that it is slower to acknowledge its corporate faults or to see anything faulty in its order and governance. But maybe we are getting around to it. Entering a new millennium, and pressed by serious public scandal, its members are asked to purify memories, and the whole institution must perforce do likewise, with consequences as yet unforeseen.

There are those who have difficulties with the style or the content of such confession and apology. How can we purify memories without first admitting that we have them? They are collective memories about which, each and all, we are asked to acknowledge our solidarity in sin, in violence, in the suffering and humiliations our people have endured, in our place in the circles of hell. Is there not to be a telling of tales, lest we forget? If we decry the reduction of whole peoples to poverty, if we decry the exploitation of African by European, of Chinese by Japanese, then of African by African, of Chinese by Chinese, of those ready to exploit the need of any race, do we not delve into the part of missionary activity played in the ruination of cultures?

When requests for pardon for past sins and faults are joined with a nice doctrinal distinction between a sinful Church (never!) and its sinful members (those absurd enough to commit sins or make mistakes within an indefectible and indefatigable Church), one is left to wonder what is precisely being said. Does the distinction mean that the Church is primarily those who do not make mistakes (especially its bishops) but who have to put up with those who do (even some bishops), or does it mean some separation between the Church and its members? Or does it mean some platonically ideal Church that exists above the fray? We need to admit to ourselves that it is the Church in its totality, in its life, its doctrines, its catechisms, its witness and structures, that is invited to purification, to a remembering and a healing of memories.

Stretching Mind and Imagination

We might learn collectively how to approach questions of ministry, authority and sacrament by taking note of what is happening in other areas of Church life and by learning to rethink ingrained positions. For example, I think of how we have come to formulate the mission of the Church in the world as both proclamation and service of God's Reign. The Catholic Church has moved through various formulations of the adage "outside the Church no salvation" and some of its past actions in this regard must find their place among the memories needing purification. What may be less noted is how we as a Church are reading the Scriptures and using scriptural resources in taking a faith-inspired slant on the Church's mission. The image of the Reign of God has in fact enabled us to get away from an identification of Church and Reign, and is now used as an image that evokes God's saving action in worldly activities that promote justice and peace, in cultural heritages from the past, inclusive of their religious dimension, and in other religions whose present-day adherence is legion.

This is an excellent example of how meaning is perceived only if we find the poetry in the text and the possibilities it opens up by imaging for us a way of being and acting. The image of God's reign is not found anywhere in either Testament precisely as it is now used in theology and by the magisterium. Nonetheless, the trajectory of poetic license and creative employment makes of it a symbol that allows us in historical memory to appropriate new perspectives on God's loving action. This historical memory has to take into account a sense of the non-continuity of events, of the disruption of linear development in history. Theologically, we would say that in discerning the signs of the times as evidenced in events and cultural upheavals, God addresses the Church through both Word and Spirit. The Word is remembered and proclaimed and the Spirit moves the Churches to creative remembrance and the foretaste of what is promised, provided we allow it to unsettle some deep-seated persuasions.

Embodying Divine Power

Many, if not all, the memories that exact purification have to do with the Church's presumptions on God's power and providence, and so with the structuring of its governance and missionary endeavours to reflect the power of God. When we think of some of the things that were done in the name of this hierarchy or sacred power, there is no doubt that memories need purification and the confession of fault. The moral standing of individuals needs not be questioned to see how the structuring of power stifled spirits. It was a matter of wanting power to get things done, even to get the Gospel preached or defended, and hence of attributing a power to God that the Church could then claim for itself. This hovers rather close to sin against the Holy Spirit.

But does not Christ take flesh and his part in history, stripped of glory, even through a Church "mistaking" but always called to take stock of these mistakes and reverse its positions? The mystery of the incarnation of Word and Son is not about one single person. It is about the Christ who lived for God as Father, the one from whom he was sent in the midst of a people, who took on a dwelling among his disciples, who were called to walk the long road of fidelity in faith. The being flesh of Jesus in his lifetime was a being in communication with others in the flesh, in his labouring and suffering, learning from his people and then doing spiritual combat with them over the things he had learned. So is the way of his being Lord in his Church through all history: God and love revealed through a chequered human history, that of the Church itself in its presence among the children of the earth—in the world, but only inasmuch as it lives of the Spirit and of Christ, not of the world, yet often falling back on the ways of the world in its claim to power and presence.

The children of Israel, when they looked back and saw their sins and errant ways, their deflections from the law of love of God and neighbour, saw that salvation was always at hand; the reign of justice was always desired and proclaimed, so that they truly grasped what it is to say that God is Lord of history. In face of the reality lived, God was known to them as the one who sustains a people, whatever happens, in their love of justice, a justice not found by them but given to them.

This people,[3] however, have now sustained the Holocaust, passed through and most often died in Auschwitz, giving us a history of victims, the memory of the unnamed, a blotting out from history that is not accounted for by their sins. And yet they hold to the name of God. They were faithful to God even when they had occasion to doubt God's fidelity to them. Relating religious tradition to historical reality, we can say that God was present otherwise: present in the camps, among victims and sinners. This is another way of being God, harder even to grasp than his being *Lord* of history: Not lord but victim. This too belongs to the memory with which the Church is charged.

Structure and the exercise of authority are sustained by ideas that we hold on to and that we need to empty out. To be poor, becoming poor, through the purification of memories, means, in humility and knowing our mistakes, rethinking how we present fundamental teachings of the scriptures, in word and deed. The penitent going to confession is asked to confess what she has done "in thought, deed and word." For all the penchant to confess having had bad thoughts (confessed even if not consented to, "just in case") among its members, the Church as a body seems quite reluctant to confess the bad thoughts that lie beneath the excess of its power and the misarrangement of its structures and community life. Even if not consented to, or not realized as wrong at the time, ideologies that shut up, abused power, stifled and hurt people with their divisions need to be confessed, memories purified of the harm they have done.

Of Traffic Accidents on the Road of Tradition

In making the transition from one way of being Church to another, not all move at the same pace or with the same vision. Hence there is considerable conflict, some of which we do not understand. I have seen it suggested by a sociologist that traffic accidents are in part the result of a clash of cultures, of two visions of the road surface that have not been reconciled. This phenomenon is a good symbol for talking about the difficulties the Church is experiencing in getting its leaders and members to adjust at parallel rates to its new situation in society.

Failure to build a bridge between people living two eras of a culture simultaneously is quite tragically borne out in traffic accidents in Tahiti. There are those who like to test their new motorcycles or motorcars at high speed, passing other cars, cyclists and pedestrians or trying to glide over the road bumps made to slow them down. Pedestrians or cyclists simultaneously spread themselves across the road as they would have done when the lifestyle was more rural and there were few motor vehicles. Taking the road was an occasion for social encounter or for getting places without undue pressure. The young in their flying machines, though, see the roadway differently and the results are terrible. They themselves, of course, carry a conflict of culture within themselves, for often even though they drive they still imbibe and smoke by the patterns of another age. Old ways of looking at death, however, seem to be alive among even the young in the fatalism with which such deaths and injuries are accepted. Death was coming anyway, it is inevitable, it is the will of God. The whole people have not accommodated themselves to new situations, and, what is worse, they see these in an irreconcilable manner. Traffic accidents are unhappily real but they are only a symptom of greater difficulties and clashes in negotiating change.

This sort of thing seems to be happening in the Catholic Church in the United States. To take one example, recriminations and offenses in the field of sexual abuse are met with the effort to bolster an older vision of the priesthood and relations between clergy and people, even though bishops make apologies. A clash between what is called a clerical culture and a culture that is more lay-centred has emerged. The laity derives its viewpoints from the vision of the Church as the people of God, with laity quite rightly playing a bigger role, not just in the sense of doing more but even in the sense of their role in decision making and in mapping out the future. The response to the crisis is not always a good mediation between these two perspectives but often a re-enforcement of a clerical view of priesthood, with emphasis on the distinction between the two states and the direct and divine nature of a call to priesthood.

We might get closer to the clash of paradigms or mentalities by using the distinction made popular by Walter Brueggemann between royal consciousness and prophetic consciousness in the evolution of a body such as the people of Israel or the Christian Church. The distinction comes from the era of the Davidic dynasty in Israel when kings and their followers had become satisfied with the status quo and tried to enhance their own power among their own people and in the face of other nations. They failed thus to understand new situations or how they needed to change. Prophets like Jeremiah went unheard or were even subjected to persecution for calling established ways of doing things into question. These prophets for their part could read what was going on, could see Israel's structural and spiritual failures that lay behind unjust behavior and its weakness as a Covenant people. The royal dynasty mistook the role of Israel among the nations to the extent that they were concerned more with power structures and the exercise of power than with the justice of the Covenant, or divine justice.

In the life of the Church today, if resort is had to the reaffirmation of established ways of thinking, seeing and doing, renewal as a prophetic people will not come about. Ministries and ways of being community emerge in obedience to charism and prophetic vision. They have to be heeded so that structures and modes of governing can change in the service of the Church's mission in the world and of its reality as the Church of the Poor. If the Church deals with the lack of entrance to ordained ministry by a new enforcement of a clerical culture, or by images of priesthood and hierarchy that bear the brand mark of Tridentine, it can hardly be deemed very open to the workings of the Spirit outside the frame.

Prophetic consciousness is said to be integral to the role of those called to what is now dubbed the consecrated life, a title that may itself be a way of compromising charisms if that term is tied into the notion of official recognition as foundation. Whether the prophetic voice comes from religious institutes of one sort or another or whether it comes from others, it can be effective only if accompanied by personal and corporate commitment to evangelical poverty. This is not to be confused with possessing all in common but is to be a real witness of being poor and being the Church of the Poor. Common possession may require asceticism on the part of individual members, but it can also be an excuse for the institute or community to keep considerable holdings that make it quite wealthy and give it a voice in the corporate world, euphemistically named "where the future of the poor is decided." This may do good, but it is not a response to the prophetic call to practice evangelical poverty. Traffic accidents occur in religious institutes on the basis of different ways of seeing evangelical poverty. As for the Church as a communion, divergence in the understanding of its mission to be as Christ's Church the Church of the Poor means quite a few upsets on the highways and byways.

The Church of Divine Holiness

The call to seek corporate pardon for a corporate past gives rise to a theology of the Church as a Church of sinners. It is paradoxical but it is within a body of the sinful, even a sinful body, that the holiness of the Church as called by God stands out. I think rather irreverently of a scene in a Bunuel film, *The Discrete Charm of the Bourgeoisie*. A murderer approaches a bishop, asking for confession and absolution. In the course of the confession the bishop discovers that this is the man who killed the bishop's own parents, whose murderer had never been discovered. He makes the sign of the Cross over the penitent, invoking divine forgiveness. Then he adds, "God forgives you, I do not," and shoots the man with a gun that lies conveniently at hand. There it is: the Church with divine mercy at hand, mediating it to others, but never up to the task of living by it itself, and at times choosing whatever else is at hand.

At the same time John Paul asked for indulgence through a purification of memories in his Jubilee Bull of the year 2000,[4] he evoked the remembrance that despite all the sins of past and present the history of the Church is a history of holiness, given through Christ and the Spirit and lived by many in testimony to God's grace. This might be read as nothing more than promoting the veneration of saints and ideal saintliness. In fact, it can offer a concrete way of doing a theology of Church by reflecting on how people have lived by the mystery made known in Christ. Those figures of history whom we deem significant tell us much about who we are. In them, we find the embodiment of a call to holiness, a witness to divine justice that the Church is called upon to give in our time.

When it presented the universal call to holiness of all the baptized, the conciliar Constitution on the Church reminded us that if we are called saints, it is because we have been chosen by God and made an elect people. Concretely, on the issue of what makes the Church a true witness to God's holiness, we think about persons who represent this holiness. Though not always of the present, these persons and the tales told of them (and at times even the image of them) address what is at odds, what is odd, and what is oddly hopeful about the times in which we live. Perhaps this is an integration of hagiography into a theology of Church.

In invoking the holiness of the Church, with its convocation of saints in calendar and litanies, I resort to what is called today a hermeneutics of suspicion. The popular devotion by which some persons were originally invoked as saints, and the later history of official canonisations, often betray special interests. What is portrayed as holiness has much to do with how the people or the official Church see their patrons or with what they want at a given time. The preface for saints in the Roman liturgy claims to find in those who are commemorated exemplars of holiness, as well as encouragement to press on in the following of Christ. This is an exemplary sentiment, but there are times when the saint in question does not bear too much scrutiny. Having guided some studies in hagiography, I know that the appeal is not simply to facts of history, and that to some extent the saint "is made up" by making use of the right kind of source material and accepted paradigms. When I was a seminary student, we were told that it was a matter of dispute among theologians whether canonisation of saints fell under the object of ecclesial infallibility. At times, I have found the negative opinion on the matter a consoling teaching.

Nonetheless, in the devotion to saints, in liturgical feast and in hagiography, the Church conjures up for itself what it sees as the call to holiness. We all participate more or less in this exercise, and when there are divergent ideas about this call and the response to it, people reveal their own prayerful ideals in those whom they particularly choose to remember and honor. Although readers might make other selections, as a kind of ecclesiology I evoke five voices and see five images from the past. They seem to beg for a place in our midst, speaking wonders about the charity of God that might touch hearts and spring revolutions at this beginning of a millennium. These are the figures of Francis of Assisi, John Wesley, Charles de Foucauld, Thérèse of Lisieux, and Helder Camera. The cameos given below are not biography but an indication of how I see their significance for the present. This is not because they made no mistakes, since in hindsight they might seem to have made quite a few, but because they took every challenge and tried to live in God's love through the issues and dilemmas they faced with others of their time. These are the kind of people of whom Stanislas Breton in his book *The Word and the Cross* likes to speak of as the Fools of Christ. Humanly speaking they are among the lowly. They are without power, or are deprived of power, yet they have done much more to present the God of Jesus Christ before the world than those who have exercised temporal or religious authority.

Francis

Remembering Francis borders easily on the romantic, and to avoid this it is necessary to remembering him sleeping in ditches at the Carcere outside Assisi and tearing down with his own hands a church that some of his devout followers wanted to erect to God's glory. Their intentions were proper, but they made the mistake of wanting it to be "their" Church, and in the face of such behaviour Francis was quite rough with his followers, as indeed he had been with his own father, who as far as his son was concerned was too fond of money. But poor he was, and a lover of the poor and of the creatures of the earth. And most of all he was a lover of Christ, and communion with him was the great desire of Francis's life. Seeing Francis transfigured even in his flesh into Christ, walking among the people, speaking of God's love and mercy, kissing lepers, talking to wolves, many thought to see the beginning of a new age in the story of the world. He was, along with his harsh side, capable of great affection. He could show Brother Leo a tender love in which the exchange between divine love and human love makes an incredible mixture: and so, he wrote to this brother, who wanted to come on a visit, if simply your heart makes you wish to see me, come. You do not need to look for other, more practical, reasons, is the implication.

In his lifetime, there was a great flow from a small beginning, but on Francis's part there was also a great disappointment, a great sense of having lost in the end what he had wanted to build. His spoliation, when stretched naked on the naked earth, was complete. He was even despoiled of the movement that took on his name.

In Francis's heart, along with his love for Christ, there was love for the poor. Some, such as the leper, are commonplace in hagiography. Historical fact points more to those newly poor, or poorer, as a new economy emerges, a merchant economy where one grabbed for oneself what there was for grabbing. It had its good side, a distribution of wealth and an acquisition of liberty by people who were not of good blood lines. People, lands, beasts, the possibilities of wealth, did not simply get apportioned to those born into them or those who could acquire them by the sword. But such upheavals carry new forms and threats of poverty, and Francis was resolutely on the side of the poor, which he could not be without being poor. His followers were not to be found among those who availed themselves of the new possibilities to gain possessions. To own nothing at that time was not simply to be without. It was to say no to what the changes in society made possible so that in this kind of self-privation, indeed community-privation, Christ might be more visible and his place in the turmoil of the times evident. Though Francis does not always steer clear of shopkeepers and popes and sultans and ladies bountiful with land to give away, his own chosen place on the earth was unmistakably the ditch at the Carcere or the cave on Mount Alverno or the pathways on which he begged for bread with his companions.

We are told the story of the chat Francis had along the road with Brother Leo about perfect happiness, a story that is an inspiration on the full meaning of evangelical poverty.[5] Seeking to know what constitutes perfect joy or happiness, and thinking at first that it would be in the success of converting and winning people to Christ, Leo is told by Francis that it is to suffer all kinds of bodily privations and then to be scorned and rejected even by one's own brothers. Then one is truly happy because one is totally one with Christ and with Christ's poor, and knows one's own human and even spiritual nothingness.

John Wesley

When recent Church teachings talk of how Christian Churches can meet through recalling what they have in common, they mention the mutual recognition of saints from different communions.[6] The struggle for mutual respect between the Evangelical and Catholic Churches on the island of Tahiti reminds me of this truth that Churches need their commonly remembered saints or holy people on the road we take together to Christian Unity. Happily among Catholics there is now a growing remembrance of the extraordinary work done in bringing the Gospel to Polynesian peoples by the London Missionary Society. This can only increase if it is the remembrance of God's work, even as we purify memories of our conflicts, that is to guide us.

John Wesley is one of those holy persons or saints of God whose remembrance makes the ecumenical enterprise sensible and imperative. Considering his life, his works and the Methodist tradition that originates with him, one sees why ecumenism must mean the reconciliation of Churches and the respect for diversity of traditions. He inspires a reading of the history of Church and movements within the Church, with all their glory and their agony, as a "history of salvation" lived under the guidance of the Word and the Spirit. In his ministry, and the consequences that he bore in faith, we see how difficult it is to make reforms within established traditions and ecclesiastical frameworks, as we also see a movement of faith that at times exacts that one step outside such frameworks for the good of sinners and the glory of God.

The content of Wesley's preaching is a return to sources, to the genuine Word of God, and a piety and zeal rooted in a firm faith in Jesus Christ, as well as a belief in the guidance of the Spirit. This is the kind of "conversion from within" that ecumenical instructions from Geneva or Rome tell us is imperative to the reconciliation of Churches, and these are the factors that more and more guide the commitment to ecumenism and mark whatever steps Christian bodies will take into the future. A reading of the life and works of Wesley brings us to a saint much needed in the quest for Christian Unity.

He also lets us see what is ordinary and what is extraordinary in the exercise of ministry. One must say to would-be prophets, do not try it unless you are as holy as Wesley, but his life amply illustrates that not all ministry is ordinary. Extraordinary circumstances bring a special call from God and ask for an exercise of preaching and pastoral care, and even sacramental ministry, that is outside the ordinary. Wesley found himself obliged to "obey God rather than men." He and others saw the fruits of what he was doing and this obliged him in God's eyes to continue, despite the remonstrances of higher authorities. This caused him much pain, but he could say firmly, "God being my helper, I will obey Him still, and if I suffer for it, His will be done."

Within the Catholic Church, we know well that in this century several who gave their lives to fostering Christian Unity suffered for it, even at the hands of the Church. Such were Yves Congar, Paul Couturier and Lambert Beauduin, to name only an outstanding few. Vatican II, in listing what it found in other Churches and communities, mentioned "martyrs," those who died for faith in Christ. We can also as Catholics look to other traditions, to pastors and doctors and women and men who were ministers of mercy, who show what it is to testify to Christ and to God's Word, at times even prophetically "against" the Churches.

Thérèse of Lisieux

Catching up with Thérèse's travelling relics as well as living on the island of Tahiti may have made me sentimental, but there is much more to devotion to her than this. While I was in Polynesia in 2002 the relics arrived there, greeted with much enthusiasm and much prayerful devotion. Earlier, when I was in Ireland in July 2001, I witnessed the visit of these same relics. It is estimated that two-thirds of the population of the country made their way into their presence, not usually with a lot of loud noise but for a quiet visit, perhaps an intimate conversation with the young girl who had lived such a short life, died a hard death, and got herself in the aftermath much talked about because she was indiscreet enough to have left a journal behind.

What did these visitors find? And who were they? For now the talk of Ireland, of the Celtic Tiger, of the European orphan made good, has not ceased to be the marvel of the hour. Much visible change has come. The hovels and slums are dwindling in number. Even where living conditions leave much to be desired, the children out on the street do not have the hungry faces and the torn pants that older generations remember from their hurried walks through Gardner Street or the Liberties. And the suburbs, as well as the farmhouses, show an affluence that some decades ago would have been hard to imagine.

As part of the picture, there are signs of greed and certainly of insouciance about religious practice. Boys do not doff their caps passing churches and priests, people do not stop in their gardens, at their tea-tables or on O'Connell Street to recite the Angelus at the sound of the mid-day and six o'clock bell. On Sunday mornings the near emptiness of the churches is striking, even while the cars along the road, off to the seaside or out to the country, are bumper-to-bumper. The Church and religion, the nun and the bishop, have lost their well-grooved place in the social and cultural fabric. No regrets, but a big change.

Does this mean the end of faith? The visits to the relics of Thérèse seem to have been neither simple curiosity nor the revival of religious practice. The summer of 2001 did not bring any bigger crowds to Sunday Mass, nor get more cohabiting couples to get their marriages fixed. So what did the people go out to see? They went to see somebody who said that she had found her vocation of love at the heart of the Church and lived this out in considerable pain, but also with considerable interest in others and common sense. Maybe she was the sign that the kingdom still belongs to the poor and meek of the earth, even in a time of newfound affluence. While very patient with her sisters of the flesh and her sisters in the conventual life, Thérèse looked outside the walls to those with whom in love she lived in communion. One thinks of the condemned murderer she followed to the guillotine with her prayers and of the missionary in Canada with whom she corresponded about his work to bring the Gospel to those outside the boundaries of that part of the world where modernity was getting a foothold. One also remembers the mark in her geography book around the Pacific island of Wallis, representing for her the most distant islands where the Gospel was still to be preached. Is there a tug in all of this on the Irish heart, as its people ruminate on the choice in the human decision between Boston and Berlin?[7] What are to be the choices about the future of the world? For whom do we care in the long run? Thérèse puts the question and points to the answer.

Charles de Foucauld

Some recent biography has called the openness of Charles de Foucauld to non-Christians into question and sees him as a collaborator with colonialism. If he strikes me as a kind of living paradox, this may be because his memory appears as a type of the future. He is a hermit who through his very real but somewhat compromised withdrawal managed to be very present in a harsh land among people of two races, the Berbers and the French. He inspired a movement that led women and men committed to the life of the evangelical counsels to live not in withdrawal, but "*au coeur des masses.*" He is a believer who is Christian among believers who are Other, and a colonial who does not colonize. Charles has significance for those who find interreligious dialogue both necessary and imperative. He lived with respect among Islamic believers. While still probably too much tied to French perspectives and the ascendancy of European culture, he stood up for the rights of those subjected to foreign occupation, denied a spot of their own on the world scene. It is always through an initial openness to others that we manage in time to overcome the limitations of what we had once imagined superior. He died absurdly, not even in a way that could be called martyrdom. He made no converts. He witnessed intensely to Christ and to the Father's love for peoples of all religions and to the presence of the Spirit among the downtrodden.

Helder Camera

Though I ran across him in passing on other occasions, my one very real memory of Helder Camera is of eating breakfast with him in the room off the Church in Recife which served as both sacristy and bishop's residence. Besides a desk overloaded with papers, there were a table and a few chairs, a wardrobe in which to hang clothes, a hammock in which to sleep, a small cupboard for victuals, and a primitive stove on which to cook the few things needed to survive.

What else did he need to live? Well, the door, of course, on which people might knock. In the course of the simple breakfast shared with him and another priest, and at which I talked Italian, my friend spoke Portuguese and Helder a mix of both, it was odd to see this champion of liberation theology rise to hand out money, food and advice to those who came knocking.

He was, it seems, a bishop twice converted in the course of a single episcopacy. The first conversion was from being a good episcopal administrator to being a pastor of the poor, from being a just man to being a man fired by the desire for justice, persuaded of the people's power to be their own Church, their own providers, their own advocates. The second was the conversion that enabled this advocate of justice and social reform to see the face of the Other at the door, those who always get left out, even from base Christian communities and advocacy groups. Work with the first and love the second seems to have been a kind of rule of thumb for this bishop, for some today a saint and for others a scandal. That is the most Christlike thing about him. He was also a leader who treasured friendships and who suffered much when his enemies made his friends suffer because they were his friends.

Together these five examples remind us what it is to be the Church of the Poor and to embody Christ's holiness. It is to live a real poverty among the poor as the age demands, it is to discover in the simplicity of one's life what it is to love as Christ loved, it is to be open to the promptings of the Spirit to new ways of ministry, it is to open the heart to the other, it is to devote oneself heart and soul to be converted to the service of God's kingdom.

Outside the Calendar of the Named

Those five apart, among my images of those addicted to Christ, despite a questioned relation with the Church, there is a young man, of no name and significance at all except to his sorrowing mother and father and siblings, who, dying of leukemia, said yes to suffering because the Law of God forbade suicide, even to the dying. He could tell me that the most important passage in the New Testament is when John assures us that it is not we who have loved or chosen God, but that it is God who has first loved us—and given us his Son. He pronounced this message at the moment when I was about to give him the Son in Eucharistic communion, a fairly rare ritual for him but a communion intensely lived in the suffering that both he and his Saviour assumed.

There is indeed a host of ordinary folk whom one remembers, persons encountered here and there in the course of a lifetime, who witness to Christ and the Spirit. I remember a woman of the Orthodox Church, married to a Catholic, who gave an excellent preparation for First Communion to her son but embraced the pain of exclusion from the eucharistic table on the day foreseen, though I believe that the pastor was ready to cut the edges. I recall a young man, aged fourteen, *and a half* as he insisted, who was preparing for first confession and communion with children much younger than himself. Telling me that his parents, nominally Catholic, had shown no interest in religious traditions, he emphasised that at fourteen *and a half* he was old enough to make his own decisions. I am also mindful of the university professor who spent her Saturdays at a soup kitchen, handing out food and washing dishes. In memory's eye, there are quite a few professionals and artisans who with their families gave several years of volunteer service among the poorer peoples of the world, of whom I think when I hear the expression "artisans of justice and peace." Paul would have had no problem in addressing such as "saints of God."

Living by the Spirit

Reflecting on both the purification of memories and the holiness of the Church through its communion with the Pasch of Christ, we gain insight into the mystery of the Church as Christ's Body and into the mystery of divine *kenosis*. It is by the gift of the Spirit, God's own divine self embracing it, that the Church lives and loves and communes with Christ. Some contemporary theologians have written of a *kenosis* of the Spirit[8] within the life of the Church: for all the love and power that the Spirit receives from the Father, its presence and action is contained and retained within a Church that is still weak and sinful, as well as often persecuted and laid low. There is here it is said a theophany, a glory, a revelation of the Spirit through self-emptying that is akin to the glory of the Son shown forth in the weakness and abasement of the judgment brought against him and of his death. It is in the spirit of the beatitudes, in the testimony of the weak which is akin to the testimony of Christ against the powers in his obedience unto death, that the Spirit is at work in the world and in human history. The *kenosis* of the Spirit is that its consuming power, its power to transfigure the world and the cosmos, is held back until the end of time, even though it is already operative in as much as the foretaste of God's glory in the world is made manifest in sacramental celebration and in witnesses to the coming of the Lord.

Because he continues to be among the children of the earth through the Spirit, one can also speak of the Son's own abasement through his identification with the Church. He is present in the world in the time between resurrection and final coming in that communion of faith that is his Body. This continues the mystery of the incarnation: the glory of the Word given in the weakness of human flesh and in the passage of that flesh through death to life. Rather than taking scandal from the sinfulness of a Church proclaimed holy in the Apostles' Creed, we need to see that it belongs to the mystery of divine love that it takes body in this weak vessel. The struggle with evil takes place first within the body of the Church itself, under the action of the Spirit and in the memorial of the Pasch, the *kenosis* of the Son in the flesh.

The weakness is not only the weakness of members, as though the Church remained pure while its members sometimes sinned, even grievously. It is weakness embodied even in the institutions and the orders necessary to its existence as Christ's Church as a communion of faith. It is only when the Church admits to its need to repent and to reform as a body, as a body holy but sinful in its whole being, that it can truly partake of the self-emptying of him of whom it keeps memorial. Only by engaging in this internal struggle and passing beyond it in witness and action against the evil rampant in the world does the Church embody divine *kenosis*.

Despite being a sinful Church, the Body of Christ is yet one with Christ and free in his Spirit, with a Name for God in a troubled world. It is a Church that strives to live by the law of the Spirit rather than by the law of the flesh. What then is it to live and love by the law of the Spirit?

Though one might well begin with Paul or with Martin Luther's commentaries, it is of Aquinas that we will speak. In Thomas Aquinas's treatise on Law (*Summa Theologiae* 1a 2ae, qq. 99-108), he made an interesting contrast between human law, the law of Sinai, and the law of Christ, which is the law of the beatitudes. Under the first, which will always be necessary, humans try to organize society and enact a penal system as well as legislation for the common good. In the second, prescriptions tell us how to act, and we learn to fear rejection, damnation, being outside the pale, deserving of God's anger. This can be salutary but all too often those who live by such religion fail to notice Sinai's twin foundational precepts of love of God and neighbour. The Christian Church has often found it helpful to recall the decalogue in order to guide conduct, to give people signposts on their journey through life, with the promise of a more benevolent future, but it knows that this is not enough. Under the third law, therefore, there are those who profess Christ as Lord and live the law of the inner Spirit, of the freedom found in Christ, of the urge and instinct to love, needing few prescriptions to keep them on the way, because the Spirit dwells in their hearts and urges then to seek the good; in other words, in the Spirit *caritas Christi urget nos*.

There is an odd victory of Christ over the observance of the first two laws, not nullifying them but making them out of date in many of their details and giving those commands still to be kept a new orientation. As a small boy, during the trimmings of the Rosary I used sometimes to kneel with my brothers and sisters as we listened to our Mother recite what was called The Thirty Days' Prayer. This was a prayer deemed useful, if recited thirty consecutive days, when one was in need of really important things, such as improvement in health or getting children through important state examinations. The prayer was addressed to the Virgin Mary, but in fact it was rather a long meditation on the mysteries of Christ, from annunciation to ascension and enthronement. One sentence intrigued me, namely the affirmation that forty days after Easter Christ ascended on high, "leading captivity captive." The phrase was pure King James and Douai Bible and is not found in exactly these terms in any contemporary translations of Eph 4:8. My request for an explanation was met with the rejoinder to say the prayer and stop asking questions. Still, the sonorous phrase intrigued me and sometimes I joke that the urge to grasp its meaning was one of the things that pushed me into a theological career.

Now of course that I am more erudite, I know that the image is drawn from the victory parades of returning generals who rode into the city with the more important hostages of the vanquished army chained to their chariots. But Christ outdid all these, leading as captive that which makes people captive. All that subjects humankind to a reign of sin and a reign of suffering is tied as vanquished to the chariot wheels of Christ ascending as Lord into heaven, to the right hand of the Father. So if captivity is captive, those who profess Jesus as Lord are free. They suffer and die, they are within the circles of hell, but in their choosing and their loving and their service to others, they are divinely free. The one who lives by the Spirit of God simply loves. Being free, choices do not impose themselves against the grain: in face of the face of the other, one simply loves, and knowing what to do flows from that. Discernment consists in being sure that it is truly the voice of the Spirit that speaks, the instinct of the Spirit that urges, and not some more carnal, however sublimated it may be, desire of self-love.

From these thoughts spurred by reading Thomas, I turn to the New Testament itself. John in his Gospel tells us that in baptism we are reborn of water and the Spirit (John 3:5). But none can receive this good news or receive life from the waters who does not profess faith in the one "to be lifted up," who does not know the difference between the temple built with hands and the temple that is the Word of God made flesh. Paul in Romans (and Galatians) contrasts the one who lives by the Law and so knows nothing but sin with the one who lives by the freedom of the Spirit, as a child of God in Christ, baptized into the death of Christ, and knows all the fruits of the Spirit, and has even the power to discern between spirits.

The reading of Paul or John unfortunately can give rise in Christian hearts to prejudices against Jews; the history of Christian complicity in anti-Semitism is horrible. Therefore, I also have to turn to the scriptures of the first alliance and to the way in which Jews live by this alliance down to our own day. The Vatican Council made some initial attempts to find the place of the Jewish people and Judaism in the mystery of salvation and of the Church. This was improved upon later in the 1985 statement of the Commission of the Holy See on Relations between the Catholic Church and Judaism. In light of this it is quite striking that books on the theology of the Church still say little of the significance of Judaism in probing this reality and mystery.

Awakened by Jewish writers such as Elie Wiesel and Primo Levi, and by the Christian theologians Johann Baptist Metz and Jürgen Moltmann, I know that a place to begin in opening minds and hearts to Judaism is the remembrance of the Shoah—both the need to remember what this says and the purification of memories it imposes. The latter tells us that we got it wrong, the former that in God's naming of himself there is meaning in what happened to this people, including fidelity even in persecution, and in memory of the horror lived out by many.

The Catholic Church has reminded its own members of the common spiritual patrimony that includes the memory of the patriarchs, the Covenant made through Moses, the eschatological and messianic vision of the prophets, and the promises given. It also reminds us that it is in the design of God that this people retains its unique character and its significance for the nations. Making all this part of our vision of history, part of our Christian spirituality, and integrating it into preaching and catechesis is an augury for the future rather than as something that is truly part of us as Church.

The Spirit Who Testifies to Our "s"pirit

The subtitle uses the word spirit twice, once in capitals and once without. Reflection on the mission of the Holy Spirit and its wedding with the human spirit finds an incomparable starting-point in the reading of Romans 8 and Galatians 5, but these chapters fit into a larger picture.

Let us begin on the day of Pentecost, with Acts 2. Full of fire, Peter tells the people of Jesus of Nazareth, raised from the dead, reminding them what the prophet Joel had proclaimed in the messianic promise of the outpouring of God's Spirit. Through this Spirit what Peter had to offer was the impossible dream, the healing of the division of tongues marked with the sign of Babel. In the light of the Second Vatican Council's focus on the image of the People of God, to which it gave priority over the image of a hierarchical society, the flow of the Spirit that makes young and old dream and sing and dance and shout forth their witness is quite appropriate.

Liturgically what the Church has constantly evoked in tandem with this outpouring is the image of God's Spirit passing over the waters in the creative act of God. The Spirit is now in travail over the sin against creation, its enslavement through the abandonment of the rules of Kyoto. But its reconciling power is imbedded in the dust of creation, at the very beginning when the hostile force of Satan caused *chaosmos* (credits to James Joyce) to take over from cosmos, but was never quite able to make the world revert to chaos, since the Lord of Alliance and liberation is the one to be named the Lord of Creation.

When we look out over the world in all its suffering, as Paul tells us, the Spirit groans within us, teaching what it is we ought to pray. It is in the Spirit that we proclaim "Jesus is Lord," from the depths of our human experience and the travail of creation, it is the Spirit who drives out fear, above all of God the Lawmaker and Judge. The Spirit raises up our mortal bodies to make them like unto Christ's, perhaps like him bearing the wounds of our earthly existence for all eternity—though Paul reminds us that it is quite foolish to ask what they are going to look like, even while indulging the desire to play poetic games that are not going to be taken *ad litteram*. There is no Church without such travail and such beliefs and hopes, since we do affirm the communion of saints and the resurrection of all flesh. The Spirit, however, is not only given to sustain hope for the future, but works now among God's people for a new order in the universe, giving the charisms that serve memory and that also serve unity, charity and testimony. It is the Spirit who allows us to keep memorial, who lifts up and sanctifies creation in our worship, who filters our laws through the filter of compassion so as to make them instruments of love and mercy, and who makes us attentive to the whisperings of other peoples, churches and religions.

Conclusion

For the Church to live out its call to poverty and *kenosis*, at the heart of the matter is the need to purify memories. In our critical and parlous times we suffer the negation of memories and the fear of remembering the unbearable. As Christians we define liturgy as *anamnesis* or memorial, made up of words proclaimed, ritual acts and traditions, and we encourage prayer in families. Our children need traditions, but in trying to assure this we come up against the insubstantiality of our memories and feelings of dislocation. Disruption of memory is forced upon us even as the task of telling the story to the world, of grappling with memories is imperative. It is not done by rote or definition. Passing on is an act of passing on the faith of a generation, interpreting what Christ means to us and who God is for a generation that follows, in the midst of what we may feel as havoc. Faith may be more naked, stripped down, but it lives by *kenosis*. The weak must indeed truly confound the strong as we cling to the one crucified outside the camp.

6

*Fidelity to Mission
in the Service of God's Reign*

——————————————— ⚜ ———————————————

It was not only traffic accidents that I saw in Tahiti. Amongst other things, a stint there has been conducive to thoughts about the Church's mission, with its good news but also with its failures and divisions. Tahiti is a place where one is brought up against the ambiguities of the story of the preaching of the Gospel, even to the farthest limits of the earth or the most distant islands. As a stranger, living here for less than three years, past and present are hard enough to take in, and it is improper to judge. Still, as I have come to know it, it is a story of intense poignancy, because of what was and what has come to be, and because that reflects in microscopic fashion a more universal experience of Church.

On the 5th of March each year, the people celebrate the Arrival of the Gospel, an event fixed on the European calendar as 1797. On that day, a boat came to harbour after a long journey from England, carrying about thirty men, women and children, members of the newly formed London Missionary Society. British adventurers, admirals and generals had taken possession of new territories, including these Pacific islands, and the missionaries wanted to bring both Gospel and the fruits of European culture and technique. There was also the auspicious reconciliation of warring groups through the witness given by Pomaré to the reconciling power of Christ's sacrifice. Yet, twenty-five years or so after Christ had come as the Living Word, with the transition from British to French control, French missionaries arrived and with them the introduction of a Catholic brand of Christianity alongside the Protestant. From then on Christian bodies were at odds with each other, the Body of Christ itself divided.

Animosity between Catholic and Protestant was bolstered by animosity between British and French. Christ has scarcely arrived among the people before he is divided, between the Christ present in the proclamation of the Word and the Christ present in the Blessed Sacrament. A small island atoll with five hundred inhabitants is divided into two communities. The people are won from their plurality of Gods to live the divided Christ. The scandal of Christian division takes on distressing meaning. The oddity of the situation moreover is that in the atolls it is hard to see the Catholic community as a eucharistic community in the proper sense, for all the devotion to the reserved sacrament. Left alone, the people practice their devotions and may see a priest a few times a year, for confessions and Mass.

In the process of the invasion of Europeans and the preaching of the Gospel, island life and island culture were absorbed into the dominant of English and French accents, with the French winning out, giving the archipelagos their present time of overseas territories. There was the usual underground resistance of unchanging attitudes and the positive retention of a religious outlook that proved compatible with believing in Christ. Unfortunately, the issue of the inculturation of the Gospel, the taking root of the Gospel in culture and the enriching of culture by the Gospel, is marked yesterday and today by the rivalry of cultures and the rivalry between Churches.

What can respect for a past religious culture still mean, provided it is known from what remains of it? In Tahiti one would need the local language to reach deeply into people's lives. The precarious footing on the island, the sweep of the ocean towards an unknown horizon, seem to be accompanied by the precarious hold of the Gospel in soil that still needs ploughing. Local authorities worry about secularization and the outlook of youth, but it is not possible to understand this unless it is clearer what is being laicised. Speaking as one less wise, there is an impression that it is not so much Christianity as an older cycle of traditions of birth, marriage and death, of relations to ancestors and to what is called the *fenua*, the home place where all the members of a large family, living and dead, are one. Even worry about secularization may require a more humble attitude on the part of Church pastors, a sense of their own weakness when it comes to an adequate grasp of peoples' beliefs, outlooks and traditions.

Being a Missionary Church

In what sense can we talk of the mission of the Church in the light of *kenosis*, as the embodiment of the mission of Word and Spirit from the Father? To be missionary means to be sent, and in the Spirit the Church is sent to speak of Christ to all people and all peoples and to tell what has been revealed of the Triune God and its presence in history and the world. When Christian communities live together in this faith, it is not only persons but the whole community that is sent, that is urged to witness. Being sent among others with such extraordinary news, one can do a lot of talking and even condemning, or one can do a lot of listening and conversing.

Gradually, from Vatican II to the dawn of the millennium, the Catholic Church, with a number of other Churches who have followed their own path in this direction, has learned to express its mission and its presence, and indeed its hope of things unseen, in terms of *dialogue*. The term is not without its ambiguities in the ways in which it is used, but at least it always bespeaks attention to the other and attention to the other's otherness.

A number of things marked the heightened consciousness of Christians that we associate either with the World Council of Churches [1] or with the Second Vatican Council, but they did not always easily coalesce. We learned to talk of the presence of the Church in the world, sharing the desires of others for justice and unity among peoples, races, cultures and societies. Different Churches learned likewise how important it was to act and talk with respect for other Churches, for great religions and for traditional religions. We became penitent about the imposition of Eurocentred culture on peoples of other cultures and so adopted a language of inculturation of the Gospel, or of the encounter of the Gospel with cultures. We moved from respect for religions because of their authentic values to a global dialogue concerned with their vision of all of reality, and even with John Paul II in *Redemptoris Missio*, we learned to speak of the action of the Holy Spirit in all religions, both the great ones and those of Africa and Oceania. Church leaders, theologians, pastors, and the "ordinary folk" are still trying to work out how all these elements may coalesce and what language needs to be used for the mission of the Church to proclaim Christ within such a mix.

The Second Vatican Council and after it John Paul stretched the use of the image of the Kingdom of God to speak to this situation. In chapter two of *Lumen Gentium* the Council took the kingdom to mean that divine action that is already at work in the world, in the Church but also in places outside the Church, looking forward to a consummation when all things are made one in Christ. John Paul takes this further in seeing in the kingdom a divine action that has to do with the unity of the human race, as the divine destiny wishes to bring it to fulfillment through God's gracious action. For him the action is present in many ways and in many places, equivalent with all effort to bring about the good, to have love and peace and justice to prevail over sin and evil, in whatever form it appears. Thus the kingdom touches all domains of human life and society. While always being faithful in proclaiming Jesus Christ and the mystery of divine love made manifest in his Pasch and his *kenosis*, the Church is, beyond this, at the service of all divine grace and human aspiration encompassed under the name of the Kingdom of God. While this stretches Jesus's use of the metaphor almost to breaking point, it also happily breaks up the Church's presumptions about itself being the kingdom. In relating to humanity's efforts towards the good and in bowing before its service to the action of divine rule in all its forms and places, the Church undergoes another self-emptying, a renunciation of claims even to the point of dying to its own history in order to take on life as a servant. Only with such an attitude, in such humility, can it engage in the multiple dialogue to which it now aspires.

The first thing to do, out of initial respect for those with whom we talk or act, is to express what our core belief is, what it says to us of God and of his way of showing humanity a divine love, in the sending of Word and Spirit, in the Son, Jesus Christ, who is anointed by the Spirit. It is by such faith that Christians, when true Christians, live, and it is this very love, implanted in their hearts, that commands their dealings with all and sundry. As John Paul II has said, the Church must refrain from imposing obligations and must respect human freedom in the face of present life and eternal destiny, but ought to be able to give a joyful account of the faith that is embodied in the Pasch or in the *kenosis* of Christ. Let others know the hope that is within us.

It requires an extraordinary openness to the presence and action of God in the world, in peoples, in cultures and traditions. If we are motivated by faith in the salvific action of Father, Son and Spirit everywhere, then there must be a lot for us to learn about God. The Churches say rather readily that they accept all that is not alien to faith and the divine, but they must be open to what they find rather than judging it in advance. Instead of starting by saying that the Gospel brings something and purifies cultures, and finds what can be accepted, we might do better to say that because we do firmly believe in God's action and presence we come to learn about it from what we hear and see. We then discern and dialogue, in action, prayer, encounter, so as to relearn and reformulate our faith by this wondrous exchange.

It is not only in the encounter of greats that most light is shed on what this means. Christianity and Hinduism, Christianity and Buddhism, Christianity and societies and governments, European culture and African culture, American culture and Asian culture, encounter one another, and indeed to great profit. However, there can be a tendency in such encounters to see things at a higher level, to deal with organisms, with ritual practices, and to adopt what can be called a wholistic view of things. This does not always make it clear how divine and ecclesial *kenosis* are at work in lived experience and how this affects towns, villages, families and rural dwellers. Looking at smaller entities, at the microscopic, brings more to light. There is special importance in the new Vatican interest in what it calls traditional religions,[2] whether African, North American, Asian or Oceanic. There is much to be learned from them about the interaction of religion and culture, of the permeation of culture with the religious, as well as of what happens when this connection disintegrates. It may also be there that we see the Spirit at work among the weak things of the world, the full extent of a lowly divine presence in the world and in its traditions, and that God shows the divine self to us along the way of weakness.

The Prelude of Eschatology

All of this talk of the reign of God and the Church's service to it shows clearly that to any vision of the Church's Mission, eschatology is prelude. This is a somewhat weak link in the theology of the Church put forward by the Second Vatican Council. In the chapter of the Constitution on the Church that deals with eschatology, the talk is mostly of living in the hope of eternal life and of communion between heaven and earth. These are important elements, but not the whole story. They give us little account of history and only feeble insight into how to measure time. There is still a hint of the mentality that despises the things of earth so as to treasure the things of heaven.

Eschatological vision of the world and of the Church's mission is grounded in the memorial of Christ's Pasch.[3] Seeing in this the advent of the fullness of time, Christians know that it is the reference point for all true knowledge of God's loving and saving presence in human history. We do not see the action of Pasch and Spirit moving forward developmentally nor even organically. We learn to live rather by the distinction between *chronos* and *kairos*, between the effort to write chronologies and the openness of heart to unexpected irruptions of divine love that alter the course of events if they are received. The tough question then is how we measure history as the time of God's presence through Son and Spirit, through Word and Love. For believers, the time that the calendar says is *anno domini* is a new time, a time seen differently, days that can be told as history because memories are enlightened by the light of Christ and by the knowledge that through *kenosis* we come to life.

The Pasch of Christ as an event in history is not the closure of time, nor simply a new era in time, but a new vision of all our days, of how in the gift of the Spirit we pass through death to life. This is the measure of how we view history and of our hope for the future, not so much of the Church as of a humanity that is moved by the impulse to unity. When the mission to the world of Son and Spirit, of Word and Love, is made bright in the light of Christ's Pasch, we come to know that creation is the work of the divine Trinity and human history the place of their continued presence and action. It is however, in the poor, in those who hunger, in the weak, in the peacemaker, in those who suffer persecution for justice's sake, that this presence is made known.

The symbol of God's reign then interprets history. It says that God is graceful and guides humanity towards a goal of unity and communion. It is the transcendent being and coming of the holy that will gather everything into itself. The symbol is a key for Christians in talking of God's covenant with Israel and of other religions because it pinpoints the importance of finality, of goal, of hope, even while seeing a holy presence in history. It is for Christians to speak in dialogue of what in Christ and the Spirit they have come to know, sure that God's covenant of love with them asks of them to do this.

If we are to take part in this effort to build human community, to serve the reign of God in communion with the action of Word and Spirit, we also have to take stock of what the witness at the core of mission needs to be. Turning back to the eschatological vision of the early Church is helpful. Nowadays, there is a certain emphasis put on the notion that early communities, Paul, even Jesus himself were mistaken in their ideas about the imminence of the end of time. It may be true that they were inclined to think in shorter terms than those of millennia, but this does not corrode what they have to say about the way to live in hope and fidelity.

Historical criticism has employed considerable skill in trying to put back together the actual sayings of Jesus about the end-time. Putting such studies to the side, it is of interest to see how the Gospel of Mark in chapter 13 presents the eschatological, or apocalyptic, discourse of Jesus. Its introduction is a kind of interruption of the story Mark is telling about Jesus himself, and is placed at the end of his ministry and before the Passion narrative. As we know, Mark presents Jesus as the Son of Man and connects his need to suffer and die with this title. He truly wishes his readers to grasp that as God's messenger Jesus had to be betrayed, persecuted, executed, though he was to rise up again. It seems that his audience, who were disciples of Jesus, were disturbed by what had taken place since the resurrection, by their own continued suffering and persecution and an apparent failure of the preaching of the Gospel. It is to give them a slant on the Passion of Jesus that will hold and strengthen them that Mark gives the discourse about end times at this point of the Gospel, the burden of which is that Jesus's disciples are to continue to give their witness before the world.

The words attributed to Jesus cover a wide range of events. He begins by alluding to wars and natural disasters, to the persecutions of his followers and to the advent of false messiahs to disturb their inner peace. But he goes on to affirm and foretell the coming of the Son of Man in judgment and in glory. The Son of Man who is destined to die at the hands of others is the same one who will come at the end of time. The end of time and the time between Resurrection and Coming have to be seen in the light of the Passion. Those who persevere in trial, in disappointment, in the disturbance of their faith, will be gathered among the elect when the reign of God preached by Jesus, the reign that in Mark is marked by forgiveness of sin and reconciliation, reaches its completion. All things will be judged in light of fidelity in witness. One might sum up this discourse—in a way very pertinent to our own times of doubt and trouble—by saying that Mark's counsel is: Continue to witness, do not be drawn from your course by what you suffer or by what does not happen. All is in God's hands, and our witness is but tributary to the witness of Christ. God is present in history, taking human suffering unto himself, in the witness of the Cross and in that promise of the eschaton which includes judgment between good and evil, victory of life over death.

Church in the World

Witness to the love and salvation of God given in Christ and dialogue with others together define the mission of the Church in the world, but dialogue is possible only on the basis of witness. What recent Church teaching has brought to the fore is that witness has to include belief in God's loving action in all the affairs of the world and that it has to entail a respect and an openness to others to which Christians have not long been wont, whether among themselves or with respect to others. Entering into dialogue, finding God in religions that once the Church allied with demons, praising God for his work among the nations, requires that Churches—and in a very special way the Catholic Church, still with its claim that the Church of Christ subsists in it—empty themselves of claims to power and to claims of possessing The Truth. It is, however, possible in humility to see things afresh, renouncing nothing of the revelation given in Christ, in the perspectives opened by such documents as *Lumen Gentium, Redemptoris Missio,* or *Dialogue and Proclamation,* a directive issued in 1991 by the Council on Interreligious Dialogue.

First of all, in discerning the movements and aspirations of our era we can see a quest for the unity of the many spelled out in terms of a sense of a common origin and a common destiny when a communion of all is realized. This may be seen as movement within the design and finality of God's creation, as stated in these teachings, and so also as the reason for seeing God's action and presence in all of human life and history. It is to this constant presence that allusion is made by broadening the symbolism of Reign of God to apply to all movements of human goodness and all inspiring traditions and practices of religions, with their books, teachings, rights and practices. A great flux and movement of God's Love is at work in the world, among those to whom in Love He has given life. It is the hope of a communion of all in the Word Incarnate and Risen, or in the Word and Spirit, that allows Christian believers to interpret this divine action eschatologically. That is to say, the final communion of world and humanity will be a communion in the Wisdom and Love of the eternal God, who is the source of all life, all love, all goodness. In its self-emptying, while it continues to announce Christ as the revelation of God's love, even to breaking-point, the Church recognizes that the final consummation will not mean the baptism of all, nor the belonging of all to the Church of Christ. It nonetheless knows that it has a mission to speak of Christ to all peoples, to invite them to belief in him, and to let others know of the divine love of which in and through Christ it has a vision. Working in dialogue with others, in mutual respect and mutual exchange, it sees as integral to its mission the contributions that it makes to peace and justice in the consortium of human communities and societies.

There is today a particular, historically determined situation, in which Christians must find their being as disciples of Christ, in the obedience to their mission. Awareness of this situation is already present in the document of the Vatican Council on the Church in the World, and in what is said of culture in the Constitution on the Liturgy and in the Decree on Missionary Activity. In the first, we see the growing awareness that as society changes the Church has to take on its own share of responsibility, in the name of the Gospel it preaches, for the poor of the world. The poverty grows more than it decreases and discriminations are rife, between countries and within countries. There is an incipient awareness in what is said at the Council of Gospel and culture, later much developed, of both the need to respect cultures in doing the work of the Gospel and of the crime against cultures to which Christians were often accomplice.

In Dialogue with the Other

What is needed now is a true dialogue of mutual regard, a serious effort to establish together what all may bind themselves to, granted that this is provisional and open to further inquiry and discussion, and approached with humility—the readiness even to ask pardon in order to build the possibility of justice, with due credit here to Pope John Paul's peace message of January 1, 2002.[4] It is noteworthy that in the apostolic exhortations following synods on the Church in the Americas and the Church in Europe, what was chosen as a point of departure in evangelization and dialogue was an emerging social consciousness that took issues of peace and justice as the point of departure for a new humanity. Among the *areopagi* of evangelization that John Paul is fond of naming, this one is singled out.

One may ask of a Christian, and of anyone who lives by a faith, whether in faith she is moved to a deeper and more concerned, sincere and even passionate discussion on the grounds of a common hope. Can the Gospel of Jesus Christ present an image of the "infinite God at the heart of humanity" that invites us to work with others towards a more profound and just community between persons and between peoples?

Though faith itself pushes us towards a positive answer, were we to think that the attachment to an ensemble of institutions, beliefs and rituals of its nature meant faith, we would be in deep trouble. All of that ensemble is only meant to support the "insearch" into living by faith, which in its core lineaments is intense and modest. Paul's (and Luther's) description of faith, and justification by faith, helps, when it emerges that this is inspired by keeping memory of how God in *his* form of justice made of his Son an expiation for sin, and an icon of the divine. Faith is to live with love for the other and in hope for the future, on the basis of knowing oneself justified by the mercy of God, given in Christ, and, by the grace of his Spirit, bestowed with love and as love, the freedom of being loved and in love. To have Christian faith is to be attached to Jesus Christ and to want to be one with him in his knowledge of the Father and in the movement of the Spirit that animated him, in life, death and resurrection. It takes effort, humility, and renunciation of secure sites, but one may come through Jesus Christ to the essentials of living, of loving God as the source, support and future of our being, and our neighbour as ourself. One finds this out by penetrating what was Jesus's faith and way of talking and being, his "little way" of making God's presence to human suffering and human hoping visible.

This is where the issue of living the Gospel call to poverty enters in anew. Of old, members of religious communities were exhorted to renounce worldly possession, and all interest therein, in order to live completely of "heavenly things." What we now perceive, with models such as Charles de Foucauld and Francis of Assisi before us, is that the leaving aside of any kind of the power of wealth, of status, of economic influence is the Christian way of getting involved in the things of earth and of society according to God's justice. If the Church is to bring the influence of the Gospel and of the self-gift of Christ to bear on the world, it has to be by witnessing to another way of building human community and even communion among peoples and religions. It is not immediately evident what the practical implications of this are, but it is by the hundredfold of the reign of God that the Church exercises its mission of here and now transforming the earth.

One's partners in reasonable effort towards justice and peace, in thinking them out and establishing them, will usually not be of this persuasion, nor need they be. Faith moves the Christian participant, in the hope of what Christ promises, to make serious and passionate efforts to dialogue, to talk out, to work out, what all can agree upon, and also to inject conversations and even institutions with a vision that comes from knowing Christ. Such dialogue will demand the witness of our own poverty and the sincerity of letting oneself be emptied, of letting go of the ways and displays of power, in one's very conformity to Christ being as nothing before others.

Witness

You shall be my witnesses, Christ says, unto the ends of the earth (as well as in your home towns). There are no confines where the infinite expansion of love ceases, by the power of the weakness of the Cross. What odd times these are to be Christians, called outside our ghettoes, urged to take on dialogues to which we are ill-used, and to be part of a humanity that seeks an order of justice and development, becoming inclusive and non-discriminatory communities in an effort to bring nations together. In the very process we find out how weak we are, both as Christians and humanly, and still we persevere. Expansive doctrines of permeating grace collide with planted crosses in the dust of bombed-out cities and grave-yards full of AIDS victims, but this is where the name of Christ is to resound. We felt called forth by the hopes of modernity, of the global, of networking, looking perhaps for the advent of the eschatological kingdom of peace and justice that at Vatican II caught the imagination even of bish-ops. Then we found ourselves caught in the muddle of the rifts of human-ity, the global tensions, the inner discriminations and conflicts, the refusal of immigrant populations with whom we network but whom we do not want to meet face to face. We saw Churches called before the bar of human justice for their failures, past and present, and challenged from without and from within to purify their own memories and watch their own language before presuming to speak God's name or to give divine directives to others. To respond to this we must be ever mindful that the wisdom of the Cross is not to be taken as a divinely planned and infinite satisfaction for sin but as the manifesto of a self-emptied and powerless God and a testi-mony to the curious power of love to so implant itself.

Followers of the crucified Christ love to excess because such is the God they have come to know in Christ and in the excess of his suffering. What they hope for is an order of divine justice that breaks all the rules of human justice about equality and retribution, with its excess of mercy, pardon and love and unflinching in its witness and practice even when refused and "martyrised." The witness Christian Churches may give from within their weakness is a constant living testimony to love, truth and justice, as well as to reconciliation, for from these flow the possibilities of another kingdom. We are to keep faithful in love and hope at all times, even though "failing." This may mean walking out of step with the "other" of good will whom we are asked to embrace in her very otherness on a common platform. Or it may mean standing together up against the railings. Much might be said about the Church of the martyrs of the present time who suffer for righ-teousness sake, or about the prophets who cry for justice, and about the falsely accused who hold silence and submit to trial, trailing Jesus's own question to Pilate about the nature and provenance of power.

In an hour that has some claims to be called the hour of Satan and the hour of darkness, no Church can give testimony to Christ without letting go of some absolutist claims made as Church. This is required by recognition of the OTHER, being humble, patient and present as a church, as a community that witnesses to their faith in Christ, receiving from the Spirit but making no claims, seeking only to be present where there is pain and need, and not "doing anything" to make things better, knowing that one cannot. Denise Levertov, I recall, asked how much humanity is able to find God in the "dry wafer, sour wine," "in the dust not sifted out from confusion," "the mere not darkness."[5] In the quiet of a place imbued with concentration and love, where nobody does "great things" but someone at least loves to "near perfection," people of faith learn to be perfect as peace-givers, just as the heavenly Father is perfect.

This is the mission of a Church brought to its knees. Even as it awakens to its participation in the human community, to its call to witness before all, to its call to work for peace and justice and reconciliation, even as it discovers that God wants it to step outside the church building into the street, to be on the street corner and in the projects, it is learning how weak it is before God and man. If we are to be true disciples of Jesus Christ in our time, it is of a Jesus who became poor that others may be rich, of him who emptied himself, the worm and no man, of the one whose glory it is to be lifted on high, outside the camp, in an appalling witness to the play of freedoms and to a love whose fire cannot be extinguished. There is new meaning to the mandate, "let your light shine before the world."

In its doctrinal teaching and in its theology, from Vatican II onwards, the Church is recasting its own image and identity in the face of the evidence of God's manifold presence and action in human history and in the world. It is doing so by changing its patterns of speech, by listening anew to the metaphors of people of God, salvation history and reign of God, even as it moves along new paths of dialogue and service to the peace and reconciliation of the human community, from centres of power to the farthermost islands.

As noted, it is the image of the Reign of God that has been used most profligately by Council and Pope to give that fresh vision of human aspiration, of divine presence, of eschatological horizon, within which the Church exercises its mission by holding to its faith in Jesus Christ and the Spirit. The reign of God is present and active wherever persons and societies are moved by a sense of a justice that transcends the human, but is never complete "in our times." It is through and through a vision, through and through a hope that may remain inarticulate but that is a fire in the belly nonetheless. What this hope is, to those of Christian faith, is the expectation of the consummation of all things in a communion like the communion of the Three. But to locate their mission and witness in the midst of human affairs they listen, learn, dialogue and act with all who too look forward in hope to a true oneness of all, founded on principles not always in evidence in how histories and history are humanly shaped.

It is within this metaphorical and so really real language of people, history and reign that the Church bespeaks its own identity as Sacrament of Salvation, an identity it borrows from the Word made flesh, hung upon the Cross. It is sacrament, for it cannot cease to testify to God's love and to the way of this love, and it is sacrament because it never ceases to seek in a way humble but true, to mediate love and hope to all with whom it lives, works and has its being.

Conclusion: Church of the Poor

A group of bishops that called itself "The Church of the Poor" at the Second Vatican Council may well have been justified in choosing such a name as an image of the Church, alongside "People of God," "Reign of God," "Body of Christ," and "Sacrament of Salvation." This name incorporates all that is meant by these more common images. It is among the poor, in the freedom from slavery and domination of body and spirit offered to the poor, in the choice of naming the divine self by reference to images of worldly powerlessness, that God is present in a special way to the world.

Some still react quite forcefully against the idea that the poor have a special place in God's design, or that for names of God one can look to the poor. Among other things, they say that the poor are no better than anyone else and that there is no reason to think that God may love them in a particular way. But there is no moral judgment of persons intended; the language refers to the design of revelation and God's presence in history, to where and how God poured out his love, and by whom and how he wanted to be named. The freedom he grants through Word and Spirit should lead to a release from grinding poverty and in that sense to a release from "sinful structures," but it is not by association with the powers of this world that God finds a name. Indeed, it is by renouncing such an association, by freeing the divine self and presence from it, that God shows "I AM WHO I AM." The poor who suffer poverty and those who choose the way of meekness and peace-making through a love like unto Christ's are more tuned into this naming than are those who exercise power over others, of whatever sort. The Church is church for the poor in mediating Word and Spirit to them and in seeking justice. It is of the poor inasmuch as it has to dwell by preference among them. It is poor in itself by choosing the way of being holy, present and powerful through the wisdom of the Cross. Hence, it truly is the Church of the Poor.

The Eucharist is to be at the heart of each community because it is the memorial of the supreme gift of Christ, and so of his *kenosis*. The *kenosis* of his obedience unto death, even the death of the Cross, becomes— through the act of the Spirit and the sacramental donation of his body and blood—the *kenosis* of his presence in the world through his Body, the Church, in the glory of divine communion and the fragility of human flesh. In the life of the Church, the truth of the gift cannot be lived unless it passes through the profound frailty of a table dressed with the simplicity of earth's most primitive nourishment. Being poor in what it brings to the table, it becomes Gospel poor through configuration to the One who became poor for earth's sake.

PART THREE

GENEROUS DESCENT:
THE DIVINE TRINITY

_____ ✠ _____

The revelation given in and through Christ, to which the Church gives
testimony in its adherence to him, is a revelation of the Divine Name. It is
God's gift of self through the *kenosis* of the Christ whom he sent into the
world, by which the Church lives in the Spirit, giving witness through its
espousal of Gospel poverty. To give himself in this manner is a *kenosis* on
God's own part.

To name God in the circles of hell is a vivid and timely challenge. The
voice of Christ, God's embodiment in human suffering, is not spoken by
way of violent reprisal, nor even in the eradication of poverty or discrimination—though this belongs to some hoped for future and has become a
key theme in Christian teaching. Yahweh is the God of the underprivileged
and of the liberated but this God is not to be identified with any of the
powers of this earth, political, economic or religious. God is present rather
among those who want to live peaceably and peacefully, respecting earth
and respecting neighbour. The option for the poor always means seeking
God in their midst, even under conditions of suffering.

Learning from the story of the Israelites we know that the suffering of
those against whom evil is done is to be given voice with vehemence, not
subjected to abstract discourse. They speak their suffering but they also
speak their refusal to take evil as the determining factor of their existence.
If the voices of those who suffer and of those who resist are taken seriously,
how can we be faithful, full of faith and open to life, by listening anew to
the word of the scriptures? What if in those places that are hell-like, we also
hear the freeing voice of Yahweh known to the chosen people? What if in
those places we also hear Christ speak of his Father? What if in those
places, we also hear him say that not a hair of one's head is touched without the Father knowing? What if in those places, we hear him say, Blessed
are the poor, blessed are the meek, blessed are the persecuted and the
scorned? When justice, peace and holiness appear to fall victim to the
processes of globalization, all Christians are compelled to open their hearts

117

as they listen anew to the Word of the Lord, while they also attend to those who speak from within the circles of hell in the present.

We see God's revelation in the *kenosis* of Christ and the missionary poverty of the Church, his Body. What knowledge of God and what communion with him is given to the world through such mediation? It is this that is asked in the following pages. The question is pursued in the light of what has been said of God's presence in the *kenosis* of Christ and of the Church. It is asked not only of the mystery of salvation but also of the mystery of creation.

7

I Am Who I Am: When God Names God

It is time to reflect on how the contemplation of the *kenosis* of God's Son made flesh leads us to the knowledge of God. Does this imagery of *kenosis*, or what we have called divine weakness, imprint the entire reading of the Bible and all that we know and say of God? The habit of bringing philosophical or popular notions about God and especially about divine power to the reading of scriptural passages must be broken. There is a deep tendency to hear God's Word in the echo of what we already believe about divine attributes. We may then marvel at the way in which such a God has chosen a people, chosen to be with them, and chosen to send a Son who would suffer for our reconciliation. This, however, is a short-cut, and trespassers will be prosecuted. We need to shed our images of divinity and lay our souls bare to what God reveals of himself in his deeds, in the words of his prophets, and through the mission of Word and Spirit.

The Word of God is unfolded for us through Law, Prophets, Wisdom, Gospel and Apostolic writings and is heard through a faith that is a gift of the Spirit. Attending to the scriptures is always the most basic way to "keep faith," but it is done in a communion of believers who keep memorial of the work of salvation and live by the Covenant of *kenosis* even as they are harassed by other memories and attentive to the sufferings of those who fall victim to history and social order. There is no pure listening to a fresh and pristine text. Listening in sincerity requires a constant purification of the memories we think we have of God's name. Since in the history of Christianity God's name has too often been married to the exercise of power, let us bring the images of God's weakness and fragility, and of the very fragility of his naming, to the fore.

I Am Who I Am: Word of Yahweh

The naming of God in Christian tradition and in the life of any community or person is deeply rooted in the celebration of the liturgy and its appeals to scriptures. It is there that texts are mixed and shuffled by diverse communities, bringing out the richness of the intersection of different texts. It is there that word and rite interact in offering gifts that come from God, allowing us to addressing the "I" of God as "thou," to forge links between the human experience of earthly things on the one hand, and the Word of the Lord on the other. It is there that Gospel and tradition meet culture in the unending immersion of Word in the earthly, in the human, and in particular histories, so that the face and voice of God take on ever-fresh appearances and tones. It is there that the testimonies of those who stand by God's name in all seasons, and especially in seasons of suffering, injustice and persecution, can be incorporated. It is there that the witness of Jesus from the Cross, and the self-emptying but living words by which he gives life and self in bread, wine, oil and water, are given their privileged moment in the act of memorial that looks both backward to the Pasch and forward to Judgment.

It is in a liturgy where it is conscious of its election and its mission that the Church is invited to be most traditional in its looking back to beginnings and most "post modern" or "post present," in not impeding what comes from the future from entering in. It is there that the proclamation of Word, ecclesial words of petition, peons of praise and ritual acts of communion conclude in the silencing of words and the quieting of bodies in doxology and its invitation to be still in openness and wonder.

By a shuffling of texts learned from liturgy, believers take up the question of God's Name. To get it straight requires attentive listening and thought. We are like Moses before the burning bush, pressing God for a name, a credential to cite to the people held in slavery. The narrative of Exodus 3 may give the impression that God was a little exasperated, faced as he was with Moses's own exasperation. "I am who I am," God says, or who I have indicated myself to be in being God of the patriarchs. That is the name.

The play with the text of this conversation records the difficult path of latching on to a name for God. When one asks of another, rhetorically, "who are you anyway," the answer may well be, "who do you think I am?" Such a little exchange, full of challenges and uncertainties, is an invitation to give some thought and acknowledgment to what one has seen of the other and witnessed in the person's life. Full name and address do not say all that much about the character and the value of a life. Whether the person is at that address because he was born there is more revealing. Whether the name is a family name, or one changed by deed poll, makes a difference to his identity. How closely an individual has kept to that mooring or how far she has wandered from it says much of the making of a life and the forging of hopes and expectations.

The God who speaks to us from within our tradition is a God who changes addresses quite regularly. That is part of his weakness: he took no vows of stability. At first, he was content to wander around with nomads like Abraham, who even as he vacillated in affection between his wife and his concubine seems to have had some inkling of the worthlessness of idols that promised the untenable. Ever on the move to seek fresh pastures for their flocks and quite unable to identify themselves or God with stable structures and regimes, these nomads looked for something to take hold of. When in captivity the people perforce took to brick-making, God took up a dwelling in Egypt, not in Pharoah's palace but among those enslaved and exploited, helping brave persons like Shiphra and Puah to save at least the children (Exod 1:15-21). Then, on his invitation, this slave people followed Moses out into the desert, where Yahweh wandered with them for forty years. During that time he took up temporary residence in a tent or on top of Sinai, where he could best converse with his servant Moses, and tell him of the Law and Alliance whereby the people might live in justice and peace. After that, Jerusalem and the Temple became his abode, but meeting-houses and synagogues throughout the land and in the diaspora proved satisfactory enough for the constant hearing of God's Word and the incantations of praise or lament that the people raised up to him. Indeed, this God who dwelt behind the veil in the Holy of Holies also spoke to them in their meeting places "everywhere and anywhere." He invited them to inhabit creation by the word of his Wisdom so that he could always be found in the simplicity of daily life and the seasons of life, even as he made it possible to feel the pulse of life in the splendour and wonders of the created universe. To find God there, however, the Wise and the Simple and the Just needed to know that the one whose face they saw reflected in the universe was the same one who had been with the slaves and had wandered the barren desert for quite some years.

When God first invited Moses to take a look, feet unshod, at the fire that kept burning but did not consume, he reminded this exiled hireling that he already had a biography and a curriculum vitae. Moses was told from within the bush that the speaker was the God of Abraham, Isaac and Jacob. This same God told this prince turned shepherd and servant that he was of a mind to add to this name by new adventures with a people whom he would like to call his own, a people who had fallen on hard times. This also said something about this God, for all his claims to sovereignty over the nations.

The people were to find out whether knowing that there is one God, who is both saviour and creator, was more important than being content with one's lot. Though under the leadership of Moses the people liked their victories and took inordinate pleasure in the slaughter of their enemies, God might be better known in defeat than in victory. Fighting over straw for bricks, or guarding flocks against intrusion, or wanting some acres to call one's own among peoples who tend to parcel up the earth and its tribes among deities, leads to warring claims. In the world of the truly divine there are no rivalries, but coming to that knowledge has its dangers and defeats.

As those who went before us, we also manage to get God's name wrong much of the time by wanting to attribute him only with victories and with power as we see these things, or by confusing gender and divinity. God "as named" then turns out to be very masculine/muscular, and quite vengeful with Canaanites, Turks and Jews alike, those inassimilable others who do not fit into the world as our claim on God has ordered it. The day's liturgy has been touched up, or sanitized, but it is rather appalling to note that Rome's liturgical calendar still harbours a feast (October 7) to mark the defeat of the Turkish and Islamic people.

Though we may think of it less, or think less of it, today God has also changed address and indeed now has citizenship in a variety of cultures. Inculturation and openness to world religions have become theological themes because we see that the openness to "other" required by Scripture means taking heed of how God speaks in other things, or lets his Gospel take root in new languages, or is working with people who have different religious systems to ours. That makes listening to Scripture more complicated, but then the book itself is quite complex in its speech about God, and this actually helps when we are compelled to live and think anew.

Reading an Unstraightforward Bible

Christians, even Catholics, are encouraged these times to read and "pray" the scriptures. They may be tempted to seek in them a very clear picture of the God of ancestors and of Jesus Christ, but God is not that kind of pedagogue. In fact, it is impossible to read the bible without the lurking thought that even the prophets hovered long on the brink of getting the divine name and identity wrong. They did, however, continue to listen and to scrutinize. Reading the bible (let us for the moment cut out the capitals of this odd collection, for wisdom's sake), commenting on the bible, praying with the bible, is a hazardous spiritual experience. Readers or listeners have to struggle with questions about God and with God, letting themselves be led to this struggle by what they read, as well as by random liturgical choices of texts and conversations that unearth disharmony.

The story of the Exodus is the story of a people's (and especially of its mediator's) struggle with God and of God's struggle with the people to make himself known. God kept on pressing them to get them to name him aright. The name was sometimes written with large strokes, attaching identity to some story or other, as when the Law was given to Moses on Sinai. It might be spoken in life metaphors such as wind and light and spring water. There is room, too, for conjuring with both male and female adjectives, lest Yahweh be made one with patriarchs and their rule. One can even risk naming the divine after the animal world, a beast roaring for its prey or a dove of peace. Following the texts, one may attend to the heavens, eyes looking upward, for the sound of a voice, ready to run with the wind, when not running against it.

It was not for nothing that the people's lore included Jacob's wounded thigh (Gen 32:22-32), given the extent of the struggle with the God whose naming is in itself a combat. Though we labour over it, it is obvious enough that the stories, the recitations, are never to be taken as matter-of-fact accounts. They rather provide interpretations, with certain points of reference, and struggle to get beyond them.

God's Action?

One of the great gains of Vatican II for Catholic theology and Catholic piety was to relate divine revelation to historical events, awakening to God's presence in human action. This made it possible to overcome the very propositional approach to truth embodied in the expression, deposit of faith. On the other hand, it is no easy thing to make the connection between God's presence in history and human action. One has to be discerning even in the face of those who claim to act in fidelity to God's alliance or in God's name. Like the biblical writer, we may be inclined to attribute everything to God's intervention, even bloody victories over enemies, and need to stand back in order to grasp better what is being communicated.

Nothing can be concluded from a biblical story without first taking into account how narratives are construed. What is told is told in hindsight, from the point of view of a writer and the writer's people. God was indeed by covenant and alliance among a chosen people, prompting them to seek the divine name and justice in deed as well as in worship but he was not doing their deeds in any narrow, causal sense—as though he were pushing them to action. With faith and hope in his presence they attributed these deeds to him, though it might be better said that they were inspired by his promise of alliance, in consequence of which they made their own practical judgments. Their failures and defeats they also attributed to him, and in so doing made abundant use of the dictionary of punishments, applicable both to themselves and to their enemies. To see the decay of social and political life as the consequence of a failure to live according to the covenant and to pursue true justice may have been closer to the mark, if we are looking for theological explanations to place alongside a good story.

A less hurried reading of narratives and prophecies suggests that in victory and in defeat, and in the seasonal and daily search for food, the, *the*, issue is one of fidelity. The Law and its pursuit is the key practical expression of what this fidelity demands, provided it is always interpreted through the prism of love of God and neighbour. When the people act in fidelity, God's Name is glorified. When they stray, it is "idolized" (made idol, idle). The Jewish philosopher and Talmudic scholar Emmanuel Levinas reminded those who lived beyond the Shoah that it is not possible to read the command, "Thou shalt not kill," without looking someone, not well liked and not belonging to the company one keeps, in the face.[1] In a broader context, this may serve as a metaphor for interpreting the scriptures and singing praises or laments while lifting one's eyes from the page to look around.

God's action is first and foremost in the hearts of those who are opened to the possibility of divine presence through events, through what they see happening. There is something breathtaking in taking one's place on the far shore of the Red Sea with the unruly mass that followed Moses, his sister, and his brother out of Egypt. They had suffered much travail in Egypt. They had escaped the misfortunes that nature visited upon the Egyptians through the plagues. They had, by the use of their wits and most of all by the strategies of Moses, found their way across the sea with considerable herds and flocks and other treasures, always in dread fear of pursuit and massacre, in fear of nature itself, for all the benignity of the full moon. Looking back over the waters, they could see the chariots and the charioteers mired in the mud, drowned in the waters that flowed over them. They had come through all this on the word of Moses and Aaron about Yahweh, about a God to be revered in a way that acknowledged his supremacy, one of whom Moses spoke with a purity of speech not common in what peoples said of gods. They had made a commitment to sacrifice the best of their flocks to this God. Standing there now, at last delivered into safety, seeing their persecutors laid low before their eyes, it seemed to them a truly awesome night. They felt that all was made new, that some divine benevolence had accompanied them, that they had been given a God incomparable, one whose name could not be spoken in the same breath as that of other Gods. Their life as a people was a new venture, their journey was unparalleled. Wander more they must, but in the hope of a safe haven, of a more blessed existence, if only they learned how to honour this God whom they saw as their redeemer.

Moses spoke of a covenant that delivered to them both the promises and rules of treaty. In the course of their further wanderings, in some awesome places marked by both the acerbity and the extravagance of nature, over a period of time of uncertainty and certain hope, he spoke with God and spelled out the conditions of Covenant. The Word at its core was a prompting to be faithful, to seek the justice proclaimed by divine covenant. The Israelites seem little by little to have been rightly convinced that only in the proclamation of the one God and his justice could truth be established and the right ordering of human affairs discovered. When they acted out of this persuasion, the narrator ascribed everything they did to God's intervention. A reader needs to be more discerning. What may be said to be of God and what of more crass human ambition? Maybe we are all Lutheran enough, or paradoxically Ignatian enough, to know that there is a war of spirits going on in the human heart that leads to actions derived from mixed motives. We need to ask of ourselves, of Christian history and of the biblical accounts, what was of God and what of the flesh?

This leads to some ironic distanciation in taking the Bible (capitals used) as the Word of God, however heartily this is proclaimed in liturgies. The Word of God is a somewhat complex term to refer to a tradition of faith handed on, with the aid of written texts, but placing us at one and the same time in front of written texts and attentive to the promptings of the Spirit, which have to be discerned. The Spirit is inside us, in hearts and sometimes heads, moving people to see things from the perspective of a desire to acknowledge God and somehow name her/him/THE. When the text is presented as the Word of God, it is about listening, reading, responding, acting, not about letters on a page or between two covers. Readers are invited to think out new issues within the parameters offered in stories and sayings, with due reference to other stories and the conditions of human life in which they are immersed. It is because in reading, worship and deed they find themselves addressed that they speak of scripture being the Word of God.

Example of an Awkward Text

Examples are worth many words. Knowledge of the process outlined in reading a text is a reminder to be prudent about ascribing things to God. Exodus 17 is a good reading whereby to illustrate the point. As the story unfolds, the people of Israel, recently released from the slavery of Israel, are wandering through the desert, seeking a place to settle. They are attacked by their enemies, the Amalekites. In answer to the prayer of Moses, we are told, they prevail in battle and with his army the young lieutenant, Joshua, slays the Amalekites, even having at hand a two-edged sword that made quicker dispatch of the enemy, two at a time with a back and forward stroke. The careless reader may well conclude that God made it possible to kill them, that he fought on Joshua's side. Except that this is a story, an event narrated, in the light of certain assumptions about God's alliance with Israel. These assumptions may well have led the author to say too much, but in themselves they still hold a certain validity. One needs to read the particular story more carefully, within the framework of the larger story provided by reference to the liberation of Israel, the alliance and the Law, and with the figure of Moses as mediator and symbol of another to come occupying the foreground.

What people actually did, as told in the narrative, may be rather crass and not in all things to conform to the demands of the divine initiative.

God chose Israel, as he chooses those of the covenant in Christ, but neither one people nor the other necessarily makes sound judgments as to how God wishes them to act. Within the range of assumptions prompted by divine election, the writer of Exodus 17 tells the story of a rather bloody battle and victory as an act of God's intervention. It seems odd to find this in a holy book, but it is none too surprising when one hears those who avow vengeance on America's enemies end with the ringing claim, God bless America. It is possible that under the circumstances, and within the horizons of the claim to know the One True God and the desire to establish a nation dedicated to his worship and his justice, the Israelites had no choice but to defend themselves in battle. Could they have done it in a less bloody manner? That we do not know. Were they anxious to be faithful to Yahweh and to rely on his fidelity? That seems clear. Did God slaughter the Amalekites through the agency of Joshua? That is highly dubious. With the background of past memories of liberation, Joshua saw himself as the champion of God. A reader might admire his zeal and yet feel queasy about the bloodiness of his action and the ease with which the storyteller puts blood on God's hands. The fitting response, however, is to look to oneself and reflect on the extent and nature of one's own commitments to the Law and one's way of judging and forgiving.

Shuffling Texts with Leviticus

One is always picking texts at random. It is possible to put the story of Joshua's victory into a dialectic with some texts that we owe to the random choices of the liturgy. The first is from the office and the second from the Mass for the early weeks of Ordinary Time.

Deuteronomy 4 and 5

Alongside Exodus 17 we can put chapters 4 and 5 of the Book of Deuteronomy, another passage that attributes mighty deeds and wondrous signs to Yahweh. Exegetes have no trouble in identifying these lines as an impassioned plea for observance of the Law and an admonition to avoid the false gods of the neighbouring peoples with whom the Israelites had contact. To keep the people faithful, the author holds up Yahweh's fidelity and the choice of the people as his very own. He asks them if any of the other gods have manifested themselves so clearly to their peoples as Yahweh did on Horeb, or if any delivered them from such plights as that of the Hebrews under the slavery of Egypt, when their God worked great wonders for them as a sign to Pharaoh. Commentators take note of the rhetorical devices of the text, which include the majestic description of the divine revelation and the might that Yahweh showed in overcoming the Egyptians. One may say that speakers and writers exaggerate with purpose. But it is the purpose that stands out, and here it is to persuade the people to follow the Law. This observance is what holds them together as a people and guarantees God's continuing presence among them, the loving choice that he makes of them as his very own. In Deuteronomy 6, we find the text of the *Shema Israel*, we find again that the foundation for living by the Law is the remembrance of slavery and God's choice of a slave people to be his elect and mark of his presence in the world.

1 Samuel 15:16-23

1 Samuel 15:16-23 is given in the lectionary for Monday of the Second Week of the Year in the Roman Liturgy, Year II. In this story Saul is reminded by Samuel that he was sent against Israel's enemy, the Amalekites, to put them "under a ban of destruction." He is rebuked for having taken some of the spoil of victory, the sheep and the oxen, into his own possession. Saul's excuse is that he preserved them to offer sacrifice to the Lord God. For Samuel, speaking in God's name, this is unacceptable and Saul will be rejected.

What is the point of this passage? Israel has won a pretty bloody victory against the Amalekites, wiping out men, women and children. In political terms, it was necessary for them to protect themselves against this people and Saul was an effective leader and warrior in doing this. The people are now free of that worry, so the command to exterminate the enemy is attributed to the Lord. But Samuel is bothered because Saul has wrought gain from the victory, both for himself and for the people. They are endangering the purity of their faith in God and their fidelity to the Covenant by trafficking in the goods of another. Furthermore, in excusing himself, Saul puts cult and sacrifice ahead of faithful observance of the Law. The words of Samuel suggest that Saul has also taken a fancy to some of the divination and sacrificial practices of this foreign people, risking idolatry. That obedience to God means exterminating the Amalekites seems to be taken as given, but even as we baulk at this we see that what is ultimately at stake is fidelity to the Law and the Covenant, to the one true God.

On the part of the assembly hearing this text on this particular Monday, there will surely be doubts about the command to kill and annihilate. The point, though, is the call to be faithful, to examine one's political and military ventures, as well as one's business dealings, in terms of how well God is served and the purity of faith maintained. From Samuel's misgivings about establishing a kingdom for the people, recorded in the same book and read in the liturgy a few days earlier, and with what we know of the kings of Israel, we may think that a good part of the problem was the identification of the Lordship of God with the lordship of kings and with military victories. In fact the psalmodic responses to the text in the liturgy, taken from Psalm 50, bolster this reading. They remind the hearer that it is above all right behaviour, fidelity in conduct to the Law of God, that counts. One can readily justify or excuse all kinds of cultic practices and in the doing thereof veer away from true religion, from the true faith and hope in God that come from living within the Covenant and as God's covenant people.

The Bedevilled of the Earth

This is not to suggest that the attribution of death-dealing to God is to be taken lightly, to be dismissed as an old-fashioned attitude or as half-savage. To grasp its why and wherefore readers or listeners have to draw their breath again on the shores of the Red Sea. They have to put themselves in the place of people running for their lives, of those who are just free from the toil of slavery and still in search of a place to live and protect themselves from even worse. They lived in their own circles of hell and were inspired by a desire for freedom and justice, led in this quest by Moses and his brother and sister. Their slant on God was first that he was a God who would liberate them, would grant them freedom, the right to be a people and a nation. This God they then learned to see as Creator and piece by piece put together the kind of Law that would guarantee respect for God, respect for neighbour and an era of peace. The way to such a regime was often bloody, but the belief in God, trust in his loving choice and alliance, was the lodestar. Memory and Law together proved a pedagogy for perfecting faith. Both event and Law were attributed directly to God's action as though they came straight from his hand, though in fact they emerged from the struggle to work out what it means to be faithful to a faithful God.

When reading such passages and their attributions of acts to God, it is not to be forgotten just how needy, poor and bedevilled the Hebrew peoples were and how threatened they continued to be even after their deliverance from slavery. What they shared in common was their hardship; otherwise they were hardly one people. Delivery, formation as a people through the Law and cult, and protection against enemies were hard won. At rock bottom what gave them their sense of being a people, one people, was the conviction of being chosen by Yahweh, of being the children of divine predilection. Keeping this sense of things alive and sustaining the peoples faith was the aim and purpose of narratives and precepts and teachings.

Putting oneself in the place of the bedevilled of the earth is part of putting biblical texts and issues in their right context. How would we talk if that was where we were? How do we expect the millions to talk who today are in a like situation? How do you enliven a desire for peace when warlords battle over your land? How do you keep alive a thirst for justice with multinational corporations on your doorstep? This is why liberation theologies take the whole Exodus literature as paradigmatic.

Hearing Scripture as Issue and Response

A procedure of dialogue, in which the text frames an issue and asks a response, is a good approach to reading the scriptures. The text presents a horizon and a question, the question being located within the total context of the book, but taking on a new life within the community that hears the word. It is not a simple question as in a catechism but an issue that is raised by story or prophecy. Readers find themselves within this context and horizon but with points of reference peculiar to themselves. The issue of Exodus is how to see God's part in the action of the people when they look for justice and set out to defend themselves and the honour of the Lord in whose fidelity they believe. Today's communities have other points of reference when making interpretations and encoding ways of behaving, in the face of issues such as defending a world against terrorism. Political and military strategies abound, but are there biblical horizons within which to judge them?

Any biblical text has to be put in conversation with others, with the whole complex story of God's dealings with his people and with those called in Christ. This is what liturgy does in its intercalation of texts, whatever the critique that can be made of how this is done at times. Indeed, when we turn from the bloody scene narrated to the prophecies grouped under the name of Isaiah we find that God wants her name, THE name, to be identified with peace and justice, to be called out among those who turn swords into ploughshares and who seek an order in which the poor have the Gospel preached to them. We might well think differently about God's part in the slaughter of the Amalekites than did the author of Exodus 17, but we feel invited to place our own concerns within the horizon of an alliance that God has initiated and through which she guarantees a faithful and guiding presence.

We know that the early Church, beginning with the New Testament writings themselves, dealt with the harsher passages of the Hebrew scriptures by giving them a spiritual and typological meaning. This still prevails today in liturgies and communities, exemplified by the insouciant enthusiasm with which assemblies respond to the story of the destruction of the Egyptian armies. The attitude seems to be that since the passage is used at Baptism it is not necessary to pay too much attention to details: the text may simply exemplify the spiritual struggle against Satan and sin and God's loving choice of the catechumens. But we really do need to pay more attention to what texts say and what they are about if we are to be instructed by them. Indeed, the international Biblical Commission has reminded us that if we are to read the story of the Israelites seriously and learn from it, we need to put more effort into understanding what they passed through and how they sustained fidelity to God's Covenant in the midst of all their tribulations, victories and defeats.

It is of course true in the end that it is the spiritual meaning that counts, but spiritual is not to be separated from temporal and earthly struggle. To have faith and hope in God is to live through these things knowing the love of God that holds up in all times. On the other hand, we may be aware that the rule and love of God lead him to an identification with the suffering and enslaved and with this we might get to the core of revelation. To show the power of his rule, the loving action of his choice and of the gift of the divine spirit, God positively separates self-revelation and self-donation from, strips himself, one may say, of any show of temporal or political power. The divine is in this world among the small remnant, the poor of Israel, the slave and the captive, the blind and the lame. Spiritual power does not mean living separated from the world, outside a political or temporal order. It means bringing a force to bear on the order of things that is not that of the powers that be. It shows itself in service, in love, in respect, in humility, in a knowledge of what is not of this world, and in bearing trials that are the way towards a deeper knowledge of God. While Naomi and Boaz (Book of Ruth) show what it is to welcome a stranger, while the prophets extol people and kings to maintain a just order, the Book of Wisdom, even as it turns attention to the wonders of nature, points to the just who suffer and are oppressed and are in this God's special children.

As Jesus Told It

Jesus was an Israelite well dressed in a knowledge of the Law and Prophets. He was of the line of Mary the prophetess, who in her song of jubilation (Luke 1:46-55) penetrated to the heart of God's covenant love for the poor. When Jesus spoke of the kingdom of God, or the kingdom of his Father, or told stories about it, he clearly did not have temporal or political rule in mind. On the one hand, he preached the grace of God, the sweetness and gentleness and pardoning love of God, which is always at work in human hearts and makes its presence felt in the ways that people seek to build life together. On the other hand, he taught of the virtues and manners of those who live by this rule, those who become testimony to it. In Luke's version (Luke 6:20-23), Jesus teaching drew attention to the truly poor of this earth, those who suffer in body and spirit, those who are left without what is needed to live, those who are crippled, blinded and oppressed by those who have the plenty of the earth and exercise rule and dominion in ordering life and society. By some odd paradox, the mighty God, the all-powerful, shows who and what he is among these lowly of the earth. In Matthew's version (Matt 5:3-11), Jesus is depicted as speaking of the heart and comportment of those who do not vaunt it over others, of those who whatever their state or their position are meek and gentle, caring of others, upholders of God's covenant and alliance, ready to suffer persecution rather than betray the divine name. In the two Gospels, two different groups are envisaged, but they are to come together in exchange and communion if God is to reign.

Thus it is that when Luke gives us the four blessings, or Matthew the eight, they point us to the forces at work in the world that Jesus found to be the forces of God, of God's justice, of God's love, of godly rule. As Mary sang in her *Magnificat*, it is to the lowly, the meek and humble of this earth that the rule of God is known. This is not to say again that we desert the world to know God, but rather that in all the ordering of human things, it is what is not of the power of the powerful that is the agent of divine presence. God empties himself of the attribute of Lordship as commonly professed and practiced in order to be active and present through those who live by the lowliness of the beatitudes.

This teaching about the revelation of God's name is made more concrete through stories told. While Jesus himself is the most interesting story, when it is a matter of story-telling, for his own part he tells some tales of God that are quite a challenge to divine naming and to ideas of righteousness and justice. They are transmitted by the evangelists not always in perfect harmony, and there are no doubt additions to his own words, but we still get the gist. When talking to those among the scribes and Pharisees who thought they had unassailable claims on the Law, Jesus identifies a God "outside the law" as they interpreted it. That is where he placed the Father, once he put his own self in that position. Talking to the poor he put the Father right in their midst, counting the hairs on their heads.

Luke, for example (Luke 15), gives us three parables in sequence aimed at placing the God to whom and of whom Jesus speaks among sinners. These are the stories of the caringly careless shepherd who wanders off after one stray sheep when there are still ninety-nine at home, of the spendthrift woman who is so happy about finding one lost coin that she throws a party, and of the Patriarch who would like to see his two sons, the one with wanderlust who has to return home to avoid starvation and the assiduous worker who is late for the party, talk to one another. In this story, the welcome both to sinners and to adherents of the Law is not a matter of abiding many mansions but of coming to one big festive hall where the righteous and the sinner dip hands into the same dish, under the eye of a Father who seeks to make the peace, forgiving them both for their obstinacy and getting them to forgive each other. The whole thing has cost him half his fortune and the loss of his reputation as a patriarch who needs only to speak to be obeyed! No wonder it is claimed that a God so portrayed is in fact beyond being named, however hard Jesus may try to give a new ring to the name of Father, even giving us a new (in some respects rather old) prayer by which to address this God, one that audaciously stakes God's reputation on our ability to forgive one another in the name of the Divine One.

Jesus also has some quite startling demands to make of his disciples, as these are, for example, submitted to writing in what the Church calls The Sermon on the Mount (like good stage directors we do like the location to be well chosen with an eye to the viewer's tastes). Everything asked is excessive, urging believers to go to excess: To walk one mile rather than two, to avoid courts altogether even in a just cause, to love and not defend oneself against enemies, to hold up shaky marriages with a sense of equality between partners and generous love, to be eunuchs should mission or testimony to the kingdom so demand. To be perfect, he says, as God is perfect, the measure of God's own perfection being paradoxically the measure in which he asks believers to be perfect.

In effect, through many ways, narrative and poetic, mythic and hagiographical, God strips himself of his Name as the awesomely holy and of his power before the nations in order to invite believers to call him by that other name of which Jesus tells. To know that name from inside the story, one must either be totally just, which is where Jesus stands, or justified sinner, which is where those who claim no justice of their own aspire to be. It is the divine stripping of powers that defies the imagination and defies a more earthly, earthbound, sense of justice, of right and wrong—the kind of justice that prevails upon nations to inflict the death penalty and allows former friends to justify the break-off of communications in the righteous sense of some unforgivable wrong done. What human can ever learn from living that it is the capacity to take the forgiveness offered and then to forgive in turn that is at the heart of divine presence and gift? The whole notion of the justice of God and of the reign of God begins in such a proclamation of forgiveness. And yet, as I have seen a writer remark, Jesus is to the right of God—in other words, however radical an incarnation of this justice may seem, it is still to the right of the divine reality. This is the knowledge ". . . That Passeth All Understanding." One may readily be prompted to insert here a few words from John Paul's message for World Peace Day 2002: no peace without justice, no justice without the granting of pardon (while of course politicians and military shout out their intention to "punish" those who harm us).

For the hard of heart it is simply impossible to be attuned to this naming of God, to this God of whom Jesus speaks. The parable of the two sons shows that it is possible to live with God and Jesus quite a long time without truly knowing them. The second son could rightly say that he had led an upright life and that he had toiled a long time in his father's fields, but in failing to welcome his brother home, he showed that he did not know his father.

Not that looking at suffering, one's own or another's, one can ever avoid Job's outrage and Job's question over suffering undeserved. Nor may one pretend to be satisfied with God's answer to Job. In the end, Jesus is the rather long-deferred divine reply, he who, though having every claim on glory, thought nothing of this wealth and stripped himself of every semblance of divinity and of humanity, to reveal the divine name in the most impossible of places, outside the camp, among the carrion.

Emmanuel, God with us, we sing every Christmas of the child made known to shepherds, the same word in all languages and dialects. Neither climate nor culture cloud the descent of this Emmanuel but it resounds right around the world and its glory always shines over us. On the atoll of Fakarova in French Polynesia I was asked by a bevy of altar boys, *enfants de choeur* as the people called them, how it was possible to celebrate Midnight Mass at Christmas in cold climates, while I of course had gone there wondering how it would be possible to do it in the tropical heat. Looking at the sky above us as we sat on the steps of the priest's house (kept clean for the few times a year that one was there), I could see the brightly shining stars, the Southern Cross standing out most luminously. Look above you, I invited these boys, and tell me what you see: do you think that when people in Ireland or in far northern regions look up they see the light of stars in the heavens on Christmas night, even if they cannot sit out on the porch steps? What do you hear read of the night when Jesus was born? Is it not that the heavens were lit up, that angels appeared, that they sang to the shepherds of the glory of God and of God's peace on earth? How do you think the kings (setting biblical erudition aside) got to Bethlehem? Was it not by following a star? Do you not think that the light of God can guide all peoples, do you not think that the glory of God shines on all, that Emmanuel comes down everywhere and anywhere, all places that humans dwell? Do you not think that people can celebrate this, however hot or cold it may be? I had to deal with many interruptions to try to make the picture of Christmas in Dublin, Rome or Washington come more fully alive, but children catch on quickly.

God Is Love

Love of God and love of neighbour, we are told, are the two great commandments, and Jesus in washing the feet of his disciples commended love to them as the divine mark by which they would stand out. If such commandments have force it is because God is Love and all love comes to us as a divine gift. One reads the affirmation in the first letter of John, 4, 8, and 16. It speaks not only of redemption but of creation as well. Hans Urs von Balthasar early in his theological life published a book called *Only Love Is Worthy of Faith*. When we take this to heart, it is such love that we perceive in the image of Christ Crucified, the enfleshment of the Word/Love in slave form abased upon the Cross. It is well to speak of God as Father, Word/Son and Spirit, but such a divine *perichoresis*, such a divine dance, can be taken to heart only as a dance of eternal love, showing itself in the one who dances before the world on the Cross, but showing itself thus as that which suffuses all things and transforms the whole of created reality.

One cannot ignore the warning that the sentence "God is Love" in John exists alongside two other Johannine aphorisms, God is Light (1 John

1:5) and God is Spirit (John 4:24), the last spoken to a woman of rather fleshly experience, shared in at least five beds. All three sayings imply triune speech and revelation, for it is in the flow of light, spirit and love that we are brought into a mystery of divine giving through Wordy Son and Worthy Spirit.

What is born of the flesh is flesh, says Jesus to some who know this better than he, and what is born of the spirit is spirit. God Spirit is not bound to any place or people but to come among us, to speak divine speech, it was indeed imperative to send the angel to Nazareth, to come in Spirit and flesh to Bethlehem and to die in Jerusalem. Without the rich background of these places, and of the background of Judea and Galilee, and the odd ramble through Samaria, God would have had nothing to say and nothing to show through his Word. But boundaries are boundaries and the Word was for all humankind and so needed transfer into other speech, to be heard in other places. But there is no cause for worry: God is Spirit and she knows her way around. Humans however are slower on the uptake and tie up the Word in other, Latin or Greek, forms, but in the flow of the Spirit the Word keeps on giving, keeps on emptying itself to excess, so as to be heard. To testify that we are still talking about the Christ, about the Jesus of Judea and Galilee, about the Word made flesh, God poured the Spirit into our hearts to convince/convict the hearer that the Word says God is Spirit, and indeed a generous Spirit who gives the gifts of Son and Spirit. Donation, giving, gift, are key actions and words in grasping the Johannine aphorism, God is Spirit.

And so it goes for the saying, God is Light, in whose light we walk. And with the phrase God is Love, and so worthy of loving faith. We know, says John, that God is Love because he gave his only-begotten Son to the world, because we have communion with the Father and the Son, because we are empowered to love one another (1 John 4:20-21), even enemies, and the gift of the Spirit testifies that this is indeed the work of Love (1 John 4:13-15). To give without calculation, to give of oneself without reserve, is the other word for Love. The Father gives the Son. The Son gives himself without holding anything back, gives himself even to the Cross. The Father and the Son give the Spirit, so that we may be sure that this is Love and that all three take up their abode in those God loves.

Among these sayings, today's theology has chosen to give some preference to the affirmation God is Love, even though all three speak of a divine giving that comes forth from God and speaks of the very nature of God and the divine communion of Father, Son and Spirit. It is quite common to associate this with the image of Christ abased that is found in the hymn of the Letter to the Philippians, a text that is large in its language of excess. Maybe this is the effort to speak the divine Word, the good news, to each age according to its need. Today's age, if it is to have a future, must live with a justice impregnated with love and suck of the sap of unprecedented, almost unimaginable, generosity. Love pours out love and abides only in the light of love and not in the darkness of hate, only where the outpouring in spirit outdoes the love of one's own flesh, and indeed turns the acts of the flesh itself into unbounded turning to the other, without calculation.

Who art thou, then, asks Moses? What is the name that I may give to those who want to be freed? My Name is Love and my address is everywhere, except in the hearts of those who hate. And I was from the beginning, present to the moment when life emerged.

Thrice Holy God

While thoughts of Christmas make the heavens gleam, naming God in the circles of hell, in those dislocated localities, brings us back to the origins of talk of God as Trinity, but from within the economy of salvation that marks the actualities of life and its eucharistic celebration. Many attempts are made by theologians to retrieve or reconstruct ways of speaking of the Trinity that may have an impact on contemporary life, in all its failures, struggles and hopes. In such efforts we find ways of relating the triune revelation of God to the life of the Church, to ecumenical dialogue, to interreligious dialogue, and in particularly poignant fashion to life in a dishevelled world.

We live all the time with Moses's question about God's Name. Who is this God who asks that we be consumed with love of him, this God who asks that we look on every other as sister, this God who leads us around the world to proclaim that Christ is victor, that the kingdom of God is upon us? God of whom we predicate, ever more dubiously, "all-powerful" and "ever-provident," Who art thou then? That thou should never release us, never let go, always prompt with a terrible desire for life and oneness— who art thou then?

It is in the distress of the Cross and in the eschatological hope aroused by the signs of an active divine Spirit among Jesus's followers that revelation of the mystery of an eternal divine trinity is first given. Believers in the hope to which they were moved by the Spirit named Jesus as Lord, the well-beloved and gift-given Son of the Father, the Word spoken from eternity, the eternal high-priest not ashamed to take on sinners as brothers and sisters. Before the doctrine became/becomes abstract God-talk, it was and is written on the tablets of the heart, even of the broken heart that is consoled, revived, reconstructed in the astonishment provoked by the signs of divine love at work in the world.

Several writers in the West want to follow the way of the East in giving priority in thinking of God to the communion of three persons. They are prompted along this avenue through reading of the Cappadocian Fathers, but find traces of it, too, in some Latin medieval writers, such as Richard of Saint Victor. The Cappadocians indeed had found a happy way to put across the Nicene dogma that proclaimed the distinctiveness and unity of three in one divine substance or nature by explaining how the three together, though distinct persons, form a communion in one divinity. No one name, Father, Son or Spirit may be pronounced without hearing it as expressive of a relation to the other two, in a perfect communion of holiness and loving. There is no distinctiveness to any of the three except within this communion. This clearly brings home the need to think of God always as a Trinity of life and a Trinity of mercy, calling humanity into a share in this communion.

We should be careful, however, not to pin unwarranted human images on this communion. For the Cappadocians, in good Eastern tradition, reflection on the mystery of the Trinity belonged within the grasp of the economy of salvation. Before Nicea, Athanasius clinched the argument for the divinity of the Word or Son against Arius by appeal to the work of redemption and grace. From his own forebears he knew that one traced the work of sanctification as humanity's divinisation to the redemption by the Son who took on human flesh, and so to the Father who sent the Son. Humans are made God's children, made like unto God, indeed made gods, through Jesus Christ, proclaimed God's Son. If this mediator with whom believers are made one is not truly God, what happens to divinisation? Rather than joined with God through Christ, we would be separated from him by adherence to a lesser being who does not penetrate the heavens because he never came from there.

Basil and the two Gregories made it clear that personhood stood for distinctiveness, for particularity, but not for separation and apartness within God. Father, Son and Spirit are united in one communion of truth and love. Each is through and through relationality, is being in communion with, in relation to the other two. They are not simply three who share an essence, but they are a perfect being-in-communion through relation among themselves. It is within the economy of redemption and divine holiness that we know this being of God because of the missions of Son and Spirit. We live together in like communion, by the light of the Truth and by the love that enlightens the heart by its own energy so that the truth may be seen and affirmed.

When European, American or Latin American writers today use this model, the accent on communion rather than on questions of personhood has the advantage of getting to the heart of the divinity and providing a model for human community, much needed today, by looking to the communion between Father and Son, even at times seeing the Spirit as that Other needed to be acknowledged by the two before they can look each other in the face. The resurgence of familial and communal metaphors and concepts in relating the distinction between them to the communion of Father, Son and Spirit (sometimes all three more femininely named) is thus tied to the desire to find in this central Christian mystery the inspiration, the moving force that leads God to embrace those who abide on this earth within the circles of hell and to bring them into the divine life. If God's involvement with suffering is not taken seriously, there is little point in baptizing in the name of the Trinity, and it is rather odd to recollect the language about the divine permissive will often taught to young theology students.

In privileging the image of communion rather than that of the processions of Word and Love, one can appeal quite rightly to the Father/Son relationship that John's Gospel brings so strikingly to the fore in the story of Jesus, Word made flesh. This does away with any sense of divine remoteness from the things of earth and from the human dilemma, as though God had sent "one of the three" to set things right on earth while remaining in the innermost divine being quite distant from it. It is in the Father's communion with Jesus that he too is intensely present among the children of the world, caught up by love and by the gift of his Son in the struggle between life and death, light and darkness in which humanity is involved. The Spirit, too, loving bond between Father and Son, is a gift of the divine self that enters the human heart and guides it in such a way that it finds communion with the Father through union with the Son, even through an affectionate bonding with him.

It is considered by several to be insufficient to speak only of the filial communion of the Word made flesh with the Father as we see it in the works, death and glorification of Jesus. What is shown in his flesh has to be something that belongs to an eternity of communion, to the very nature of the relationship in the Godhead between the Father and the Son. Hence they take the metaphors of *kenosis,* self-gift, self-abandonment, to have their origin in the Son's eternal relation to the Father and the Father's eternal relation to the Son. Neither holds to his own glory, his own life, but each yields before the other in giving of self. The question inevitably arises as to whether the suffering which the Father endured in abandoning his Son to death belongs within eternal communion, or whether the pain the Son feels in being abandoned is already somehow present before taking flesh. Answers differ considerably, even as authors vie with one another in imaging God's involvement with human suffering and human destiny as something that intimately affects the Godhead.

In line with this argument that the Trinity of the economy is the eternal Trinity, some push further and look for images of communion that may express the life shared between Father, Son and Spirit. Some propose the image of the family, three united in one love and one shared life. Others speak of three wise persons in communion with each other, and still others propose that a perfect communion in shared love requires a third, pursuing a line of thought found already in Richard of St Victor many centuries ago. No small part of this quest for a model of Trinitarian love is the desire to propose in the Trinity of persons an image or model for human love and interaction, at interpersonal and social levels.

In looking for an iconography of the Trinity, there is renewed interest in the image of the three seated peacefully at table under the tree of Mamre, where they are visitors given hospitality by Sarah and Abraham. When looking more keenly at that image, whether in the iconic representation of Rublov or on a Mexican *Retablos,* one sees that at the table of the three guests of Abraham and Sarah, the tree of Eden and the tree of the Cross—the tree of life and the tree of the knowledge of good and evil—cut a slash right down the middle of the picture. There are some who see in the cup at table's centre the slaughtered lamb, the necessary recollection of the death of Christ, outside of which the Godhead is not to be named. The tranquillity of the image is somehow disturbed even if the life of the Trinity is kept intact.

Nonetheless, there are still those, in whose corner I find myself, who think that such efforts to reconceive the divine relations in communion has multiple risks, and wonder whether a renewed appeal to the processions of Word and Love can serve the purposes sought in the appeal to the communion of persons in one *perichoresis.* One risk is always that of hovering on the brink of tritheism, of a retrieval of some sort of polytheism in order to get beyond explanations that make the One, True and All-powerful God too placid, remote and finally unconcerned. Another risk is that of staying on too good terms with Hegel, even while criticizing him, and not entirely avoiding the notion that God becomes God only through involvement with humanity. Of philosophers none made more effort than Hegel to think about the mystery of God and the mystery of the world together, and to take all economic, political, social and ecological efforts seriously. All has to be placed within the divine and the divine condescension, so that the mystery of the Absolute is that of an unceasing effort on God's part to find himself, even as he takes cognisance of the world he has made, comes to terms with all its defects, embraces all its restlessness and all its evolutions, and so, as it were, knows and fulfils his own being more completely. The effort to think about the Trinity as one thinks about the world and vice versa remains a challenge to Christian theology. It is possible, however, to come all too easily to terms with the sense that God needs the world and can be God only through the world.

Nothing is lost of the sense of God's embrace of human life and human suffering in sticking to the Western imagery of the procession of Word and Love within the Godhead, provided one comes to the knowledge of this mystery by healthy attention to the economy. In fact the Cappadocians as well as Augustine, when they discoursed upon the Trinity, spoke of the concomitance and harmony of Word and Love and its manifestation and operation within the economy of salvation and of creation. Speaking of the Word as Son, whatever its ultimate ramifications, belongs in the first place to its earthly incarnation. Being the likeness of the Father in human form, as the Word was sent to be, meant knowing, acknowledging, praising, and living the Fatherhood of God. It meant being to him as a Son and in the

Spirit inviting all who were and are in communion with him to live as God's chosen and beloved children. Transposed into speech about the eternal relations of Father and Word, Sonship underlines the affinity in nature and the likeness of Word to its origin. In reverse, looking upon the Son in human flesh and in his self-emptying as the image and likeness of the Father, requires the complement of seeing him as God's Word in its plenitude, always accompanied by the outpouring of the Father's love that rests upon him—and that rests, too, on those who are children and likeness in the Son and in the Icon.

The discussion about models of communion and procession invites first and foremost a meditation on the immanence of the Father through Word and Spirit in humanity and in its history, and has as much to do with imaging human relations in their origin, destiny and exemplarity as does a social metaphor of three persons in communion compared, for example, to the unity of a family. Humanity has failed to reconstruct and redirect human history on the basis of reason and creativity, of human rights and international convention, and of the spread of a civilization of manufacture and democracy and good merchandising. And so it seems it will continue to be. In such a foreboding of the future, how may the paradoxes of a divine presence on earth, in a broken, divided, self-hating and struggling humanity, find a place for a *theo-logos,* for whatever word is spoken about God? To find its place in the world, the Church needs badly to recover how God speaks to the world of the divine intent that existed "from the beginning."

Even as the Greeks, and in particular the Cappadocians, are invoked for their emphasis in Trinitarian theology on the distinction between persons and on the communion between the three, the West also needs to be alert to what they say of the apophatic, that is to say of knowing the limits on speech and thought in the silence of worship. There are limits of mind and heart on what we come to know and say of the eternal mystery of this God, who in his being and communion transcends the world, even while lovingly entering it through the mission of Son and Spirit. The apophatic way of the Cappadocians, Basil and the two Gregories is to keep their eyes turned to the economy for the figure of Christ, the Word addressed to us, the symbols of divine gift and the reality of the gift of grace in liturgy, knowing that there is no other way to ascend to God. The Church may worship the mystery while knowing that God dwells in silence, beyond our ken. Dogma spells out the contours of this economy in carefully chosen affirmative statements but of course it could never surrender what is given through the economy to reasoned ways of thinking about reality. The Church Fathers believed that through the gift of Christ's body and blood extended under the figures of bread and wine, with the eyes of Christ turned to us through the gaze of icons, the mind and heart, open to this advent of God, could move in contemplation beyond all concept. Even the numbers one and three supersede any counting in the *perichoresis* of the divine, since the relations between Father, Son and Spirit describe a perfect unity.[2]

We share by union with the humanity of the Word made flesh and through hearkening to the movements of the creative Spirit in the universe and in the Church. We are bidden to keep silent about God's innermost and eternal being, the eternal proceeding within the truth and the good of divine life. The concept of the personhood, the *hypostasis* of the three, does not spell out the mystery of the Trinity but only the grammar for those who must perforce speak. Even then it seems to me the mystery of God is better not compared to a communion of human persons, though divine Trinity may be found in sincere efforts to be communion, however blemished the image may be.

What this tells us is that one does not do theology unless caught into the movement of the Trinity at work in the economy, especially through liturgy and under the gaze of the icon, remembering the incarnate pain of Word made flesh. While the East has often put much store by the glory of the Word Incarnate (and his mother), at the heart of this glory there is, as well as the Tree of Mamre with its Three visitors, the image and icon of the descent into hell, or, in other words, of the *kenosis* of Christ. This fits well with the Gospel and letters of John in which we see that it is on the Cross that the glory is revealed (John 3:14-15). There is no capturing the glory unless one moves through the passage of the divine self-emptying. There is no uttering the name of Father, Son and Spirit except from that place and through a liturgical memorial that the disciples of Jesus dare to keep even in the circles of hell.

It is quite extraordinary how in this Gospel we are invited to look upon Christ affixed to the Cross to see his glory and the Father's glory, illumined inwardly by the Spirit. It is as though the cloud of Yahweh descended upon him at that moment and not on Tabor as in the Synoptics. In the passage John 3:14-21, where the reader is invited to look upon the glory of the Cross in faith, she is also given, with Nicodemus, a discourse on light and darkness. One can imagine the scene of the crucifixion as a Cross around which there is a circle of light and beyond that oceans of darkness. One may enter that light and stand there with the few women, or one may stay outside, preferring the darkness to the sombre brightness of the glory of the Crucified. The glory that radiates is the total communion of the Son with the Father, the obedience of the Son to the Father's way, the completeness of the gift of self, the emptying out for the salvation of the world. Blood and water flow from the side of the Lamb: nothing is left of life within that body, which nonetheless is paradoxically upon the Cross the sign of the risen One. It is a terrible gaze to place oneself beneath.

On the Shoulders of Augustine and Aquinas

Let us return to the tradition inherited from Augustine and Aquinas. Even without access to libraries, writing on a small island in the Pacific, I still had my scientific as well as my poetic references for reflecting on the God who gives by gifting of the divine self. Like most of my generation, I was schooled in the reading of Augustine and Aquinas and never escape referring back to them in theological reflection. I am quite convinced that we must still know them, for on their shoulders we stand.

Augustine

Despite all the words he used in his *Confessions* and his treatise on the Trinity, Augustine was quite reticent in speech about God. It was in grateful response to what God gives to humanity in the economy of redemption that he endeavoured to speak of the Trinity through its imaging in grace, for then he would speak only to the gift, and of the gift, that God gives. To do this he rooted his thoughts in considering the life of a single human person, configured to the image of Christ. A most opportune and indeed necessary prelude to reading Augustine's work on the Trinity is a reading of the *Confessions*, where memory, intelligence and will are at work in the narration of a life perceived under the light of divine grace and love.

Granted Augustine's platonic persuasion that all ideas dwell in the essence of the soul and await the encounter with experience to be expressed, I think nonetheless that one can appreciate the enduring nobility and appeal of his explanation of the Trinity only when one has had a moment when everything seems to come together, memory focusing on some present moment and pulling together both past and a vision of the future. This does not have to be a great moment. It can be as simple as watching the sandpiper making its way forward and holding its place in the sand by the edge of the sea, as celebrated in Elizabeth Bishop's poem. We live what has been given to us; we make our lives where we have been placed by a variety of circumstances and influences that we ourselves have not posited, but all comes together when we keep striving to go forward, to trust, to hold firm. We consent to the past, we look forward to the future with hope; in a moment of apparent unimportance life makes sense. What is casual then becomes significant, a moment of light whose rays illumine everything.

The key moment of Augustine's life, that moment when the whole story of his life came together and a future replenished with the good seemed possible, was in a garden when he heard a child bidding him to pick up the book and read (*Confessions* 8.12.30). On doing so, he read the words of Paul: "Not in riots and drunken parties, not in eroticism and indecencies, not in strife and rivalry, but put on the Lord Jesus Christ and make no provision for the flesh in its lusts" (Rom 13:13-14). Now he knew where life had been leading him, despite its vagaries, now he knew where all knowledge and affect must centre, now he found an answer to his yearning for the good and the profound. He was led to a vision of his own self as the place of God's dwelling, of a soul still beautiful though tarnished, a storehouse of all ideas and effects of good and beauty. It is in Christ, the very image and icon of the Father, that he saw the mirror of his own self illumined by grace, it is by adherence to Christ in love that the action of life was given both its source and its direction. God revealed himself to the one who read the book of the scriptures by his indwelling, by his light that shines on life, by his love that turns the soul to seek the good that it sees in the Son, the Father's image.

Now everything holds together in a promised, if only half-accomplished, unity. This is a unity, an image, an illumination, an attraction, that may give some measure of insight into the Divine Trinity. God dwells within as source of all truth and good, God expresses himself in his Word made flesh received in faith, God prompts us to seek the good and to love by the gift of the Spirit. May not this coherence of the inmost self, of the word that believes and focuses, of the love that seeks, yearns and moves, give us some understanding of God's own eternal self? And so Augustine presents (*On the Trinity*, chapter 21:40-42), almost tentatively and apologetically, the analogy of memory, understanding, and love as an intimation of God's eternal truth and beauty, as the perfect divine coherence, whereby Self, Word and Love are a perfect coherence and unity, three in a oneness that could not be more perfect.

While such explanation comes from personal conversion and experience, it is sustained by Augustine in his approach to many things of a more communal nature. In the sacraments of Baptism and Eucharist, he finds the seed of Word and Spirit, truth and love, sown and nourished, coming forth from the Father and leading to the Father. In these same sacraments, he finds the truth of a communion of all members of the Church as one Body in faith and love through the gift of the Word and Spirit. The human history in its eternal movement towards consummation, when good and evil, life and death, will be separated, when God will be all in all, is also to be grasped in faith as the movement of the Word and the Spirit, now embodied as witness in those who are children in the Son, who are one with him in the sacrifice of mercy and love. Creation itself, for all its suffering and travail, for all the violence and agony which spew forth from incomprehensible energies, is to be seen in the light of God's eternity, as the cosmos which in the splendour of six days comes forth in God's Word and is directed by the energy of God's love. It has its origin and its destiny in the very eternal self of God, and is writ as a story whose beginnings we do not see and whose destiny we can bare imagine, and yet may be seen whole in a still single moment of illumination and yearning.

Present to oneself through a memory that draws the whole of a life, in its prospects as well as in its past, into a unity beyond "timing," a believer in Christ sees a life totally transfigured by the image of the Incarnate Word. This is ground for that work of intelligence that draws out in thought, and in speech, the meaning of such an existence. Such beauty and form shine forth in this vision that love it one must and then act out of love of that which has been seen and is so faith-fully possessed. It is this roundelay of memory, intelligence and love that provides Augustine with an analogy for presenting some moderate insight into the mystery revealed through the advent of Father, Son and Spirit in their giving of themselves to the soul they inhabit. The mystery of Trinity in God is thus the mystery of the inter-action between total possession of self, speaking of self, and acting from the love that pours forth from the divine perception of—and the word-ing of—the divine goodness.

Memory is not simply a looking at things that went before, but it is being in touch, as yet inarticulately, with what is at the core of being and existence, with the inner depths where the mystery of origins and the mys-tery of what is in time to become, dwells. The indwelling of God by gifts of grace was well-evident to one who wrote the story of a soul in the *Confes-sions* as well as his work on the Trinity. But the metaphor may be drawn from what humans share and are together, rather than simply from the soul of one person. The gift of divine indwelling, in the oneness of Father, Word and Spirit, is a gift of communion and is to be known from the communion with which it gifts those who live from the depths and do not keep paddling in the shallows. Being in touch with whatever moves us from the centre, from life-centred yearnings, helps us in our God-talk and godly living.

Thomas Aquinas

Saint Thomas is nowadays often subjected to the criticism that he gave priority to the notion of one essence or substance over that of three per-sons, so that it was in view of the substantial being and unity of the God-head that he wrote of relations and of relations of origins. In the same vein it is said that he gave priority to the individual human person rather than to a vision of the collective and the social and that this provided him with his perspective on divine persons. Several things are, however, to be noted. In the first place, he taught that revelation shows us that the God who is the source of all being and who creates, both exists and creates within the relational mystery of his being in three persons. In other words, while rea-son may tell us of God as Pure Act of Being, revelation tells us that in this very being he is triune in the interrelation of Father, Son and Spirit. In the second place, his emphasis on relationality meant that nothing could be said of any of the divine persons except as related to the others, so that within the one essence there is eternal and constant relationality. In the third place, when it came to the economy of salvation, he was able to relate the missions of Word and Spirit to the inhabitation of the three in the soul, as did Augustine. This allowed some human but graced grasp of the divine mystery.

The nature and context of his discourse were of course quite different from that of Augustine. His purpose is both a systematic presentation of the mystery and an effort to relate faith and reason in a way that respects both the transcendent character of revelation and the power of human intelligence. To begin with, apart of course from the genuine theological insight involved, it is helpful for our own sakes to ask why Thomas chose to speak of God as subsistent being, the very core of Being, without discharge or limit. He was faced by two audiences, one philosophical and the other, at least remotely, the common people, more prone to imaginative reconstructions of truth.

Among the first audience, problems arose on two fronts. There were those who clung to some kind of platonic emanation to explain the existence and order of the universe. In such a vision, creation was necessary to the divine being, and at the same time the eternity and everlasting vision of human beings was called into question. Once the divine being came to its own self-expression and self-realization, created beings, including the human, were no longer necessary. If God's own self-fulfilment required creation, it seemed to Thomas, all being is limited, including that of God, and this did not seem to fit well with the God of the burning bush, who had exhibited a peculiar and very free freedom in face of human realities, and had also shown signs of a wondrous transcendence of earthly being. The God who provided names such as Saviour, Holy, Father, lord of history, could not be seen to belong to a world of limited and finite beings, simply bigger and better, even infinitely, than others. He lived and moved and had his being in its own sphere, even as he gave out to the created world the gift to be and the urge to strive in being towards ultimate good and perfection in being.

Some of the intellectuals of his first audience lived by some idea of divine revelation but thought that reason and revelation construed two quite different worlds. One might learn to straddle both, even quite successfully, but one could not make them converge. For Thomas, this seemed to belittle the harmony of the universe and God's creative act, as well as diminish respect for human beings. While Christians live by faith, they are endowed with intelligence, and even in face of revelation, reason can offer a perception and understanding of divine action and of the world that God created. If God in Trinitarian condescension created the world, how could thought of redemption and thought of creation not interlock?

The second audience that Thomas may have had in mind, and of whom his writings show him aware, was those more attuned to mythic language and story, who express their sense of reality more by image than by abstract thought. In staking a place on earth, they were often puzzled and perturbed by evil and found it hard to square thoughts of a good God with what they suffered, day to day and year to year. Those who led these people astray by easy-to-grasp answers, offered myths and rituals that allowed them to separate the two worlds of good and evil, each with its separate source and origin. For these, Thomas proclaimed the world good at the core because made by the good God, and ventured to explain what God does about evil within an overriding perception of God as ultimate goodness. While there are chapters on a divine permissive will that can make a modern reader shudder, overall the point was twofold: first, sin is human, and second, what God does is done out of his goodness, to lead humans back into good, and this is done through the sending of Word and Spirit, both in their distinctive ways abiding in human flesh.

With all of this in mind, Thomas may show us that in explaining the presence of the triune God in common and public life we may be better served by attention to the interlocking of intelligence and will, or understanding and love, than by anthropomorphic social metaphors of three coalescing in one. The names of Father, Son and Spirit describe both what God is for the world and what the divine is unto itself, in the essence of their relationality, once analogous anthropomorphisms are cleared away. But Sonship is a proper name for Word because of the likeness to the source. Hence the Son is the perfect image and icon of the Father and there is no Word that is not accompanied by the breath of Spirit. The infinite God, in whom Word and Love perfectly cohere, when taking flesh through the mission of this same Word and Spirit, appears among us in the form of one who lives a perfect Sonship in all adherence and address to God. This fitted for Thomas with his vision of God as being through and through, without limits, necessities, or compulsions. As a current Benedictine writer, Ghislain Lafont, reminds us, the theology of Thomas is to be connected constantly anew with the narrative of the Christ and of the Church that lives by belief in him.[3] Mindful of that, we will not separate the eternal procession of the Word from its fleshly form in the Son and in his followers.

If of course I want to think with Thomas, rather than simply think what he thought, I have to place myself within a Church that has a different audience, that has to speak in a different location, a different time, in the face of different issues. But I believe that this can be done by an analogy with the harmony of word and love, combined with a worshipping and divinely inspired reluctance to go too far in analysing the life of the divine Trinity. Granted its limits, God-talk is then well served by analogies provided by insights derived from the ways of being of a human person, and beyond that of a human community, who with intelligence, wisdom, and good will struggle to reach for the goal of good and truth. Rather than centre simply on an individual, this metaphor may, nay must, take in the efforts of humans to be social (if not always sociable), to live in harmony and community, to work together towards a goal, *and* to keep faith in times of decline, in worlds where evil abounds. Even there, there is the super-abundance of grace in the body of Christ and in the eschatological currents of the Spirit that do not run off into gulleys and drains.

One would then very inopportunely expect to find third millennium whole-cloth in the works of Thomas Aquinas, but one loses nothing in following up on some of his leads, weaving the threads picked loose from his garments. Thomas related the revelation of the Trinity to the mystery of creation, for it is in the relationality of persons that creation is done. He connected it, especially in relation to the Word, to the story of a humanity where some always struggle to establish an order of divine mercy rather than one of human distributive justice. As far as social life is concerned, he found its law in the freedom of the Spirit and the pursuit of the beatitudes, rather than in codes of law, be these ever so sublime. In all of this, God is relationally present, but this relationality comes alive, lets itself be spoken of, from the signs of divine presence in those who live by the beatitudes, who follow the example of the obedient and crucified Christ, who identify with him on the Cross. Present visibly in the world and in humanity, God is present in the relations of Word made flesh, made crucified flesh, calling out as Son to Father, and of Spirit poured out from the Father and drawing back into life with the Father, through communion with the One proclaimed and blessed as Son.

This way of talking of God, which even in these times of ontological retreat is inspired by Augustine and Aquinas, does not present a model of divine communion and harmony between three that humans are to copy. It says that we must "inscape," "insight," catch in its movement the interrelation of the Three in the forms and signs of divine presence in the world, always with a hawk eye to the iconic representation of liturgical action. This brings us back to *kenosis*, to the antinomy between glory and humiliation, as the core of the revelation of the mystery of God and Trinity. God is ever-present in the care-worn flesh of Christ's Body, in the movements of the Spirit towards compassion and hope, in a humanity that struggles where evil abounds by wise ordering and the good will of love to seek and pursue the end of divine justice, of the righteousness that by Word and Spirit God offers to the world as an act of self-donation. The three are one in relationship as we see it working out in the mystery of grace, and, beyond our seeing, in a communion where relationship and oneness merge in such a way that one stops counting. One steps into the silence of faith before the divine face shown to the world, in the marvel provoked by that table that sits in stillness even as it is pierced by the blade of the root of an inordinately ambiguous tree. The harmony of divine mission of Word and Spirit, and the harmony by which humans are invited to live, is the perfect harmony between what is said and what is done, between the sense of order and the inner instinct that leads to the implementation of this order.

This order by which Christ lived and died, and the order by which in communion with him the Spirit moves us to live, is the order of total self-gift, the order of the excess of love, the order of an excess of mercy that is ready to renounce all show of power and control such as that by which societies tend to define orders of justice. It is an ordering through communion that comes from God's Love, in the self-gift and self-communication of acts of creation, redemption and justification. In this self-gift, God appears in ways and in forms that seem to us lowly and are alien to habitual human notions of power and control.

Kenosis of the Spirit

It is often pointed out that Latin theology has problems with accounting for the presence of the Holy Spirit in the mysteries of salvation and in the life of the Trinity, paying as it does most attention to the relation between Father and Son. Applied to Augustine and Thomas this is questionable, though unfortunately true in the main. In efforts to learn from Greek theology, there have been many who have tried to make up for this lack. The best advice is to make sure we start with what we find in the books of the Scriptures and what we know of the experience of Spirit in the life of Christians and the life of the Church.

What we experience of Spirit is what leads us into the mystery of God as communion, where both Word and Love have their place. Following up on a line of thought opened by Karl Barth, Walter Kasper writes about the Spirit as possibility of revelation, in God and in humanity.[4] As scripture has it, the Spirit is shown forth, felt, as gift, gift of love, indwelling, who gives to know, remember, speak, and remain attached to Jesus Christ as Word and Son of the Father. Kasper also points out that the Spirit is the experience of a freedom, a freedom to love and to be creative. This experience of freedom through the Spirit says something too about the Spirit in God. There is a freedom in God that allows gift, speaking of the Word, incarnation, and inculturation. Gospel and remembrance of Incarnation/Pasch take root in many humanities and their stories. And in us, it is an inner breath, a breath of freedom, a sense of gift, an impulse to be open both to receive and to give, in happy remembrance of Jesus Christ.

Some write of a *kenosis* or self-emptying of the Spirit, complementing that of the Son. This image can be depicted in several ways. First, there is the work of the Spirit from the beginning of creation, moving without name through all the energies of the created universe, and in particular within the human spirit in a search for life, for a communion and reconciliation of all through acknowledgment of a common origin and common destiny. Then there is the Spirit at work in the prophets, giving voice to the divine word, hiding under the vague but forceful designation of the spirit of God. With the incarnation, there is a deferment of the Spirit to the Word

Made Flesh, to the Son who is the icon of the Father, now making all the energies of God's love flow towards the embodiment of all that is good and true and beautiful in the Christ and in the embodiment of Christ in the communities and peoples and cultures of the world. Finally, there is the way in which the Spirit ties itself to the Church, holy yet sinful. Though continually working in other ways, the Spirit faithfully works in and through this sinful and vagrant reality of the Church to make of it the sacrament of the reconciliation and community of all humankind.

Almost "because of" this self-limitation of the Spirit coming forth from the Father, so far at least in the lived story of the world, the harmony of the triune life of God has not shown itself in our ecclesial, social, political and economic patterns, despite such iconic glimpses as liturgy and the lives of the "fools of God" offer us. In the divine action and presence in the world, God is still struggling with evil and suffering. The only way that the divine is manifest is as *agape* in *kenosis*. Our common movement towards the eternity of God is only through this movement, where the gift gives itself, and where believers in the hope of things unseen live within this giving, and must still live by the mystery of divine self-emptying.

Conclusion

Attention has been drawn anew to the matter of continuing to name God in divine holiness in the circles of hell. If the names of God as Saviour, Creator, Spirit, Love, Truth, and ultimately Father of the beloved, Jesus the Christ, do not ring true when pronounced in desolation, the effort to name is better silenced. Today, as in the history of the people of the Covenant with Israel, there are persons and communities who invoke these names with trust and hope in the midst of their alienation from the fullness of life on earth. The names echo most genuinely as assurances of God's presence and as revelations of divine holiness and mystery when connected with moments of divine self-emptying in face of what humans might expect of power, and especially when revealed through the *kenosis* of Jesus upon the Cross, outside the camp. Lastly, this act of divine gift is situated within an analogy of the Divine Trinity as procession of Word and Spirit from the Father, pointing to the implications of this for understanding the economy of God's presence in the world, when both processions and missions are viewed as the origin and mode of God's loving gift. The mode and meaning of this divine self-gift is most strikingly presented to us in the *kenosis* of Son and Spirit, the root metaphor for all understanding of God's self-communication.

8

The Divine Dance: The Work of Creation

Knowing Yahweh as Saviour, the Israelite people also came to know this All Holy One as Creator. In one of his hymns, Paul (Col 1:15) invoked the Christ as Creator and first-born of creation. Liturgies based on ancient texts, as for example the second Eucharistic Prayer of the current Roman Missal, which is a reworking of the prayer from *The Apostolic Tradition*, readily look to him as the Word through whom God created the world. Thus our traditions invite us to think together the divine trinity, the work of salvation and the work of creation.

To write of creation and the flow of history on an island in the middle of the Pacific is to see reality from a curious perspective, almost like looking through a kaleidoscope that causes forms and colours to whirl and dance. In these Polynesian islands, especially on the smaller atolls, one loses a foothold on earth. Directly within one's gaze there is the blue, green and silver of lagoons and out some measure the white-horsed waves where the ocean, appearing black even in the sunlight, runs up against the coral reefs. Where one stands there is sand, some brush, a few coconut trees, the fragile dwellings of the islanders, a cemetery. A giant wave across the island and all would be washed away. At sunrise, the sky and sea are tinged with pink and red and at sunset the fierce amber and ochre yield in minutes to the blackness of night. As light gives way to night, sun and moon look for an instant at each other across the sky and the heavens are filled with stars that hang down, begging to be caught in the hand. From the insecure footing that one has on earth one is transported into that vast expanse, invited to retrace in the convergence of sky and ocean the unmapped path traveled by those sea pilgrims who plotted their voyage by the stars of the night and let themselves be carried by the flow of the waves to whatever island it would lead them.

An ocean of another kind opens up to the imagination, one whose beginning and end is untraceable. Floating on this ocean one ever risks being cast out upon the shore of the island of the day before where the unfamiliarity of location and odd traces of the past commingle. Humans are only specks in this vastness, whether they are rowing their pirogues across the seas or have planted a house on the flats of an atoll or on one of the volcanic islands, somewhere on the shore or up in the hills that rise precariously from the ocean's level, conveying the impression of being in danger of tumbling out into the void. Humanity is such a small and discardable part of this entire wonder and its foothold is so insecure, and yet God chose to make of it the more fulsome reflection of his own being. While the terms were used by Pablo Neruda of a sojourner on Easter Island, faced by the remains of its monuments of stone, there is a sense in which one is always on the face of the earth a "starry-eyed blunderer," a "transient," a shipwrecked traveler.[1] Or like Henri Matisse visiting Tahiti, the traveler is blinded by the light that seems to suffuse everything, even the most immediate objects, and must take some distance before being able to paint again.

In Polynesia, of time the most urgent and poignant sense of its transience is evoked when one stands in a crowd of mourners next to a newly dug grave and hears the people address their dead, not in the language of the settler or of parliament or of court of law or of commerce but in the heavy and vibrant tones of the tongue inherited from their ancestors, in which vowel sounds far outnumber consonants. Placed in the earth from which they will stand up to face the rising sun, the dead are committed to their ancestors, and bid to bring the memories of their kin and friends with them into the abyss across which they are to travel. One is ever before death, the death of place and the death of the other and the death of self and in these days the even more terrifying death of cultures. Time ends and the possibilities of time; one is face to face with the fact that all will either disappear or be changed within that bright light of the sun as it blinds us in a way that corrects our vision of all other reality.

In the vastness of this world and cosmos, and in the flux of time and ages, how can the human race be said to be "master" of the universe, or even have its place on the sixth day of creation as its crowning achievement? The human person is rather more like the sandpiper on the edge of the Atlantic Ocean,[2] preoccupied and obsessed, moving forward watching the grains of sand between its toes. It makes little progress, yet knows that only in moving will it keep its footing and not be swept away by the vast ocean that advances and recedes. But it is not without vision, it is not unaware of beauty: mid the grains black, white, tan and gray, there is quartz, rose and amethyst.

What and why God created and how he keeps in touch with us are constant questions and the stuff of many myths. Faced with these questions, for many, even learned people, the world of reason and the world of faith stand apart. Those who know about the scientific exploration of the universe and look into the origins of species can still quite naively accept a six-day creation and a God who is going to step in by revising the patterns of nature at will. All of us know that in pastoral work religious teachers find it problematic to respond to a common belief in divine providence as getting things done and the harsh disappointments that people feel when God fails to intervene to make things change. It is hard to come to grips with the fact that the God of small things is in the small things, not to change their movements but to make it possible for us to live with them and through them and into a beyond. It is hard to keep in mind that while we are invited to admire the wisdom of God in the universe, this wisdom is more finely made known in the fact that the privileged place for the divine presence among us is the one who suffers unjustly.

Apart from the daily disappointments that people have with God, in our age many are troubled in spirit, at least subconsciously, by awareness that we live in what is called an ecological disaster. They are also aware of the move towards the globalisation of the world's peoples in trade and politics and of how some have begun to claim the end of history, while at the same time vast multitudes live in the midst of cruel injustice. What can be said of the doctrine of God as Creator and the Lord of History when things are in such a mess? Surely some rethinking of doctrines of creation and providence is needed. Can it be aided by an appeal to the image of divine self-emptying? Looking back from the Cross, do we get a better grasp of the beauty and bounty of creation?

To ponder these matters, I follow in the wake of writers who point out that creation is a salvation story, and that in fact the question about a creator is originally a question about a saviour. In that light, I go back to the belief in creation professed in the Creed and to what it is to look for a divine presence in history.

Creator God[3]

Caught in the turmoil of an obstreperous and contentious humanity, and wondering where humans fit in a galaxy that seems without spatial limit, each generation is left with the question of how it all began. Even people without religious faith tend to speak of "creation," maybe because the term "story of the origins" is less catchy. Jewish writers and prophets help us to frame the context within which the issue of beginnings may be placed. Living under the sign of divine alliance, they tried to say where this God of treaties and covenants came from, and so they link him with patriarchs and matriarchs, Abraham and Sarah, Isaac and Rebecca, Jacob and Rachel, with their striving and often jealous offspring. God is thus given beginnings with the wandering Aramean of Deut 26, among nomads in need of pastures or trying to settle down somewhere more permanent, and escape the constant warring between rival peoples. But it is God who has the initiative and shows Abraham and his descendants the way to peace, in the recognition of this God with whom they wrestle for a name.

But where did all the others come from, all those other peoples, this earth that we all cherish and war over, the stars that excite our admiration, the sand on the shores that is beyond counting, the new moon that gives bright nights, the sun that rises every morning without fail, the vast expanses of water and the springs that quench thirst even in the desert waste? Hence come the stories of the beginnings of "everything," but in which even the beginnings of human fratricide and genocide and warring kingdoms must find a place. These become the story of creation, which Christians have so mishandled that they ended up with a six-day divine effort that did such things as put Galileo under house arrest and spawned odd ideas of original sin that consign millions of unbaptised infants to a place designated as limbo, where they never have to grow up but do not have much eternal fun either.

Reading Genesis

As some biblists have pointed out, it is the unit of chapters one to eleven of Genesis that gives us the story of the origins. The stories within the story, including the creation narrative, are to be read in the light of the salvation promised by Yahweh and never forgotten, whatever humanity's aberrations. These chapters can indeed be fancifully read backwards (as when for one's peculiar enjoyment one reads a detective story from the last chapter), beginning with the Tower of Babel that sees humanity divided, peoples caught in an interminable linguistic, ethnic, cultural and contentious divide. Continuing to read backwards, there is the disharmony between generations featured in the story of Noah and his sons, the quest for self-interest and pleasure that brought on the flood, and the fratricide in the story of Cain and Abel. In the middle of this human muddle is the story of the destruction of the earth itself by flood, to emerge anew only under the sign of the dove and the olive branch of peace. The effort to give all this root and origin gives rise to the story of Adam and Eve's irresponsibility and their desire to be themselves the criterion of the difference between good and evil, the human hubris that is the root of all evil. But it also gives rise to the story of a gradually be-spoken world that God saw to be good.

Reading backwards, what we are first given is an elaborate account of a reign of sin, that sin from which the God of Abraham and Moses offers salvation by way of divine justice. But the creation story tells us that this same God promised redemption "at the beginning," once the serpent came out from behind the tree, and that it is he who made everything but made it all good. The God who redeems Israel is then the God who made good and who is Good.

Creation and Providence

In spelling out dogmas and doctrines of creation, Christian teachings have been most concerned with this vision of an initial goodness. They have kept God's name clean and made sure that evil, however it enters the picture, is not seen as God's doing. We have the "facts," as it were: a good creation and a human race destined to be a divine image, to live in God's company, and on the other hand a reign of sin and evil in which humankind will not even leave nature alone but thwarts its growth and beauty, along with their own destiny. But redemptive love cannot be killed, and so God's constant action and intervention favour the intent of good.

In the history of Christian theology and devotion much of what is thought of as God's action, seen as a necessary follow-up on the act of creation, has been gathered under the umbrella of divine providence. One can be left with the disconcerting image of the God of Providence as a watchman on a tower correcting the order of the procession of creatures passing beneath. If, however, the teaching on God's providence is valuable and incontrovertible, it is simply that the saving and creator God is always present to humanity's striving, to the earth's yearnings, and especially to the suffering. God is present both where there is life and where there is death, always pouring out the Spirit without calculation (John 3:35). Situating our belief in the present era, this means for Christian faith that God, the Father of Jesus, is present in the circles of hell of this our world and on the land or upon the oceans laid waste by human emissions. It is there that we hear him utter, perhaps in a whisper, "I am, who I am."

How can we address such a God, take account of this naming and the need to take some ideas apart? The God of Creation, we pray, Creator God, all-powerful. The "all-powerful" is the part that sticks in the throat. Is his omnipotence that of doing mighty and marvellous things? Is it really something that reason itself, from which can be seen a way of explaining the origin and movements of the world? If he is all-powerful, why does he not intervene more often? Trite questions, maybe, but common sentiment for all that.

With scientific explorations into space, with the mapping of the human genome, with increasing knowledge of insect life, there is a tendency to revive the old argument from design for God's existence, finding an intelligence as vast as it is minute in the making of the universe, the microcosm and the macrocosm. This might seem to have gone out of vogue with Isaac Newton, but not quite so. Still, I suspect that there is not much point or much harvest to such argumentation, however erudite it sounds. What of all that comes and goes, of the vast universes that come and go, of the species that have disappeared, of the destruction and violence inherent in the emergence and disappearance of life or of quantities of mass? Is that "intelligible" and intelligent, on the evidence alone?

Certainly what we learn from scientific research or theory enlarges our sense of the universe and allows us both discovery and wonder. For those who have faith in God it may inspire praise, but it offers no argument from design. It is true that some may wish to appeal to science itself to speak of God in terms of the inexplicable beginning and the infinity of what it discovers, the infinity of space and the infinity of even a minute molecule but it is done with caution and Christian believers need to do likewise. Recently I read a story that claimed that Pius XII was inclined to take the data of astronomy and science as a way of arguing the doctrine of creation, even of a moment when God created, until a couple of Jesuits convinced him that this was not a very engaging line of proof. Papal stories of that sort are actually quite consoling, since they show popes with human foibles, and in this case one a bit too anxious to get proofs, even as in another matter he was intent on finding Peter's bones beneath the dome—in both cases, however, smart enough to listen to wiser counsels in the end.

But God the Creator is not quite rightly seen without more ado as the God of beginnings and endings. If Israelite prophecy made him the God of beginnings, this was because he was already there, as the God providing redemption for a rather desolate and insignificant people and a God who could be better known only by peering into the future. Rather than being taken for an engineer, God is more likely, likeably (?), seen as the ineffable in whom the universe is grounded, or a mighty breath who breathes through the universe with some vast yearning for being, for being not nothing but something. We do not need to know anything scientifically or factually of a moment of beginning, nor project any decipherable signs of an end to history, to profess faith in a Creator God who out of bounteous love sustains all things in a being of unfathomable desire.

In the thomistic teaching on creation, the movement to an end or finality was as important as the question of origins in spelling out the act of creation. Something could not participate in the Being of God, as creation and all created things were said to do, without an inner force and dynamic energy directed to the consummation of all things in truth, goodness, beauty. To locate belief in a Creator God one might think of a vast aspiration to being which God has given to the world, an urge to live, a great creative and exploratory memory in which all this mystery of existence, replete with its miseries, is treasured. Creation and providence affirm a presence and a desire to finality that escapes us, but which remains alive in the worst of times. Scientific explorations, while they show the extraordinary fabric of being and of the emergence and disappearance of species and of universes, might just as readily bespeak carelessness as order, readiness to let what is or has been disappear into nothingness, leaving hardly a trace behind. But it is much wiser not to confuse areas of discourse, muddling science with theology, or theology with science, and let faith speak to us of a God who is in love with the universe.

If God's answer to Job means simply "you do not understand" rather than "see what extraordinary things I have done," it makes more sense than would any set of explanations. There is a presence of the divine in all that is or has been, but there is no mapping its intelligence for us by the way of reason. To find some aspiration, some yearning for being, some great unsatisfied impulse in the world, is more striking than the "intelligence of patterns" and speaks rather of the hidden God than the infinite power and wisdom of scholastic theologians. To reverse Anselm's argument, there must be a wisdom hidden in all that we know, but think it we cannot, unless we go outside the camp where Jesus hangs between two thieves. As Hans Urs von Balthasar put it in the title of his small book, only love is worthy of faith.[4]

In effect, the Apostles' Creed expresses just this point in the first article, which says, I believe in God, the Father Almighty, Creator of Heaven and Earth. Creation, salvation and divine Fatherhood belong together. In professing belief in the economy of salvation, the Creed begins by associating creation and Father. This is to affirm that God is the origin of all that is, and that it is in the generation of the Word and the spiration of the Spirit that he breathes forth the universe. The love that is the love that forgives and saves, the love that sends Word and Spirit into the created universe to dwell among humans, is the same love in which the world is created and which continues to move all things towards a common destiny—just as they have a common origin. Hence the Creed ends by professing faith in the resurrection of the dead and life-everlasting, that marvelous metaphor that says that the life that comes from God will outlast death and transform all, even mortal flesh.

God Ever Present

As noted, within the horizon of faith it is necessary to rethink the doctrines of Creation and Providence and the ever-recurring liturgical address, "Almighty and Eternal God." Such rethinking must take place within the circles of hell, among those who suffer most from the impasse of evil and who hope even in such places.

What we call the doctrine of creation is firmly grounded in the story of Genesis, all seven days, where it is told in the light of the belief in salvation. It has been affirmed by the Church, as in 1215 at the Fourth Lateran Council, in the face of those who would answer the questions of evil by positing two principles and originators of life, the one the life of the Spirit and the other the life of Matter. This idea, too, can find some roots in Genesis, or in Job, considering the serpent in the garden and the scope the "good God" allows to Satan. However, the profession of faith in the one God, "creator of heaven and earth," says that answers are not as facile as ideas dubbed heretical would have them. As it happens, we don't know if there were heretics giving blossom to such ideas, since records were wantonly destroyed or hidden. There was it seems a great fear that even a parchment on which bad ideas were written could contaminate the world, as is so extravagantly portrayed in the figure of the old librarian monk in Umberto Eco's *Name of the Rose*.

The doctrine of creation, of the one unique God whom all must revere, does not stand alone. It goes with the doctrine of the incarnation, of the dwelling of God upon the earth, where the Son takes on combat and seems to lose, and in this apparent loss wins. Integral to the doctrine of the Word made flesh is the imagery of his Second Coming, of his judgment on all things human made in love, and of the revelation that humankind in its variety of histories must learn to live totally by God's promise that there will be life and that there shall be a new heaven and a new earth. To possess eternal life, life with all its possibilities, the life of which we speak when we profess that there is but one God, is to believe in the Son, on whom the Father has poured out the Spirit without calculating the discharge. Self-emptying takes on the tone of emptying out to such an extent that everything overflows with life and abundance, and that out of fullness comes fullness. The story of liberation and scandalous victory is what calls forth the story of creation. Israel is a sign for the nations, of God's law, covenant, redemption for all. Are there really many gods, guiding differently different nations under the one sky? Or is there but one God?

This story of creation, mythic though indeed it is, has a different ring to it than creation myths of a pre-biblical past or from more recent ethnological resources. There is no suggestion here of one thing coming out of another and all finally proceeding from God, with many intervening spirits in between. Here, all is done by God's word. It is a very free word. He speaks as he wills and goes on with the work when he finds pleasure in it. Nothing seems to compel him, except his care for his creatures. It is not good for man to be alone, so there must be woman. By this sexual union life is put in place by God, with whom humans share the task and the joy of passing on life.

One of the things that we Christians learn from interreligious dialogue is that peoples of other faiths sometimes have more vivacious images and expectations of creation than we do. The belief in creation that is our heritage is enriched by theirs. Looking back, it is not to be overlooked that the Israelites, living by a divine alliance, met up with peoples who had more definite images and stories of a creator God than they had. It was in part through encounter with them that they learned to think about the origin and end of life and of the cosmos itself. In that sense, we might in today's language say that they took what was good in other religions and integrated key insights into their own, but always with an eye first to the fact that God brings salvation and good and makes alliance with the faithful.

The God of alliance is then a/the God of creation, the very origin of life in a divinely free act of divine pleasure. There is no compulsion here but the pure bounty of good will and act. The alliance has a foundation beyond pacts made with nomads. It reaches back into (or deep into) the very origins of life and cosmos. But then, if humankind so enjoyed the company and the benignity of God, what happened? What happens today when things go out of joint and possession of the things of earth and space on earth is contested among peoples, and, within peoples, among races and genders? So to the mythic story of creation is added the mythic story of fall and sin and expulsion. To tell the truth, stories are needed.

The story tells of a mythic time when all was in harmony and humankind, in its original coupling, knew of but one God who could be lauded in the work of his hands, and who yet inhabited a rest that was not confined within the time and the space of his creating. But then the storyteller—whether single or composite is left to the exegetes—must perforce continue, given the experiences of evil: sin is already present in the time of the creating, there is tension between man and woman, between human and the other beings of God's creating, a fatal lack of harmony within the order of things, and an unsatisfied desire to outwit God in the human heart. Yet, beyond the tension, the strife, the lack of harmony, there is the one God, the God to whom the whole of creation looks for life and for reposeful peace.

Scientific theories and empirical observation are not banished from sight by faith, but faith has its own way of looking at the universe. To allow for lurking evil, there is a mythic tale joined to the story of the creation of the universe, distinct from that of the story of the sin of humankind, even though it ties in with it. The serpent in the garden ties in with myths of angelic fall and angelic warfare that have to do not only with human evil but with opposing forces at work in nature and the cosmos. Alongside the Genesis story of the good creation, these tales also speak of the origins of the world and of its destiny. While creation is good and has its destiny in living the glory of God, there are negative forces at work that produce conflict. Nature has its own demonic forces that produce havoc, and prevent harmony and peace. Hence we are given the mythic drama of combating angelic powers that affect the order of the universe. In faith, we cannot supply answers to how things work out, but we may see in hope Sophia's hand at work. The triune communion of Father, Word and Spirit is at work in the whole order of things and embraces all things in love. To speak of Christ in his *kenosis* as creator (Col 1:15-17) shows that divine reconciling energies are engaged in the universe's destiny of participation in the glory of God. We believe that these energies are kept alive in the power of the Spirit that hovers over the waters from the beginning. The promise of Christ's resurrection tells us that the reconciling gift of the Cross continues at work in the whole of creation, until the time when in him all things are submitted to God and become the kingdom of his rule of self-giving love.

Looking Back from the Fullness of Time

To say that there is a divine permissive will that allows evil to be in order to test human freedom, we have done little more than fudge. Some explanations are best silenced, or left to gather dust on library shelves. What God chooses to do in the abandon of divine freedom is more to the point. It inevitably brings us to the fullness of time when he pitched a tent in human flesh and met the world face to face, on its own terms but willing to challenge it precisely within that quadrant. He saw a young maid called Miriam in an out-of-the-way town, in whose face, as Rilke has it in one of his poems,[5] Gabriel could read the perfect expectation that resides only in the waiting of God's coming. He later met a woman at a well who needed to be healed of memories, and a blind man begging by the wayside, and two stressful sisters bewailing a lost brother. To these unlikely conversation partners, the Word that comes forth from God, with a strong urge to live, offered in himself, living water, unquenchable light of life, and the final victory over death that makes of things still life. And there was Judas, "who would betray him," dipping his hand with him in the dish. Is God's hand always in the dish with those who betray their sisters and brothers? Is that not the providence that bestows peace, not as the world knows it?

The providence of God is to be present to all and in everything, as a God of love, who gives his Spirit and who in his very creatures aspires to the fullness of life; to be present in the workings and the unworkings of the universe as a great aspiration for being, for life, for wonder. To be present to the suffering, and indeed to the sinner, and to where love is transgressed. The knowledge of God as Trinity comes from the economy of salvation and the indwelling of God in the human heart, and from that we come to believe in God's presence in history and in his creation, even in the circles of hell.

With his early and youthful work on the theology of hope, Jürgen Moltmann initiated a vast theological programme that led him through the mystery of a Crucified God into the experience of the Spirit of Life in the world, with its pointers to eternity, along the roads of creation and ecology, and right into the awesome communion of Father, Son and Spirit. But the starting point is always the fact that even in the memory of concentration camps, even in the concentration camps themselves and in all those places where earth and water are despoiled and made unlivable, some people live with an inextinguishable hope, not only for eternal life but for this world itself and its ongoing history. If today one is to get back to beginnings, if one is to speak of providence, if one is to harken to a God with one name multiplied as Father, Son and Spirit, one has to begin with this hope, and begin where it is located. And God does not enter the picture without self-emptying, *kenosis*.

When we read in Hebrews 1:2 or elsewhere that God sent his Son in the fullness of time, we tend to think only of the story of salvation and of a chronological sequence. As with the Book of Genesis, we can gain insight from reading the hymn in Col 1:15-21 backward. Read in sequence, the hymn proclaims Christ the image of the invisible God and the one in whom all is created, then it proclaims him the head of the Church and the first born from the dead, and finally the one who brought reconciliation and made peace by the blood of his Cross. If the hymn is read from end to beginning, it is seen that because Christ reconciled all things with the Father through the spilling of his blood, so he may be seen as head of the Church and the one in whom God created the universe. As James Dunn put it, in the shedding of his blood to make peace, Christ revealed the character of the power behind the creation of the world.[6]

The point of the proclamation is that as Redeemer, Christ, raised up from the head, is head of the Church. He is the person in whom humanity is saved and reconciled with God so that even now its members live with God in the kingdom of the beloved Son. The hymn, however, has larger horizons. Those who sing it look out upon a universe in which there are rebellious forces, powers at odds with each other, which now through the blood of Christ are reconciled. Not only is humanity made safe but the entire universe falls under the dominion of Christ, the beloved of the Father. It is in light of this reconciliation that he is proclaimed one with God in the creation of all things. A lordship that wishes peace and harmony for the world, a lordship that reveals its true character in what God does for the world in the Cross of Christ, in his self-emptying, is the power at work in the world's creation. This bespeaks both origins and destiny. The whole of creation comes forth from such a loving God, ready to mingle the blood of the Son with the sufferings of the universe, and in such a God it will enjoy eternal peace.

There is a sense in which the hymn recommended by Paul to the Colossians puts us back into the Book of Wisdom. The readers of this book are asked to look out upon the vast universe and to see there the work of Divine Wisdom. They are to observe the rhythm of the seasons and the rhythm of human life. They are to ponder the lilies of the field, the birds on the wing, the beasts in the forests and also the splendour of the galaxy above. But lest they should think that this alone manifests God's wise ways, God's delight to be with the children of the earth and all the works of divine hands, they are also to consider the lot of the one who suffers innocently and unjustly. That is the privileged place of God's wisdom. It is God's loving care for such people that reveals the true nature of the power that is at work in the creation of the universe. Not only that, but it is as children of God, as his special beloved in the world, that these suffering, who keep trust even in their human nothingness, appear as a more perfect image of God's relation to the universe. This prepares us for the revelation of God's image and his wisdom in the shedding of Christ's blood, in his humiliation before the powers of the earth, in the strong love that overcomes these forces that are inimical to life, and in the divine destiny that leaves its imprint on everything.

There is an inkling of this not only in Colossians but in other books of the New Testament as well. In Romans 8:19-20 Paul depicts how the groanings and futility of creation are tied up with human sin, just as its hopes belong with human hopes for the gift of divine freedom. In the Book of Revelation and in 1 Peter, the eternal salvation and life of human beings is to be found within the transformation of the universe, in the emergence of the new heaven and the new earth.

The challenge to faith in today's world is to bring to the needed reconciliation of humanity with the forces of the universe, the same love and humility that we are encouraged to bring to the reconciliation of enemies and cultures. The elements of nature are not at our service. We are at theirs. We are to live in the name of Christ and in the name of the Father, in the strength of the Spirit of wisdom, in peace with them. It is not possible for Church or humanity to give voice to the praise of God inherent in the work of divine hands unless they are at work towards universal peace, with respect and humility.

Concluding with John of the Cross

In the wake of these reflections, I find myself drawn into a poem attributed to John of the Cross, a romance on the verse *In Principio erat Verbum*, some lines of which I give here in my own rough English translation from a French version I found in the library at the Papeete seminary.[7] John presents the very act of creation as a love affair between Father and Son, joined so intimately and profusely in the love of the Spirit that it requires even a created beloved and lover:

> A spouse I would like to give to you, my Son, my well-beloved,
> A spouse who thanks to you would deserve to live with us.
> One who would eat with us at table, of the same bread of which
>   I nourish myself,
> So that she would know the good things that I possess in such a
>   Son,
> And so that from your grace and strength, she would find joy
>   with me.

Theologians may discuss whether creation is the work of the Word-Son or of Love-Spirit, of divine intelligence or of divine goodness, but John makes them both one, for God himself in his uttering is an eternal love affair. And of this being and love, he makes the world and holds it in being so that it too can, as a spouse of the Son, be absorbed into this love. As the Father wishes, may the world indeed be partaker of such love.

9

The Spiral of Time and Eternity: Eschatology and Trinity

---⁂---

In its thought on creation and on the link between creation and the sending into the world of Word and Spirit, theology today is working within an expanded sense of history that looks to human development even in ancient times, or what is scientifically called homogenesis, itself posited within the orbit of cosmogenesis. If people worry and even demonstrate in the streets about the "ecological problem," it is because at least in broad terms they see a link between all that goes into the making of human history, the development of the human itself, and the fate of natural and cosmic reality.

The Revealing of an Ungodly God

To be more evangelical in what we say of creation would be to allow the Gospel its transparency, to let the words of the kingdom and the figure of Christ stand forth, as spoken of the God who creates. In the interlocking of the mysteries of Creation, providence, history and divine Trinity, it might be a good idea to draw more on the New Testament Johannine corpus that speaks of God as Love, Spirit and Truth, while continuing to take God's revelation through *kenosis* seriously.

To commune within the mystery of this dynamic divine being, we live by the gift of the Word Incarnate and of the Spirit who makes us cry out, Abba, in communion with the whole of created reality. It is gifted/gifting Word and Spirit that bring God to human history and to the becoming of creation. By Word and Spirit, history is taken into an upward spiral towards an authentic espousal of the alterity of divine Spirit, Truth and Love. Moved inwardly, we aspire upwards, beyond loving by the desires of the flesh (even in religion!) and narrow criteria of true or false, and beyond the confined service of narrow ends, becoming through fidelity to Word and the animation of Spirit totally self-gift and appreciative of all that comes to us by gift.

162

Naming this God of eternal and ever-present triune communion in the circles of hell means looking to the experience of the gift of God that pervades even there. This is the presence of the suffering servant, the Son, who identifies himself with the wounded, the suffering and the dead, and of the gift of the Spirit that moves to fraternity and love, even in their absence. Such an experience and knowledge of God, by grace, is not reducible to formulations of divine essence and activities. It is within the anomalies and aporias of the affirmation of the divine within the world that one comes to God. The way of the apophatic, the non-knowing of affirmation, is for those who wrestle their way through these anomalies, and believe "despite sin" and "because of the superabundance" of the gift of Christ and the movements of the Spirit.

History is sometimes said today to be anthropogenesis, that is, a matter of the human race developing and evolving in an ever more complex system of communication and exchange, beyond boundaries of human distinctions and with a sense of shared beauty and destiny with nature and cosmos. When this seems too limited, it is complemented by saying that it is also cosmogenesis, once the human race comes face to face with the fact that its destiny is linked to that of all things and over which in its sin it has tried to exercise an inordinate magisterium. What happens if this anthropogenesis and cosmogenesis is read as "theogenesis," not to explain how God becomes, but as the story of a God who is truly triune in a dance of love upon our earth, where the meek and poor in spirit beloved by God are the movers of history and all creation groans and aspires to freedom?

History is not a chronology of facts. The most mundane of human stories cannot be measured by clock and calendar. The relativity of time to space, to speed and movement, has worked its way into our perceptions of history, not only of cosmic wonder. It is stored up energy that makes movement and passes from capacity to act. The capacity to suffer, to be "patient to" what is done unto one, increases the capacity to act.

When we talk of God in history, we resort to speaking Greek and measure by *kairos,* not *chronos.* That is to say, we leave our clocks on the mantle and our calendars on the wall and look around us for signs of life vibrating, for the breath of a Spirit blowing. Seize the day, seize the power to love and move, provided by those moments that stand out. This is the measure of our lives, not calendars, not even millennia.

How to think this through within all the complexities of anthropogenesis, of cosmogenesis, of economic, social, cultural, artistic, political movements, in an age of globalisation, when humankind is measuring itself out in its capacity to act, to take stock, to turn things around, even to change climates, oceans and the fashions of procreation? In the midst of this, who are the ones who make history as a revelation of divine patience, love, sending forth? Where is God, where is the divine dance? Blessed are the peacemakers, and indeed the martyrs of our time, including those children in forced labour, or who die beneath the bombs, or who explode themselves for what elders have taught them to believe just and right. If God is "all-powerful," it is in Christ, on the Cross, in the combat between death and life, hate and evil. In him we are assured of the hope of life to all, whatever their suffering and their misfortune, a life that resides in the power to love, to serve.

In the past, the Church was at times quite stubborn in turning the doctrine of creation and providence into opposition to the findings of science about the workings of the universe, or even the working of the human body, in the name of the Bible or in the name of one who controls everything in minute detail and enters the picture at will. In the beginning, however, this notion of the all-powerful does not seem to have been the one that mattered. More telling was the acclamation before the Cross on Good Friday: O Holy God, O Holy Strong One, O Holy Immortal One. Who hangs upon a Cross.

It is good at times to invoke prayer traditions rather than doctrines to get at the roots of belief. Thus in the Roman liturgy, the appeal to God, creator and provident, is a quieter matter, an expression of the trust that God will let his Church live in peace, that he will harmoniously grant it space to breathe and above all to worship, in the midst of war, of tempest, of sin, of persecution, of invasion, of earthquake, of flood, of pestilence. A provident God is the God who is able and willing to support his Church in the midst of all that, who orders things not by making them happen but by the gift of peace, the gift of the Spirit of peace, and the gift of obedience to the twin commandments of Love of God and Love of neighbour. In that peace, in that love, is the true dwelling-place of the provident God, of God the provider. Later, the Church claimed a powerful God in the name of its own claim to power, a God who managed all things, great and small. Which may indeed be an image that sometimes even occurs in scripture but is outwitted by Prophets, Wisdom and a Gospel that is more interested in the lilies of the field and in counting sparrows to watch for spring.

From certain explanations of divine power one returns to the sayings and parables of Jesus and especially to his beatitudes with a sense of relief. "Denken ist nachdenken," to think is to think after the Word has been addressed to us, as I believe Eberhard Jüngel, a German theologian, has it.[1] The beginning is the word, not our rational thoughts about God. Hence, it is with the conflicts and ambiguities of the naming of God that occur in the Bible that a Christian believer begins in earnest to think about God, rather than with the theodicy of Descartes. Sort out these ambiguities, or better still, abide (in) them, and you may be on the road to open your soul to the divine Name given on the Cross. Note that everything that refers to creation, to the Lord of history, to providence, to the expectation of God's kingdom, refers to the alliance, the covenant. Were humankind to live by the covenant there would be peace and justice throughout the world. In the meantime, there are those who suffer for righteousness' sake. In the meantime those who know God are those who live by such righteousness, even in a perverse world. God does not promise to deliver them from this sort of trial, only from a trial to their faith or to their hope in the future of the kingdom. One may live, even when living for the present, in the hope of a life that endures in the love of God, so that in fact it is the weak who know God, and it is in weakness that we know his goodness and his power to save.

Death

Ultimately it is in the weakness of death that we will know God. We will be finally taken over by the totally gratuitous and superabundant grace of Christ and will surrender ourselves totally to divine gift. Beyond this prospect of human death, however, there is a sense in which we can say that God makes his true being known in death and through death. We know God in the death of Jesus and when death is entered in communion with him we will know God in our own death.

In contemporary theology there is some stress on death, or facing death, as a final moment of decision, affecting all that the person has been and is before God. More basically we can see it as the moment when one is truly justified by faith, when one knows the grace of God freely and lovingly given, when one will behold the fullness and truth of all that is revealed in the Pasch of Christ. Some of the more eloquent passages on death in the scriptures come from the farewell discourses of those parting this life, such as Jacob (Genesis 49) and Moses (Deuteronomy 33 and 34). In the New Testament, there is great poignancy in the farewell discourses of Jesus (John 13-17) and Paul (Acts 20:17-35). It is the moment when they can no longer continue in the companionship of their friends, when they can no longer act for others or carry out their task, the mission they received, Jesus from the Father and Paul from the Jesus whom he persecuted, the Christ of God. But it is in this moment that they enter fully into divine communion with the Father. In the death of Jesus, God's Son and Word, we see the limits of God's presence in the world, in human life, in human history. The fullness of divine life is not contained within this form; instead of God becoming God through this presence among creatures, God empties himself of all form in order to take creation into his own fullness. Theology has often wrestled with the human, the religious and the philosophical issue of the inevitability of death. It has been one of faith's fantasies that without original sin humans would not have died, that they were created immortal but by sin lost this gift. Paul himself says that with sin death entered the world (Rom 5:12ff.). But death has always been, and is always the one inevitability of life. In being obedient, not only unto death but to death, Jesus subjected himself to this inevitable and embraced the tragic of human existence. This tragic is not reducible to the impossibility of realizing my own plans, my own possibilities, but it includes the awareness of being unable to remain in communion and companionship with others, of not being able to know more of the wonders of nature and the universe. It is an awful and awesome closure, the final bowing to one's limitations. So we find Jesus embracing this condition for the sake of humanity and Paul for the sake of being configured to the Son.

In coming as Word and Spirit into the world, God took on the origins and depths of human being in its efforts to go from the one to the many and to bring the many into one as an ultimate destiny. In theological speculation or in the protestations of believers, God finds himself told that he could have saved humankind from death, that he could have abolished death even in the aftermath of sin. There were even those who thought that with Christ's Pasch they could keep on living, that at least some would bypass death. What a wonderful fantasy to imagine that with Word and Spirit calling forth and breathing out life in our midst nothing would die, all would be immortal, without the limits of space and time. Then indeed God would show his power over life and death in the very act of revealing this eternal trinity of life and life-giving Spirit. It is not so. In the face of continuing decay and death, theology has tried to pardon God and stand up for justice by calling it punishment, God's self-assertion and the assertion of divine justice in face of the impudence of sin, of wanting to be the arbiter between good and evil, between life and death. The simple fact of the matter, however, is not that God reveals his just self by not saving from death, or by a justice that imposes death as a penalty. The true justice of God is revealed in the passing of Word and Spirit into death in their earthly appearances in Christ and in his Body, and through death into the fullness of eternal communion with the Father. Nothing saves from death but death, and in this we behold the face of God. The divine freedom is not to punish, to hold humankind to being mortal and decadent, but to choose to reveal its own love for the world, its own lovely self, by accompanying humankind through death. This is a better revelation than exercising a power that would put a stop to mortality.

The entry into communion with all reality, even for Word and Spirit, is possible only in laying aside mortal flesh. Their incorruptibility appears paradoxically in passing through the corruption of death, in breaking all the bonds that dying demands of one so as to open up the passion for others, the gift of being gifted beyond one's measure. It is not only that we pass through death to be saved from mortality by the resurrection of Christ, but that God passes in Word and Spirit through mortality to take on all flesh and bring all being into communion, to infuse all reality with the magnificence of communion in divine life. In this passage through death life prevails, because the yearning for life, the desire for the good and for communion, the embrace of what is not the self, expands and enlarges the capacities of the heart.

Reflection upon the place and power of death in human history cannot be restricted to the issue of individual death. Paul saw death as a cosmic force that pervaded all reality so that it is a constant part of our experience. Everything is touched by it. In truth, for each and every one of us, death is first encountered as the death of the other. Someone passes from our midst, our bonds with the dying and dead are broken, the familiar surrounds that give comfort or at least spell out the periphery of our existence are no longer. On the other hand, the passing of another means entering into a new relation with them, one made possible in their passing on. Commemoration of the dead in prayer and liturgy expresses this. Not only do we profess that we remain together in the love of God and the communion of the saints but we assume the rule of piety to keep memory. The dead remain a part of the human story through the memory of the living. Those whose deaths appear senseless, those who have not had the chance to live, are given a life when Word and Spirit remind us that in the *hodie* of God, in this day which is God's day, even the dead live among us. Passed on into eternal life, they still walk through this life as members of the living community. Some cultures talk of the "living dead." They means those whose memories and presence are kept alive, as distinct from those best commended to oblivion.

Beyond personal death and the way in which it is experienced as an expansion of the desire for life by those who remain, there is the death that affects peoples and cultures. Languages die out, peoples die out, cultures recede and wane. These too keep some place in human history to the extent that they are remembered and valued as heritage with which we go into the future. Faith in the power of Word and Spirit tell us more. Here too they speak to us of this day, this day which is God's day when all is kept alive through remembrance, through being embraced in love.

In the death of Christ, his willing death to sanctify the humanity he took on, he passed through death to a greater communion of this humanity with God. The descent into hell means symbolically that he entered into death in the fullness of its harrowing. He harrowed hell by being harrowed first by it. He encountered this death as a cutting off from life in his meeting in Hades with those of earlier covenants (1 Peter 3:19). He suffered the pains of abandonment and of loss. But in this passing over he brought humanity into a fullness of life that cannot be experienced within the mortal limits of any human flesh or mind. It is a gift that only God gives by the final action of justifying, of introducing a divine justice that is beyond calculation.

Creation, Ecology, and Eschatology

Some theologies develop a vision of death as, among other things, an entering into a new relationship to the material world, to the whole of reality. We experience this in limited fashion through the communion with the

Risen Christ that is ours by Baptism in hope. To enter into God's vision of humankind and of the universe we pass in him through death, or God himself in Word and Spirit passes in us through death. No eschatology and no theology of human destiny or history can content itself to treat solely of the human realm. It goes further by considering the oneness of human destiny with that of nature. Since this belongs to hope, how can we even now view nature in light of this common destiny?

Reading the Book of Wisdom quite placidly, we have always looked to creation as God's work, even as his wise work, and in the prayer of the psalms blessed him for all its marvels. Earthquakes and natural disasters, and one thinks of the furor over Lisbon, give non-believers the chance to question God, but the Church does not seem to have been unduly perturbed, to have continued to indulge arguments from design, and to work such matters into theologies of providence.

Blessings for creation may come a little harder today for two reasons. First, being urbanized we see it second hand on our plates and in flower pots; we get the produce of earth with clean hands. More tragically, when alert to what happens around us we see the ruination of forests, oceans, lakes and rivers, and know such phenomena as global warming and listen in on the quarrels over the Kyoto protocol. This drives home the realisation of how intertwined humanity's fate is with the fate of nature and that the ecological problem is largely of human making, though to what degree we are unsure. What does this have to do with the blessings of creation, we may ask, with thanking God for creation, with asking the saints to protect us against the demons that inhabit things, or simply with imploring God to be beneficent in regarding them so that we might benefit from them?

The traditions of liturgical blessings can be quite instructive on God, humanity and ecology and on how humans have always struggled to relate harmoniously to the things of earth, and often feel that demonic powers are at work to make the realities of cosmic cycles humanity's undoing.[2] This is most noteworthy in how blessings changed in the course of time. In their table blessings the Jewish people always blessed God for the land, for food and drink, and for all the works of his hands. The early Christian Churches did likewise and the eucharistic memorial or the blessing of oil for anointing were both praise of God for the things of earth and thanksgiving for the work of redemption. Indeed, a eucharistic action could include a blessing for first-fruits of the harvest, for God has made them grow and "commanded the earth to bear all its fruits for the joy and nourishment of humans and animals."

Nonetheless, humanity's relation with earth was not always pacific and many enjoyed little enough of its fruits. The history of ritual blessing can be invoked to show how relationship to things of earth was part of human history, even of a difficult and painful history when humans and earth together struggled for survival. This ritual story shows us how blessing moved from thanksgiving to exorcism and petition, reflecting how whole societies lived their relation to the things of creation. People who lived in want were inclined to see nature demonised or inhabited by spirits that prevented field, flock and forest from being fruitful. Thus the thanks of blessing gave way in part to exorcism and folk hoped for a better return from earth than they were getting, "if God so willed." In what we call the Western Middle Ages, there was a vast array of such ritual prayers and actions and frequent appeal to the priestly power of exorcism and blessing. Anxiety about what nature might or might not do took over from blessing God in thanks.

When we examine the cultural and social milieu, we see that those who had resort to such blessings-turned-beseechings were people with little power, people who enjoyed little enough of fruits of earth, and were worried about what the morrow might bring and about the fruition of what little they had. Not only individual families but whole communities were subject to poverty and hard labour, to the weary toil to bring forth something for their sustenance. Blessings in the desire for something better became a prime expression of whatever hope they could muster and of their religious devotion when they looked to God and his saints. One of the reasons why Francis of Assisi is a striking figure is that he could willingly share the lot of the poor, even become a beggar with his bowl, and yet look out from San Damiano over the land and praise God for all that one could behold, by day and by night. The difference is that his poverty was willed, not inflicted from birth, though his canticle invited rich and poor alike to look further than their own holdings to see the Creator God mirrored in his works.

Those who had power, both then and later, were inclined to their own reading of the Book of Genesis. They underlined the command to master and to work nature. They forged practices and philosophies and theologies of dominion, bringing about what has been dubbed "the death of nature." We can see now that the ecological problem is an ethical issue and requires a new attitude to the things of creation, one that recognizes coexistence and the call to respect nature and its own workings, to work with rather than dominate, knowing bonding in our common future.

Retrieving a sense of wonder and seeing all as gift of a giving God would help, a giving God who cares for all creatures and their future and not only for humankind and who in divine love is everywhere present. We may wonder at nature in itself and at the divine force of life therein. We are called to bless God not because we have it but because it is there and we are set down in the midst of it, to share the gift and to cohabit and respect. God has placed humankind in the garden of paradise and human hands are still not to touch the tree of the knowledge of good and evil. In other words, we are not to claim to know all the workings of nature, nor to claim a new dominion over those areas where we have penetrated the secrets of mass, of life, of ebb and flow. To claim too much knowledge, to want to dominate and use as we will, is another way of wishing to be arbiter of what is good and what is evil.

We most often associate eschatological vision with humanity's future but we have been taught by the Bible that all creation groans and that God promises a new heaven and a new earth. Eschatological hope must perforce include ecological hope. Expectations for a blessed future for the communion of humanity and creation, beyond our doing and imagining, are grounded in God's covenant and promises but they require fidelity and humility. The promises give the possibility of looking beyond travail and tragedy, of trusting in God's action for a reign of justice and peace, yet to be brought about but at work even now among those who live by the Beatitudes/Blessings of the kingdom in relation to the things of nature as well as in relation to earth's dwellers. Our hope needs to be larger than human community and to encompass in God's name the cohabitation and communion of humankind with all that makes up the vast wonder of the universe. The whole is God's loving creation, the outpouring of his triune love, and the future is God's loving concern. We cannot claim to respect humanity if we do not respect earth, ocean, waterways and heavens, and we cannot hope for ourselves without hoping for them. It has often been said that in its prayer the Church gives voice to all of creation in praise of God: it must learn to give voice to hope for all of creation. The events and history that led us to look to God's gracious action through Word and Spirit includes what becomes of all creation, not just the human race. Integration of two perspectives, not opposition, is called for.

It is in ways rather a pity that the calendar revision of the Roman liturgy has set aside the Ember Days of Spring, Summer, Autumn and Winter. Of course there is no point in celebrating them simultaneously in both hemispheres since they mark the rhythms of nature, and it is also unfortunate that they may have been given more attention than feasts on the calendar of God's salvific *kairos*. It is quite interesting to see especially how Ember Days of December and Advent clashed, and no doubt the calendar revision was made to make sure that Advent prevailed. However, attention to the ebb and flow of life in nature is not alien to Advent hope. It prepares us for the birth of the child who is the Daystar, who is hailed as the earthly manifestation of the Word through whom God created heaven and earth. His Incarnation is the work of the Spirit that hovered over the waters and brought back the olive branch to the ark and who in Christian mysticism is identified with the feminine Wisdom of God that graced the universe. How can we hail the child if we do not know creation?

Many other things in prayer need to be reclaimed: blessings for food, blessings for animals, blessings for the seasons, blessings of the God of dry must and sour wafer. The internet of sacramental action was meant to be highly respectful of the things of earth and season but the Church in the

West lost sight of this. A faith tradition teaches us that if the living and tri-une God is not blessed for bread and wine it is impossible to see the Body and Blood in the elements. It tells us also that water must flow or there is the risk that the life of grace will be as stagnant as the dirty pool, and it tells us that it is by being pressed down that olives gush forth oil, for happiness, for commensality, for healing and consoling. True bread, true wine, true water, true oil bespeak all life, at times its abundance and at times its want, but it is only so that they are sacraments of the gift of God's Son and Spirit.

In God's Name

From prayers and parables and the thought of creation we go back to the name of the Father, the Son and the Holy Spirit. The power of God in biblical revelation resides in the revelation of God's loving desire to choose for himself a people, to make alliance with that people, to make them hanker after a Messiah who would restore a reign of justice and peace, not just for humanity but for all that is the work of God's hands. One or other of the prophets, and those whom we call the "poor of Yahweh" (people like Miriam of Nazareth) got a glimpse into the fact that this Messiah would turn out to be ugly and would be found outside the camp. The power of the Christ, the well-beloved Son, and the power of the Spirit, gift above gifts, is to keep faith and keep people faithful. It is to keep hope alive when all is crumbling around, to have the grace to know that God is Father and this for all eternity, in a way of life that is beyond the limits of human imagination. When Jesus did cure or heal or make see, it was in virtue of the question, "do you believe?" In faith, we do not expect God to put an end to wars, to let the righteous win, to prevent accidents, to heal from cancer, to stop earthquakes. We expect that the grace of the Son and the Spirit may keep us faithful, because he is faithful, "for better or for worse, in health or in sickness," in peace or in war, in nature beneficent and in nature threatened, for death will "never us part."

The creative power of God as affirmed in faith has little to do with beginnings and endings, though it has been confused with that even by great theologians who got Genesis mixed up with historical narrative. Nor is it the belief that God may providentially prevent disasters and death. It is the belief in a sustaining energy, a life force at the heart of all existence and all movement. It holds aspiration in existence, in balance and in a vital, often disturbing, move towards gathering in the infinite and extending the finite. It keeps alive a sustained desire for being and co-herence, and co-invergence of all forms of be-ing. To believe in providence is to believe that this force to be, that is not self-sustained but always gift, is at work at the heart of things and shows itself at its core in a tranquillity of heart before good and evil, and in unexpected and (humanly) uncontrolled external manifestations that interrupt the order of things.

By temperament and by education, I am not much inclined to give great credence (which is to abstain from belief, not to be persuaded, rather than not to believe) or importance to miracles, apparitions and sanctuaries. They seem to provide too much fodder for the idea of an interventionist God and to a sort of apocalyptic prediction of hell and damnation for the masses who fail to be devotees. On the other side, while seeing no need to offer an apologetics of the marvellous, I see that such things do keep alive a sense of a greater and unmapped energy at work, which fits into a belief in a creator God and into the persuasion that all things must converge. It asks us to commit our hopes and desires to the ultimate pronouncement of divine judgment on how we inhabit our universe and treat the things of earth, including the weak and the sick in our "stately" midst. It is no wonder that apparitions erupt in a time when human enterprise claims the power to control and direct, asserting an autonomy of thought and action, or in war when human energies are geared to destructive ends. Lourdes and La Salette, Guadalupe and Fatima, are all testimonies to this. The Spirit of God is at work, it seems, in such popular turning to what comes from God alone.

But it is the God of Jesus Christ who is creator and provident, and thus the life-force; what sustains existence is the gift of Love. It is therefore a freeing providence, one that does not submit the force of love and the power of creative imagination to a simple conformity or to fatalism in the face of giant and cosmic forces. It may call for limits in the folds of the discovery of DNA patterns or genomes and their promise of greater human power to control life. The God present is the God who empties himself of all display of power and majesty in order to be with us, to show his true self to us, the God present on dusty roads, in the middle of suffering and in bread and wine at the daily table, to which all the ultimately uncontrollable forces of water lead us. As Christians, we are both cosmically attuned and domesticated, provided as true believers we have no pretensions to control the universe.

Nothing But Gift

For a long time Christian writers and philosophers were fascinated by order and its underlying and creative Word in and through whom all things were made. What was not ordered was marginal or evil. All things and desires were subsumed thereunto. Whatever the critique of medieval theodicy, rationalists who still wanted God alive contributed to an equation of the divinity with order.

Today we have run up against disorder in the ordering of things. There is a great desire for a common humanity, for a fraternity, but the reality is terribly violent and fractured. And all is not explicable by the tower of Babel. Some scientists even look for a big bang, for a moment when life started among the marvellous, explosive, but not life-bearing planets from which all might start. Scientists and cineastes might both conjecture myths and images of cosmogenesis, biogenesis, anthropogenesis. Eschatological, I hope, awaiting a divine coming, a promised hope unplanned, not built into the ordering of things.

Images of triune creation have their place in the reflection of theologians. I believe that Thomas Aquinas addressed the mystery in both sapiential and theoretical terms. When he describes God in his *Summa* he seems at first to give priority to being and intelligence, and there is no doubt that he describes the procession of the Son as the uttering of a Word, and Word in the uttering. But he quickly points to the overflow of divine goodness within and without, and to the uttering of Word as itself an act of Love, the Spirit proceeding and joining the Father and the Son in eternal union. And then, having fixed the realities of goodness, utterance and love, he shows a wonderful discretion in refraining from further attempts to describe the persons. Is it not enough to know that the mystery of God is a mystery in relation to which persons hold their entire personhood, and that in such relationship they are constantly engaged in the wonder of expressing eternal truth and infinite love? This is what God wanted the world to know in giving it his Son and pouring out his Spirit on the Son and on his brothers and sisters, without calculation.

Why do some philosophers want to say that in his Goodness God is "beyond being," when Saint Thomas has said that he is Being itself, without limit and confinement? It is I think because when we encounter beings and think about being we see it as limited, and risk putting God within limits, making him whole and entire from the fabric of the stuff of the world. Can you think about God only by thinking of the divine in terms of the world? What happens when you try to think beyond such terms? The apophatic is one answer, the apophatic of silence and keeping silence, an inner self that seems to leap beyond the self into an abyss. Or there is the answer of the Cross, an answer that God has given us to make us cherish and contemplate, through the agony of withdrawal and the ecstasy of absorption, a God about whom no being can reflect the truth and the goodness, a God who refuses to be thought of and discussed in terms of the wonders of creation, of what nonetheless he has brought into being out of an eternal love affair.

One becomes contemplative by learning how to receive gift, wholeheartedly. We shall never open our hearts to God, we shall never be able to say from the heart anything of God that rings true, that rings to the truth of God, unless we can open our heart to the reality of gift. Any culture reveals its innermost self in its rites of the exchange of gifts. All the relationships of a society, from the social to the familial to the personal to the shared intimacy of affection and mutual regard, are expressed in the richness of polysemy, in the ritualised exchange of gifts. Cultural exchange sometimes breaks down through the failure to grasp the procedures of gift-giving. One of the stories told of the British occupation of the Polynesian islands is that when the first ship arrived, a strange craft to those accustomed to the pirogue, women went out to greet the sailors and offer bales of dyed cloth. The British responded by an endeavour to barter, showing that they did not understand what was exchanged through the medium of gift. The report of the women to the islanders was thus negative about the mores of the newcomers.

God too relates through an exchange of gift that is highlighted in the exorbitance of the exchange of divinity and humanity in the Incarnation, which in liturgy is given the name of sacrifice. Christianity has often side-tracked itself in dealing with the images, practices and living metaphor of sacrifice. Much in the literature on the death of Christ, on dying in Christ and on the Eucharist is the attempt to arrive at a definition, a conception, of sacrifice that may be applied to the temple rituals of Israel, to the death of Christ, to life in Christ and to the Eucharist. The attempts are often victims to univocity, allowing of difference only in degree and not in kind. Thus humankind, having failed to satisfy the divine hunger, or the divine justice (species *quid pro quo*), can now offer the greatest sacrifice, which is the death of Christ. Christ offers it himself as representative of a race struggling in the compost of sin and death, and the Church offers it in his memorial and in his name and person. We have yet to retrieve a more fulsome sense of sacrifice, grounded in the exchange of gifts coming from God.

Even in the traditional ritual sense known to the Hebrews one should not dare offer sacrifice through the priest unless totally aware of what one has received and one's forebears have received through liberation from slavery, from the state of being "no-thing" (Deut 26). However, to release God totally from the structures of blasphemy, let us acknowledge that in Christ there is no sacrifice in any traditional ritual sense. What is intended is gift bestowed and gift received, as Irenaeus has it, "with thanksgiving." It is the abolition of sacrificial attempts at the offering of gifts to God, and not just the abolition of some Old Testament rituals, some rather bloody and bloody-minded, some harmonious with the beauty of creation, that is the inner sap of the living metaphor of naming Christ's death a sacrifice. Christ is the Son who receives all from the Father, and is nothing other than the being from the Father, a condition revealed in his word/Word made flesh. He lives from nothing but gift. There is no giving back, only acknowledgment, a being in the totality of an active receiving. In this "being given" he lived himself as gift from God, offerer of this gift to his hearers, gift himself to them in his own existence as divinely given, and gift even unto the testimony of his death that there is only God and what lives of gift from God. The transfer of the title "sacrifice" to such an adventure in gift receiving and gifting of self as given (not to the giver but to others in need of gift), is a reversal of all that we seem to try spontaneously to do in order to settle accounts with God. What sense can we make of living with a God who is all-giving but never gift-receiving, except within the intimacy of the divine circle of goodness and truth? We spend an entire lifespan in coming to a point of complete openness to gift, to attain it one supposes in death, when everything else has to be let go. As a Church, we still need to celebrate many Advents.

Self-emptying and self-giving are key to divine gift and divine naming, as well as to the world's participation in the divine, to its deification. As has been noted, John Paul II invited theologians to reflect upon the image of divine *kenosis* as key to the proclamation of the Gospel in our time. When we see the communion of the divine persons made known as gift and invitation in the economy of salvation, we behold the dance of *perichoresis*, a constant interaction between Word and Spirit that draws humankind and creation into the communion of the divine life-force poured out as a communion of love, ever coming forth from its unique source, ever moving toward its consummation in God. In Godself, there is nothing that the Father retains for himself, there is nothing that Son and Spirit do not refer back together to the Father: all is gift and communion. This serves not only as image of a triune God make known, but as key to a knowledge of creation, providence and history, where God is present as emptied-out in the interaction of communion, a presence revealed in weakness, in the midst of turmoil and confusion and the imbecility of all those atrocities that lead to precisely nothing. But in the weakness of God and in God's weak presence, we affirm that, rather than no-thing, there is much-thing. This much-thing is a communion of self-emptying and gift to which mortals are inspired and moved by the gift of Spirit and Word that they receive. Beyond the many, each striving for its own fulfilment, there is the One, the one *perichoresis*, where each is in and for the other, where individual concern and satisfaction are no longer an issue because no one is anything except in and through this communion.

Visions of History: Continuity or Discontinuity?

We will readily enough agree that Christianity looks at history from the perspective of Christ's resurrection. It is in this, in conjunction with his death in shame, that we see the power of life over death, the saving hand of God at work in the universe. We will also readily enough agree that memory is the essence of history. We do not live for the future unless we remember the past and discern in it both the forces of death and the resurgence of life. Beyond that, believers and the Church's writers go in rather different directions on their pilgrim way.

If apocalyptic persuasions have remained alive through the centuries it is because people wanted not only to anticipate the end of time but because they wanted to assign a meaning in God's eyes to persons and events. If an emperor divided up the church, gave away lands and bishoprics, took dominion from popes, could he be the Antichrist? On the other hand, could a pope who was too worldly or who led the faithful astray be Antichrist? Could a holy and renowned person like Francis of Assisi be seen as the witness and the prophet who was the sign of the coming age of peace promised by the proclamation of God's kingdom? May movements like dualism, Aristotelianism, secularism, be given their spot in the continuity of the struggle between good and evil that belongs to apocalyptic vision?

Some avoided such an apocalyptic outlook. Augustine and heirs to his thought on the place of the Christian in history find no particular significance in historical events and personages, except to the extent that they foster the peace of the Church and the possibilities to give oneself over to worship and contemplation. Those who live by hope in the resurrection of Christ live in an anticipation of eternity, and despite the flux of life endeavour to keep minds and hearts focused on the eternity of God. To live in time is to try to live outside it, above it. Apocalyptic discourse, the endeavour to attach meaning to historical events, disrupted the tranquility of such a vision.

Even ordinary people often lived by this perception. In my boyhood days, elders would tell us that they hoped for a reward because in life they had kept the commandments, done their duty, were honest in human affairs and worshipped regularly. They could not dream that their conduct had any effect on how things happened, not even when they went to the ballot box in election time.

The work of the Second Vatican Council and political theologies did much to make us think differently about human history as well as about ecology. Small clans of poor people were encouraged to believe that by living together in true Christian fashion and by working together for a common good they might bring about a change in structure and infrastructure. There were others, however, whose mind turned backwards towards the dead and the circumstances of their living and dying. After Auschwitz, Jewish thinkers asked very poignantly whether the dead belonged in history and to the future or whether Fascism had truly succeeded in wiping them out. They talked of remembering lest we forget and saw purpose in storing memories. They also began to rethink teachings about messianic signs and about what it means for history to witness, even in dire travail, to God's covenant and promised kingdom. Christian thinkers took up the question from them and began to ask whether we could see the imprint of the Pasch on human life and what might be the role of the memorial of Christ and the perseverance of witnesses.

In all of this we seem to have gone in two different directions as far as the impress of the Resurrection is concerned and what it means to the expectation of the fullness of God's kingdom. One way is to find the mark of the victory of life over death constantly present and the energy of this presence as a continuous force, or a force of continuity. What is revealed in Christ's Pasch is the love of Son and Spirit always at work in human history and in the universe, giving life victory over death. The discernment of human event will be to discern such a power and a love in operation.

Another direction is to see the sign of the Resurrection together with the expectation of judgment as signifying the divine force always at work in life on earth. This means discontinuity, it means being alert to the irruption of divine judgment, perhaps in the words and acts of witnesses, so that continuity is broken. This seems more true to how things happen. It also means that in all human endeavours we need to be open to, and to ask others to be open to, a judgment upon actions that is made evident in the *kenosis* of Christ and the *kenosis* of the Spirit at work in those who give witness. Remembering the past in Christ's hope has a twofold outcome. First, it means that in faith we can see victims brought into memory and abiding in the love of God, living a life denied them in time. Second, it means taking in testimony from the past, allowing the testimony of victims and prophets belong within the fabric of how we do things and of what we fabricate for the human good. In this sense, the testimony of Christ kept alive in eucharistic memorial is also alive in the witness of those, past and present, who resist evil and hope totally in the liberating power of God. The concern is not with a simple telling of the past but with "making history" by the force of testimony, often "against the grain."

The fullness of time in which Christ came is not a matter of chronology or of how God providentially prepared his coming. It is rather a fullness in which God acts by his freeing word and love, even when it fits into human affairs but awkwardly. It is in that sense that it is a fullness by which believers live always and in virtue of which they dialogue with others and seek to serve true life and true communion in the affairs of the world. Despair has no place even if hope demands a constant revision of perspectives, calling for a change in the way in which history is remembered or made, and hoping against the odds.

We might well adjust the vision of ourselves as a pilgrim people by adding the terms nomad, refugee or illegal immigrant to suggest just how unsettled we are. Today pilgrimage is quite facile, with airlines and hotels booked in advance, perhaps at cut price when done through Expedia or hotels.com. Pilgrims of early centuries or of the Middle Ages set out towards Jerusalem or Rome or Compostela not sure they would get to their destination. They depended on hospitality along the way and might just as readily meet up with brigands and thieves. They might not even be sure of the pilgrim path to follow. If they persevered it was because a vision of what they would find at journey's end kept them going. Such is our status as pilgrim people walking the narrow path.

New Heavens and New Earth

How then may we imagine this promised communion in which the whole of creation partakes? All of creation is already suffused with the power of the Spirit and anxiously awaits its redemption in the appearance of the glory of Christ. But the reign of sin is not yet under dominion, all things have not been subjected to God in Christ. There is not yet total harmony between love and meaning, between desire for unity and our understanding of the wisdom of God's triune creative work. The glory of the Lord, sacramentally expressed in the liturgy of diverse Churches, is hidden under a veil, known through its traces and its witnesses.

The eschatological or apocalyptic discourses of the Bible, most powerfully expressed in the Book of Revelation, speak of a time of human tragedy and cosmic catastrophe before the end. The last act will be the judgment of the Son of Man and the revelation of the glory of the Lamb, the full harmony of all things within the breath of the unrestrained Spirit. As the Spirit hovered over the works of creation, as it descended upon the waters of the Jordan, as it showed itself in tongues of fire in the Upper Room, as it prompted the young to dream and the old to see visions, so it will be cosmically and universally made manifest at the end and for eternity. In the breath of the Spirit, all reality will take on the appearance of the Word of God, it will become like the Word, like the Son, the icon of God, the divine image in which the love and glory of God shine forth.

There are many who mark on their calendars what is said in these discourses, fixing a time for the rapture (1 Thess 4:18). There is even a Rapture Index on the Internet, programmed as a copy of the economic index, to help people know how close or distant it may be. But this is visionary literature and there is no need to see it as speaking only of an end to time or of years that still lie ahead. On the contrary, as in the vision of the seer of Patmos, it gives both a caution and a hope by which we are presently sustained. We live now through catastrophe and tragedy. Whatever the intimations of a common origin of all humanity, or of a common origin of all things in the cosmos, humanity included, humans are divided and exploit and harm the riches and splendour of nature. Whatever the imperative of the common good, whatever the feel of a destiny in which the cosmos and all its inhabitants share, people vie among themselves in subjecting this common good to particular interests. The catastrophe is upon us in wars, struggles, in disease and illness, in the pollution of earth, sky and waters. It is not yet the approach of the end but still we are under the judgment of the vision held out before us, of the Word and the Spirit that hold out this vision to us. As counterweight to condemnation, the vision gives us a hope whereby to live, the hope in the God of Love who is always, and will be always, at work through the Word and the Spirit in bringing all creatures into the communion and dance of love that is the eternal mystery of the divine.

A Hope for the Present

Christian theology has always had difficulty in explaining how the life of the Church and the life of the world, of the city, of the earthly realm, meet or converge. There were some quite shocking medieval claims on the part of Popes who wanted to dominate the secular realm as well as the spiritual. There were also quite shocking claims on the part of emperors and kings to be able to dictate to spiritual powers, in the interests of their own fiefdoms. On the other side, there has been the tendency to see city of God and earthly city coexisting, with the thing that ultimately mattered being the spiritual.

Apocalyptic visionaries, down to the present day, have never been quite satisfied with that. Hence they have always spoken of a period, a "millennium," when Christ would reign, the whole earth would be transformed, and all things, spiritual and material, would coalesce unto the glory of God. In this of course they found and find support in what Paul says of the rapture to the Thessalonians (1 Thess 4:13-17), in the Book of Revelation (Rev 20:4-6) and in the retrieval of Old Testament prophecies. While such vision can be seen as a kind of imaginative excess, it does raise the question whether the reign of God has anything to do with the transformation of society and the transformation of the earth within history, before what is envisaged as the final consummation.

As mentioned earlier, Christian Churches these days rewrite their mission statements to include an evangelical commitment to the establishment of a reign of justice and peace among the peoples of the earth, in the name of God, of Christ and of the Spirit. It is permissible to retrieve some of the messianic prophecies of the Hebrew scriptures and find in reading them a promise of an earth that is changing, of a human community without boundaries that respects true justice. The desire of the people of Israel to see an earthly divine kingdom is not to be dismissed as a mere preliminary to the advent of the spiritual reign preached by Christ and proclaimed in his Pasch. Such expectations are not to be taken in favour of theocracies. They may, however, give us hope that as we live our common quest for life here on earth, for this generation and the next, living by faith in the reign of God can guide humans in their work for the transformation of human community and ecological equilibrium, provided they give proper weight to the language of divine *kenosis*. The visionary prospect of a new heaven and a new earth, of a New Jerusalem that outlasts Babylon, confirms such hope, rather than leaving us like patients in a waiting room, with nothing to do but dream and browse. By virtue of Word and Spirit, prompting us to look beyond our own capacities to find God's actions here in our midst, we act as people who have an ultimate hope that must include hope for the here and now.

The Vision of Final Consummation

All vision of the end is dominated by the knowledge of the gift of God. What brings finality can only be the mercy and love of the Trinity of God in the communion of Father, Word and Spirit. What the consummation of all things shall be when they are drawn finally and fully into the communion of the Trinity, we can only imagine in a manner that defies imagination. We go back in narrative to the divine promises, the promises given to Abraham and Sarah and their descendent, to Moses and the pilgrim people in the desert, to Israel and to the nations through the prophets, to the promises given in the Gospel in the Beatitudes of God's kingdom, upheld by the vision of the coming of the Son of Man in judgment and revitalized by the gift that Christ made of himself in taking the form of a slave and emptying himself out by his descent into hell. They are all promises of God's creative love, promises that cumulatively embrace the whole of creation and all created things, the heavens above and the earth below, ocean and land, and all the wondrous beings of the six days of creation or the canticle of creatures.

Is it possible to imagine a fullness of being beyond human finitude, beyond my finitude, beyond the finitude of the race? The incongruence is that of imagining a duration beyond earth-bound time, and of space beyond what vision beholds, even with the aid of the technology that can explore Mars and other planets. When the imagination is stretched like that it is difficult to find place for the small story of individual land masses, of individual even if singular peoples, to say nothing of the very small tale of each individual person, be that person hero or one of the little people. Therefore even some theologians today suggest that we should simply say that persons and ages, as well as cosmic marvels, are carried forward into the great movement of life, and think no more of the eternal survival of the individual person, being able indeed in this to call on the perspective of other religions, or even on some theories of science that examine the minutiae of life and energy. Others, however, think that this too readily dismisses the promises and the blessings proclaimed of the poor and the meek and that we need to allow for the interventions of divine love that do more than we can ever imagine and that bid us not be anxious.

In writing to the Church of Thessalonica, Paul felt himself confronted by those who pinned their expectations on the great rapture that would augur in an era of messianic peace and justice on earth, and worried about what would happen to those already dead and so not present to await the Lord (see 1 Thess 4:13-18). He bade them not to reckon with signs and calendars and to put all their trust in the risen Christ, in whom all had died to the life of mortal flesh and in whom resurrection was promised to all. The disciples of Christ are not to grieve over the dead like the rest of people.

In writing to the Church of Corinth (see 1 Cor 15), he seems to be pressured by those who wanted to know what the risen body would be like. This is a very normal question for those who did not have Hellenic conceptions of the fragile union of body and soul and could think in terms of the immortality of the whole, even when the body is decayed. The disciples at Corinth, and certainly Paul himself, could envisage a human being only as the full unity and harmony of what they dubbed the flesh and what they dubbed the spirit. For them there could be a future only for a fully constituted human being, but since they saw bodies decay they had their questions about the risen body and felt deranged by death itself, coming in any form. Paul's answer was to put off senseless questions and to look to the risen Christ for assurance and for the nourishment of the imagination, if need be. Christ had passed through death into the fullness of life and abided now "in the heavens" yet was nonetheless present to all those who have faith in him. The grain of wheat dies and emerges in the beauty of the ear of corn. What then of the future state of our mortal bodies? Senseless question! For those who live by faith and hope, that is.

Paul himself seems to have been unsure about the state of being of those who die before the *parousia*, of those who die before the coming of the Lord. He does not think of a full existence for separated souls so he simply imagines them in sleep, from which they shall be roused at the resurrection of the body when all shall rise up in Christ. Talking about eternal life in Christ and in the communion of Father, Son and Spirit, we can probably do no better than this. Whatever our intelligence and our insights into the evolution of life may tell us, we are invited by Gospel and Creed to await the resurrection of the dead and to have confidence in the hope given to those whose lives on this globe have counted for nothing in human reckoning.

Imagining and thinking of life brought to fullness we consider a human life as a story, a story to be brought to completion through God's creative and transforming love. This is hoping beyond hope for those who are witness in their generation to efforts to wipe out not only persons but their story, and beyond that the history of what we would call a people. If they and their lives are nonetheless the object of God's love, creative and redeeming, we may expect that the visions of the parousia mean some redress, some exceptional showing forth of their story in Christ and in the love of the Spirit, under the gaze of the Father. Communion in love is not merely a counting of heads, a numbering of the many who are given a part in this love. It is precisely a communion, a being one of all persons, peoples, races, ages, a communion that does not cast aside but takes in the wholeness of human being, passion and action. In the divine memory all is contained, loved, embraced and given zest, shown forth in glory, in the communion of life that for the present is best imaged in the Christ who has been raised up because he surrendered himself to die for others.

That exacts of us that we be serious about the risen Christ. We must needs reckon with the fullness of his being and his communion with earth and mortals, once he has passed in his fleshly reality through death and into communion with Father and Spirit. In reading the Passion Narrative, beginning at the story of the Supper, we see him striving towards communion with the Father and towards communion with the generations that went before him, with all of those for whom he was giving himself, as well as with those to whom he was giving himself in the sacrament of the bread and wine. Passing through death, in being raised up, he has reached that communion. This is the reality of the Risen Christ who lives by the Spirit, in communion with the Father and with all those for whom he died, and desires the reconciliation of all things in God.

Hope and Kenosis

Where revelation through *kenosis* comes into play in this is that through being in the form of a slave, Christ transformed the possibilities of all relationships, be these to God, to humanity, to nature, or to time. This is not, however, to be seen as taking place only after the Pasch. It is anticipated in his ministry. Through the stance that he took before the powers of the world, through his compassionate companionship with the poor and the meek of the earth, through his willingness to relate to the finite existence of material being by passing through death, Christ exemplifies a transformed relationship to the world in which he lived. We may also note, though it is less often emphasized, that in his ministry we see a new way of relating to the things of earth which is appreciative of their beauty and is non-manipulative. Commentaries on the Gospels at times find in his wonders, in his stilling of a storm or in his walking on the waters, a manifestation of his messianic power and lordship even over nature. Certainly in these stories we see what the evangelists saw after the resurrection as his relationship to the universe and his way of making it possible for those with faith to relate to the natural forces around them. But we should also take note of his parables and metaphors, which show his perception of things large and small, finding in them the splendour of the loving care of the Father. In short, already in the time of his ministry we see bodily transformation, in that he introduces a way of humanly relating to the things of this world that befits the kingdom. There is a continuity, as well as a discontinuity, before and after his Pasch, in the way that Jesus transforms human being's bodily communion with nature.

To account for the relationship through life in God that Christ has with the world, we could give a twist to the doctrine of the eucharistic change of the elements to better express Christ's communion with humanity, and with each assembly, and the communion into which we are sacramentally drawn. The Catholic Church is wont to speak of the substantial change of the bread and wine. We would do better to start with the substantial change of Christ in passing through death to newness of life that allows him to give himself in communion to all, in all times and places, configuring his being to the realities of their food and drink, to the realities of their mortal bodies, to the realities of their stories and histories. In our technical language, we say that he is substantially and truly present. In the language of the imagination, which stretches much further towards the true, we can speak of him as present in the gift of himself and his new being to those whom he draws into communion with Father, Son and Spirit.

This is an immense presence because so many and so much are in communion. It is a humble and very real presence because it is constituted by a table sharing, the eating and drinking of baked bread and vintaged wine, the being in communion with those together in the table gathering. Unless the community of disciples pass through the death of being truly present to Christ in the immediacy of presence to this gathering, they cannot enter into the fuller communion into which Christ wishes to collect them. The humanly, historically, culturally insignificant story of these people belongs in that communion, finds its ultimate truth in that communion, and is opened in its own mortal and immortal existence to the communion that results only from the transforming power of God's creative love.

Book of Revelation

Only with all of the above in mind may we venture into the poetry by which the communion of humanity and cosmos is spoken when all things are handed over to God. The scriptures are primarily concerned with human salvation, justice to the poor, and the reconciliation of all in Christ. But they place this humanity on earth, on land and sea, and within the cosmos. To see what images we may take of the communion with the earthly and cosmic to which God in love calls us, we could turn once more to the Book of Revelation, to its description of the New Jerusalem.

The Book is written for communities passing through a present, very historically determined struggle, in which the power of corrupt human effort dominates the community of nations, in which the weak suffer, in which the faithful disciples of Christ endure persecution and martyrdom. They are promised vindication in the prophecies concerning the end of time and what will precede the end of time. The vindication, however, is given its spatial setting, in the New Jerusalem. This is a city of God's creation and imaging, an ideal place as yet, but promised, and it is set in contrast with the very earthly and now present city of Rome, Babylon. The victory of the Lamb, the reign of the just with Christ and in his light, mark the whole reality of this promised city, but there is much to be seen in it, where history and nature are found in their final perfection as given by God.

If the seer of Patmos describes both wickedness and the abode of the just in terms of a city, this is because his readers were used to life in cities and towns. They know the awfulness of life found in Babylon, they could be won over by the ideal beauty of life in the New Jerusalem. The most extraordinary thing about this city is that it is the abode of the Lamb, of the glory of God, of all those who reign victorious with Christ over sin and death, over the sinful and the death-dealers of Babylon or other cities. It is also extraordinary how the imagery of the Book represents an ideal communion between humans, who build cities and think of their story or history in terms of cities and city states, and earthly and cosmic reality. The waters of paradise flow through the city, it is a place of rich vegetation, and of rich pastures and their flocks.

In its own way, the Book speaks to what we think of as the ecological problem, that is, of how human ingenuity and its fabrication can affect the realities of earth and cosmos. It says that whatever humans have done, by God's doing there is to be perfect harmony and communion. This stands out all the more tellingly because the end when this comes about is preceded not only by plagues and wars but also by cosmic catastrophes. Now, in the New Jerusalem, all that is at odds within earthly experience is at peace.

To revert to the Eucharist, in it the reconciliation that is to take place when we receive what is promised, the establishment of a reign of justice, the overcoming of conflicts between human ambition and cosmic reality, is held in image and in memory through its celebration. It certainly holds up an image of an ideal whose being can come only from God's love, but it does not on that account encourage passivity. It bids us live by vision and live together on earth in the light of that vision. Since it is memorial, it exacts a memory that embraces the remembering of all those whose story and history is taken up into Christ. In Christ, the communion already exists. In his Body, the human reality of earthly existence, it is on the way towards being and asks the love that strives to be as large as the Christ who gave and gives, without calculation.

Remembering toward the Future

We probably do not realize what an exercise in memory the Churches are called to, what reconciling memory, what purification of memories, by declaring their presence and their identity at the eucharistic table. That is really the challenge of all that vaguely and ideologically passes under the heading of inculturation. It is not a matter of translating the Latin properly, though respect for a past culture will at times exact that. It is not a matter of giving place to the sounds, music, choreography, the oral and poetic expression of diverse peoples, though this too is required. It is not even just a matter of accepting and affirming all that is of true value in their cultures. It is at root a matter of incorporation in Christ of their memories, their stories, their vision of earthly and cosmic reality, their sense of communion between the living and the dead, their feeling for oneness with all of created nature. We are up against finitude and the need to let ourselves face it and be challenged by it. Our imaginations, our poetry and prose, our music and our art, are nourished by the miniscule that is but a small part of human and cosmic reality. Even in eucharistic communion, most of all in eucharistic communion, we die to this in order to be drawn towards full communion in Christ, towards the New Jerusalem that is our destiny. Our hearts open in expectation of the advent of the glory of the Lord, in evangelical poverty, in being totally for God and those whom he loves and for whom Word and Spirit were surrendered.

Eternity and Time

It is the veiled revelation of Word and Spirit in our world that we are bidden to heed if the vision of the city in which the Lamb is the light is to be our own sustaining light. The Spirit who hovered over the waters, descended on the Jordan, came down in tongues of fire, is still at work but with conflicting spirits amidst us, it needs to be discerned. The glory of Christ, Word made flesh, is always being shown to us, in his sacraments and in his witnesses, fools of Christ. It is daily placed before our eyes but in the humble bread and cup and the invitation that the bishop, as described by the Pseudo-Dionysius,[3] raises before the sight of the assembly. We depend on this glory and the hope it holds forth. We live in the hope of it. We know in faith that the communion between mortals, and the communion between human and things and seasons expressed in the one loaf and cup suffused with the glory of the Son, are moving by the power of gift towards their consummation, with the promise that all things will be surrendered to the love of God and its everlasting communion. If we are blind to this veiled glory, we are already judged, we have no life in us. If we are humble and grateful, taking what is offered in companionship and respect for the Christ and for the creatures that he has united to himself, we live in the power of the Spirit that moves all reality to communion and so to consummation. The apocalyptic vision with which the scriptures bless us is the eschatological affirmation of hope, the divine assurance of the belonging within the communion of the Trinity itself, of the first fruits of a consummation in oneness where as with the Three themselves there is "no more counting."

Since eternity and time are on two different plains and it is quite inadequate to see eternity as a prolonged life where nobody dies anymore, there seems no need to banish all measured duration from this eternal communion, however paradoxical it may seem to breath eternity and time in one breath. For humans we are inclined to think of eternity as the cessation of becoming after time has lapsed or exhausted itself. Of God, however, it has always been said that in his eternal being and act he dwells in human and mortal time, not only in the Incarnation of the Son but in the act of creation and providence. Conversely, could we not say that for humans in the glory of being in divine communion there is a double dimension, the eternal bliss of knowing God and the measured reality of being caught in the desire and expectation of an expanding communion with all human persons, with history and cultures, with the complex and transformed universe itself. This would not be a self-centred communion but a forgetting of the self so that one exists and expands existence in and through being with, existing no more outside such communion, and finding communion for the now according to the pattern of the *kenosis* of Word and Spirit.

Empathic communion through the work of memory, which after all concerns future as well as past, may provide some analogy for this. At the centre of the memory of a person or a community sure of its being and its identity, there is a constant, a harmony and a peace. But this same memory is always at work in expanding the possibilities of knowing, communing, creating. This is particularly important when the remembrance of what should not be forgotten, of the memory of victims, is concerned. Our lives are joined at the marrow: honour must be given to their names and stories and we are not ourselves unless we allow them to be part of our remembered and projected being in the world. There is no justice without reconciliation and no reconciliation without remembering, which includes imagining a future in which there is redress and a being together in peace.

Living in our own small corner of the universe, there is an immense expanse of becoming and spacing of which we have not even an inkling. What we project as ecological justice and communion has to make possible an expansion of mind, affect and imagination. We ought to be conscious of having a narrow outlook, however hard we try to be greater than ourselves, and in this way feel called to die or to lay low our own perspectives in servitude to all that is other.

How may such analogies provide some anticipation for the resurrection of the dead and their reign in glory with Christ? At the heart of memory, the dead are in Christ, they are in the communion of the Trinity, they are at peace and at one. But they are also related to all that God does, to all the pouring out of self of the divine being into the goodness of created being. Maybe in life everlasting there is something like the action of memory when it takes in new realities, and in this case all those realities that have their being from God and in God by the power of divine gift.

Conclusion

Once a young student, not of the rap generation, asked me if there would be time in Heaven for listening to Beethoven. Choosing to be whimsical, I replied that since the New Jerusalem allows for harps and song and hosannas and incense and maybe liturgical dance, I would expect that there may be a place there too for Beethoven. Now I might tell him that there would be so much else to take in, of the song of the universe, of peoples and cultures, of stories of the poor and simple, of the lot of victims and those who stood witness, so much to hear and see and touch with the senses of Christ, that I would not be sure where exactly Beethoven would fit in, though there had to be a place too for the *Eroica* as its strains co-penetrate with other melodies. But to be fanciful about details is to be as senseless as the Corinthians who aroused Paul's ire by wanting to know too much about the risen body. As in the end one is apophatic about the communion of Father, Word and Spirit, so it is better to practice apophatic restraint in talking of an eternal life of participated communion in this *perichoresis*. In this earthly life, the three abide in us and through a superabundance of gifts give us life through the economy of creation and salvation. This already asks of us a self-emptying and an openness to a communion beyond measure. For what lies beyond it is *enough* to trust oneself to the promises of the God who out of love gave over his only Son and poured out the Spirit, without calculation. And paradoxically the measure of the incalculable is found in the emptying of the divine self in Word and Spirit that was necessary to encounter the world of creation, to withstand the hubris of claims to dominate, to witness against them, to suffer death for the sake of liberating humanity and the cosmos and bring them into God's full love.

POSTLUDE

10

O Wondrous Exchange: The Church at Prayer

⸎

The Church's liturgy sings of a wondrous exchange, one brought about between God and humankind by the advent and the Pasch of the Word, the Son, and by the outpouring of the Spirit. Caught in the contemplation of this mystery one places oneself at the table of communion in Christ's flesh and blood and in the earthly realities of bread and wine, before an image of Christ's descent into hell where the exchange between divine love and human mortality was perfected, as God gave himself in total self-emptying.

To pray, to pray incessantly, to pray as one who looks and hears, to pray as one looked upon with love, is to be caught up in wonder. It is this sense of wonder that I want to highlight in the following ruminations on prayer, as a kind of postlude to a theology of *kenosis*.

Counting the Ways

There are many ways of expressing the relation of humans to God that are called prayer or praying. There is saying thanks, there is asking for help in need, a looking at images and icons, a slow reading of words, the repetition of prayers given to us by God in the scriptures, and the exuberance of Christian liturgies. But prayer is God catching us off guard rather than us being on guard for God, necessary though this latter may be as a manner of disposing oneself attentively to God's approach. The essence of prayer is to be caught up in wonder. One could compare it to looking out over the ocean on a bright night, making the effort to take in everything: the path of the moon, the stars that dazzle the gaze in their multitudinous paths and patterns, the sparkle of the heavens on the surface of the waters, the expanding horizon of heaven and ocean that appear without limit. And then being captivated by one star that seems to hang down out of the sky, that in its watching asks to be watched, looked at, offering itself even to the hand's grasp. It contains all else that is beauty but in its offer and its promise exceeds them all. In its intensity, it is greater than the whole firmament. It gazes down, and it offers to the gaze, an embodiment of the galaxy and a beauty that exceeds all the beauty that the eye has taken in through its wandering across the sky, from horizon to horizon. What is hidden is given to the spirit that is caught into the wonder of this celestial unveiling.

Finding the truth of prayer is like the one who climbs up into the mountains, hoping to find a good foothold from which to look out upon landscapes, sea inlets, valleys and rivers, but at a certain point is enthralled by a spring of water coming out from beneath a rock. Or, to use a more urban image, it is like one visiting an art gallery rich in the treasures of great painters like Rembrandt, Van Gogh, Turner, Picasso, and being stopped still in front of a frame that shows a still life attributed to an unknown name, a still life whose scheme of light allows the hidden or obscure to stand out more clearly than what is in the forefront. Or it is like a mother who after months of caring for and nurturing a young child, one morning in rousing her from her bed awakens to the beauty of life and form that this daughter brings into her daily existence.

It is impossible to be a Christian without being in wonderment, without being bedazzled by the form of the Word made flesh, from whose being all the beauty of the human drama, in its various eventualities and manifestations, emerges. While it is in prayer that one is bedazzled by wonder, one can pray in all kinds of ways provided one is fixed by the awe of divine initiative, by the God who first looks upon us and does so in such hidden and humble ways.

Falling into temptation and falling back on the theologian's habit of spelling things out, one may risk counting the ways. There is the showing forth in symbols and rituals, the responses drawn by a heartening proclamation of the Word, the repetitively inarticulate words and actions of what people like me call popular devotions, and the ways of silence near a river, on a mountain top, in face of a crucifix, in listening to Mahler (or perhaps Rap), in the catching of breath inspired by a poem, when one has to be careful to breathe out as well as in. There is the being still in the inner room of some dwelling place where one sits, squats or lies in the quiet of the Spirit.

Beyond the Preceptive

We tend to turn religion into precepts, laws to be followed, whether we are Protestants or Catholics, and even turn prayer into the proper observance of rubrics, often indeed rather arbitrary, and, from the point of view of what they first intended, out of date. We can be very busy about doing the right novenas at the right times for the right intentions or making sure that Evensong is at the proper hour, and still fail to let the Spirit give us voice.

The preceptive seems often to dominate the ways in which the religious-minded look on divine/human relations. Perhaps this is because rules are at least clear, even when hard to observe, while wonder is beyond telling and is incalculable and so makes it hard to keep one's feet on the ground. Even when not dealing specifically with rules, people look for monitions that trace out things to be done. In this age when the Sunday celebrant is expected to give a lectionary-based homily, its quality is all too often judged on whether or not it puts forward some moral teaching or practical inducements about "what to do." When he simply wants to make people wonder, to quietly contemplate or shout out in praise the marvels of God's being in love, then the homilist will find some of the congregation inclined to moralize the theme for him.

Rather to my regret, I remember as a young priest telling retreatants that in dealing with themselves and the world they needed to follow the maker's instructions, as one would in driving a car, but it was easier in those days to induce youngsters to stick to the law, for better or worse. In the end there is not much there on which to feed the soul and when fear gets outmoded, there is no guiding light left. No star has looked down with its offer of a beauty beyond telling. The young person who confesses missing Sunday Mass (if she bothers) might simply have given up because in the way in which it was celebrated no stars ever twinkled, and perhaps she had found forms of beauty offered in other places. But that is one of the big issues of liturgical reform, not much helped by too much noisy guitar playing, nor by efforts at rigid control.

Wonderment may often be missing in sacramental celebration as in other moments of life. Two people get married. They do so maybe because they believe themselves in love or maybe because the union is practical and seems operable. Sheer amazement, the wonderment at being loved and being in love, might be what is missing in all too many nuptials. In the divine nuptials of God with humankind, of Christ with his Church, of the Spirit with the human spirit, if this is missing one might press on but without much energy, short of turning into a fanatic about what is morally right (as much for others as for oneself) and about liturgical rubrics (the guilt in this case being not that of the congregant but of the priest, who here and there misses out on a genuflection).

De Profundis

The enigma of this prayer of wonderment is that it is *de profundis*. Even today, every time I finish celebrating Mass I think of the custom in Ireland before the Council of priest and people reciting the *De Profundis* psalm as the final act of the ritual. We were told that it was in remembrance of the many who died of famine in the mid-nineteenth century and who departed this world with neither bell, book nor candle. This was a deep wound on the Irish soul and a remembrance of a tragedy that left a mark on population and psyche. Not only were the dead in the depths but so were the living.

It seems to me that at the turn of the millennium many people and peoples are marked by such sickness of soul and ask when humankind will rise up from the dark pit. It is vain to compare our age with previous generations which we know through selective memory. Nonetheless there is truth to the saying that the whole world, in its establishment of the network of communication and commerce across the globe, is marked by the sign of God's absence. One of the things that globalisation reveals is the location and the depth of the circles of hell in our universe. We also carry memories from the twentieth century of humanity's cruelty and vain pride, which seem impossible to assimilate and in which it is nigh impossible to discern signs of the kingdom of God. When we pray, therefore, we resort to the tones of lament, even of complaint against God. When we praise as the text bids us, we still sense in the pit of the stomach a feeling of horror and a query: how long, O Lord.

Oddly enough this itself can mean finding wonder anew, not in old ways but through a different inspiration or breath of Spirit, caught off guard by a love that takes on suffering. It is rather like Job's situation. When he was down and out Yahweh was able to ask him to look around and behold the marvels of earth, sky, sea and mortals. Before that he was too busy thanking God for all that he possessed, from lands to flocks to children, and offering sacrifices that would keep his offspring clean and righteous. When Christians get busy in offering Masses in satisfaction for sin, when their gaze on the Cross allows them to count up how much satisfaction Jesus, Son of God and Son of Man, offered for how many sins, they are in a bad position to see the beauty of the face of the one turned worm. When divine calculations are the order of the day it is hard to be open to the revelation of the One who pours out his Spirit without calculation. What is it to look upon Christ or to call God Father from within the circles of hell? How does one pray when one has nothing, when one renounces any ground to call one's own and stand upon, however wobbly the foothold? Such questions are at the heart of much praying today.

Liturgy praises God for the wondrous exchange given in the Son of God made flesh, in the wedding between human nature and divine nature in Christ, in the outpouring of the Spirit without measure. But the wonder goes deeper when the exchange is seen to be between the divine and a humanity trodden under by death and sin and God asks of the Son that he show himself in his glory of being with the Father under those conditions. *De profundis clamavi*, out of the depths I cried, and then beheld the beauty of the face of the Crucified Christ. And then looked out on the universe and saw it held together by this bolt, this bolt of the Cross, as one called John

Damascene named it. Though we might make our way upwards towards
God through a vision of intelligent cosmic order, when we get to the top of
the scale divine order looks nothing like what we see at first glance as cosmic order. For all our haggling about divine arrangements the nub of the
matter is that divine order works outward from where a loving good within
the heart of God clashes with evil. Thus the starting-point for the hope of
order is a divinely uncalculated initiative of mercy and justice that finds
itself at odds with human calculations of ambitious construction.

Leaves from a Book

I want to ask how we can learn to pray from liturgy's embodying of
God's Word and Christ's memory. It seems a good idea to move through
one small masterpiece, liturgy being replete with such creations. To open
the book at the calendar day's prayer is to play a kind of prayerful Russian
roulette in saying things about liturgy. So to start I open my book for the
Liturgy of the Hours, which it is hard not to keep calling a Breviary. I open
at the Mid-Day Prayer, this Wednesday of what is called the seventh week
in Ordinary Time, the year 2002, three days after Pentecost. The book is in
French, put together for Francophone countries, given where I am at this
precise moment of composition.

First, I find a hymn that I know will be quite nicely chanted by our
local seminarians. In it we are invited to sing that the Gospel shines forth
like the noonday sun, not as in wintry Ireland but as in the tropics, a radiance of justice and love. It seeps, says the hymn, deep into our lives, purifying and transforming our hearts with the transcendent clarity of the
Cross and bathing us in an immense sea of peace. This is rather startling
when one is on a small island in the Southern Pacific, surrounded by ocean.

Moved by the hymn one asks what then is this radiance shining forth
from the Cross? The three psalms of the hour invite us into the depths
where that Cross shows forth its glory. Some verses from that never fin-
ished Psalm 118 praise the lamp that enlightens our ways, however dark
they may be, the word itself of divine commandment. Though the singer
has suffered far too much, the word will make him live, if he exposes his
life to this brilliance. To let the singer know more clearly what this bright
word may be, the antiphon paraphrases a saying of Christ, "Whoever follows me is not condemned to walk in darkness but shall be guided by the
light of life."

With this turn to the Word of God, and indeed to that Word made flesh
who is Christ in all his brightness, Psalm 69 calls those who pray down into
the darkness where, as the antiphon puts it, we are poor and unhappy, crying out to God from this misery. There is some hearty cursing of enemies
here, of those who have dishonoured our lives and laid them waste, but in

the middle of such cursing a confidence that obliterates even such anger cries out. God shall be the joy and happiness of the poor who turn to him. God being inclined to dawdle, the psalmist adjures him to make haste, not to delay any further. Following a verse of the Gospel, printed in italics at the top of the psalm as one might read in the Hebrew Psalter that this song is the choir master's offering to the king, composed for lyre and harp, one is allowed to sing this psalm in response to Christ's invitation to the weary and the broken (Matt 11:28).

At the top of the next psalm, Psalm 74, the italicised verse invites us to turn our eyes to the just judge who is the Son of Man who was glorified in being lifted up by the Father (John 12:23). Eyes turned to this Judge, the antiphon entertains us to a song of thanks before God's marvellous works. It is not the rising or the setting of the sun, proclaims the psalm, that brings judgment, nor is it the days spent in the desert, but it is God himself who will be judge. There is a cup to be drunk to the lees by those who have turned their backs on love and justice, whose eyes are so firmly turned to gain that they never see the Son who is lifted up, a cup no doubt of self-recrimination and self-directed anger. It is those who have looked to God, or to his Son, who shall announce the wonder of the divine exchange with the suffering and the just, singing it out with hymns and music.

To finish out this tuning in to the wonders of divine justice, the reading for the day is from Col 3:14-15. It tells us to put love before all else, for it is the meek who shall inherit the earth and the peace of Christ will reign in the hearts of those who walk this way of love and divine justice. To make sure that the matter is rounded out in just proportion, the final prayer puts the congregants into the arms of Christ stretched out from the Cross, where he takes the part of the suffering and pours his heart out in love and mercy upon the world.

Exegetes might be rather troubled by the way the liturgy uses the psalms and other biblical texts, accommodating them to the Christian mystery, and translators of course like to correct the accommodations and "errors" of the Latin Psalter, being concerned with text and not often, it seems, with context. But that is their metier and maybe the charge given them. The faint of heart may also find cursing out of place. For all such ephemeral problems, throughout the liturgy's poetic framing and inter-texting there is a recurring charge of wonderment before the mystery of Christ and his Cross. When I say rather than "pray" the hour, being in a hurry to get to lunch, I miss this poesy and its invitation, experiencing little wonder since what can be said in five minutes needs a much longer time to savour. If it is possible to take fifteen, why take five? The *onus* of the office keeps us far from its *opus*, the sense of being obliged or burdened to pray closing our hearts to the work it unfolds and praises.

Lessons from the Bible and Its Literary Genres

The example of one short hour may open the way to larger considerations. Praying with the Bible leads into the variety of the ways of God's coming, provided one is ready to play divine games rather than worry about prescriptions. One might meander through the Old Testament books, taking heed of the various genres or types of work that it contains, and find that it initiates itself the sort of patterning of texts that the liturgy pursues, even maybe beyond measure at times. A little ugliness of style may be forgiven when it serves as counterfoil to beauty, as in village stagings of Italian opera even the ugly is beautiful because it is done in a generous spirit.

The Hebrew and Sapiental Books, booked together in the Bible, in effect catch the mysterious name of God in a variety of images, stories, and kinds of literature. It seems aeons ago that I was a novice, but the cold of that study hall and its bare, unvarnished wooden floors, with its desks set in battle array, is quite vividly remembered: we were "heroes" facing challenges and so not much bothered by this uncouth setting, provided our mothers never got a glimpse of it. In that time and place I set myself the task of reading the Bible from cover to cover, from Genesis "in the beginning" to the apocalyptic "come Lord Jesus" of the final page, never skipping or omitting or indeed leafing back. It allowed me, no doubt, to get some sense of the contents, but now I have grasped that this is no way to read all that is contained therein. Muddling the texts, shuffling as one may shuffle the tunes of a CD on a computer media player, is more revealing and entertaining, or more likely to let us enter into the ways in which what is hidden between the lines, or between the books, is revealed. That is the way in which the liturgy, Jewish and Christian, treats the texts and I think the coexistence of the texts between two covers itself invites us to unbind the book and scatter the pages around the setting in the pleasure of seeing what results. There is a bit of James Joyce's motley use of words in a good reading of the Word of God, for it is that kind of book. Hard on the eyes and on the ears, but comforting to the heart that allows preference for this motley over the motley of its own sin.

Fundamental are the stories that one must never forget. One called Yahweh enters into alliance, an alliance between "you and me" but grounded in historical events grasped as acts of God. On this condition the alliance gives birth to prophetic words that call back to fidelity and peer into a future where justice reigns, as it also translates covenant into the formulation of a law that gives light to the path trodden and inspires to all kinds of songs, called psalms and canticles.

Then there is the wonder of naming this God of alliance and forgiveness as the God of creation, the one from whom existence itself and all the *chaosmos* of the universe springs. But it is all good and beautiful and gift, until humans look behind trees or within their leafy branches for things to call their own, for a self-beginning that can be set over against what is pure gift. And thus to add to songs of praise we humans must ask God to give us songs of repentance, a repentance, however, from a divine heart that reminds us of how good we were made and can still be, made to the image and likeness of the covenant God.

When God is acknowledged as the one who made all things (even "man") good, there follows the meditation on wisdom, the naming of God as wise. This God of wisdom speaks from within the human heart where she dwells, and as artist draws forth from the universe and things great and small a vision of beauty. So the name of Wisdom is to be mixed with that which comes from history. Wisdom however challenges herself in pointing to the heart of wisdom in those who suffer unjustly.

The book of psalms to sing is placed in the Book as a unit but when the binding is broken it can be scattered throughout its pages and even given new titles. That is precisely what the liturgy does in appending different psalms to different portions of the scriptures. It is a collection that speaks to every mood and situation and working its way into the soul evokes changes of mood and perspective, configuring the reader or the singers to the mind of God and the play of the divine Spirit. Augustine in his commentaries on the psalms is still a good guide on how to pray them as would Christ and his Body, but going into that would lead me off the path.

The Hebrew Covenant was already mindful of the need for rites to keep the people walking the road toward the Pasch, the new year, the feast of tents, the days of repentance, or the day the Maccabee brothers stormed the gentiles in the temple. There are also the rites for the God of wisdom, rites for early rising and late slumber, for harvest and sowing, for the days of the new moon, for birth, marriage and death.

Jesus was in his own way extravagant with ritual acts, especially when it came to healing body and heart or casting out demons. At the core, however, he placed the very simple ritual of table exchange, of breaking bread and sipping wine, and this is the everlasting medium for the gift of his body and blood, his life and his death, his rising and his expectation. It is the place where the Spirit gathers into one, not only those around the table but those of all times and all places, all tongues and all peoples, as well as heaven and earth and flowing waters. It is in the flow of the blood from that Cross that the Church lives and awaits and thirsts for justice, "even now," in some moments impatient in the exclamation, "how long, O Lord, how long!"

Being Gazed Upon

In liturgy or places of worship one might have a sense of gazing upon something or upon what is happening, or even on divine revelation in minor key. Some enter more easily into prayer by the sight of the eyes than by the sound of the ears. At some point it might dawn upon the worshiper that more properly she is being gazed upon. There is a lot of Baroque profligacy in the Catholic devotion of the post-Reformation centuries, as though something needed to be proved, but it might be in a text of the Pseudo-Dionysius that we get to the real sense of the "devout look." After the great prayer that invites to contemplation of the Incarnate Word, the bishop is instructed to hold up the bread and wine to the people's gaze and invite them to communion in the Lord's Body and Blood. They are not so much invited to look for something as to behold what is being unveiled to them under these simple symbols. The Word looks upon the gathered with love and desire and they are invited to accept this gaze and make their own the love that asks for communion. It is very clear that it is the Word who is unveiled within the symbols of loaf and cup, the veil gently removed so as to let the Word made flesh shine forth. It is the Messiah, the teacher, the shepherd, the care-giver, who handed out bread and fish to thousands in the desert place, who gazes and gives at the eucharistic table. It is the Christ who with tears and words caused the hands of his disciples to scatter, flying like crows from the crust offered at the table of the supper, as the scene is imaged by Rilke, scattering with fear in the knowledge of the taking to the death that the offer intended. Eat this bread and drink this cup and you shall be one with me, says Christ, as I and the Father are one, and you shall have life, a life shared as closely as lovers who break bread and drink wine together. Yes, but one must die to so much else to accept this communion, and that is what makes our hands flee the table and our eyes look above and around, but not at the one who gives, for how can we support this gaze?

Since post-Renaissance Catholicism could not be content with the revelatory loaf and cup it hid them beneath the extravagance of the monstrance, the "monstrosity" of gaudy power and glory. The appeal to the senses is indeed of the essence of religion and piety, but what is strange and disturbing is that Catholic practice despite all its extravagance has been so parsimonious in its use of sacramental realities. People have been deprived of the earthy and fleshy realization that Christ and the Spirit, sent by the Father, come to them continually in and through bread, wine, oil and water, generously shared among believers, even if perforce eked out when scarcity prevails. Ritual all too often, even to this day, knows nothing of flowing fresh water, of sweet-smelling and fragrant oil, of loaves broken to feed the many at the eucharistic table, of bottomless cups that hold the never-ending drop even for the last comer. Church buildings need their icons and their images, the visual brightness of light streaming through stained-glass windows, the cross or crucifix looking down upon the congregation. At the heart of the matter, however, the theophany, the appearances of God coming to a chosen people, is given in the offer of a loaf, the offer of a cup, in the bath of clear, fresh, flowing water, in the sweet balmy anointing of the head and the senses of the body. What can be more wonderful, more wondrous than that? Jesus of Nazareth, the only-begotten of God, the prophet thrust forth into the desert by the Spirit, bolted to the Cross in his outrage against injustice, empties forth into a broken crust and the lees of a cup. And reveals the beauty and the truth of eternity.

The Icon and the Dove

When Christians gather for worship, God's gaze looks down on them through several iconic representations, not necessarily in their best-known artistic renderings and perhaps present only through vivid narrative recall where the image has taken its dwelling. From the centre, in the light flowing from the east, there is the icon of the Cross, through which divine wisdom is made manifest. Alongside it, there are the icons of the baptism of Jesus and the descent into hell, the abode of the dead. Somewhere in the vicinity there is the icon of the child sucking from its mother's womb, as there is also the nativity scene in the manger, the eyes of ox and ass intent upon the babe. Looking at them from the future that God alone gives, somehow centering all these images in counterbalance to the Cross, is the icon of Christ in judgment. Surrounding these icons of the Saviour there are the many icons of Mary, of saints and of angels, eager to make known to us their communion in the wonder of the eternal mystery of the All Holy, revealed through the flesh of Jesus Christ, on which they were nourished in faith and hope through the word of the scripture and the sacrament of the table.

And in the gathering place is the living icon of Church members, not primarily in grand basilicas and cathedrals but in simple rural church buildings, in mud huts where the poor are at home, or under trees or alongside streams and rivers. Into this assembly, however this is brought about, are to be invited those who are the victims of injustice and suffering, those who cry out to God bathed in blood and sweat. Wherever the gathering is assembled, it can find its place within the gaze of the icons of the Saviour and alongside angels and saints only when it embraces those who are proclaimed just by God's justice in the Beatitudes of the preacher, Jesus, these being the poor who cry out and the meek who inherit the earth. Placed in such a setting one is reminded that Christian liturgy and Christian prayer is what the ancients of Greek tongue called *mimesis*, a present dwelling in the eternal mystery of divine Trinitarian love. Still on earth, living the vicissitudes of time, failing often to find a history that can claim impossible events, believers are already heavenly dwellers, they are caught up outside of time in the eternal communion of God's *agape*.

But they are returned to time by keeping memorial as they are taught.

The Dove hovers restlessly over the scene, as it hovered over the waters of creation bringing them to life and to life-bearing, as it descended upon Jesus at his Baptism driving him out into the desert, as it came down as a mighty wind and with tongues of fire upon the apostolic band of the upper room. Indeed, some of the icons themselves give the divine Spirit the bodily forms that she assumed. First, there is the dove over the waters, the dove going out from the ark, the dove over the head of the Baptized, and the dove over the Cross of Christ that Christian piety has added to these biblical images. Then there is the fire, the fire that sets ablaze the minds, hearts and tongues of apostolic witnesses, the fire that cleanses and purifies, the fire that burns the heart with intense love, the fire that destroys all that is not love. The presence of the Dove and the burning of the fire call to mind that prayer is not only *mimesis* but also *anamnesis*. In faith and hope, we are to keep memory. We are to let the icons show the outward look of God's gaze move from suckling child to the youthful Messiah sent forth to bring the Gospel to the poor. We are to walk with the preacher fired by the Spirit given him by the Father to the Cross on which he hung outside the camp and yielded up the Spirit with a loud cry. From the Cross we are bidden to descend to the pit of Hades, and from Hades to look upward to the one who as a Son of Man stands before the world in judgment, proclaiming that unsayable and unknowable future when God's love shall abide in all and burn out all that is dead and death-giving. It is in the breath of this divine Spirit and with a mind that lives from the manifestation of truth through the fleshly imaging of Son and Word, looking forward to the promises that they contain, that Christians seek their place on earth. For all their participation in the wonder of the eternal divine, they dwell fully in the city of humanity, in the civilizations that show forth human ingenuity in all its marvelous accomplishments, but always walking that dread earth made bloody by victims of the ingenuity of human injustice and through such blood not fertilized but made barren. Asked to express by what attitudes, by what precepts, by what values, they live and move and have their being, they can only mumble over and over again the Beatitudes, first of Luke and then of Matthew. They have heard these from the mouth of the Saviour who was sent by the Father through the gift of the Spirit, who poured out his blood, who emptied himself before the powers of the earth of all lordly claims as they knew them, who descended as far as possible into death, who in virtue of this judges all that is in heaven and on earth. Their hope is that in such memory they will discover the meaning of these blessings, that they will live by them, that through them as his Body they will serve the transformation of the earthly community of humankind, making of the earth a fitting place for God to dwell.

When they come to prayer, Christians are given the Dove and the Fire, the Spirit of love and peace, and moved by this they place themselves always newly before the gaze that shines through the icons. They have all from God and in the name of the Son they are to be gods, the living testimony in all things human and earthly that God never ceases to pour forth love, without calculation. For themselves they claim nothing: all is godly gift, wondrous exchange.

CONCLUDING WORDS

O Holy Strong One

———————————— ❦ ————————————

The paradox of the divine provides the concluding word. The text quoted above is an antiphon sung in the Roman liturgy on Good Friday. It is chanted before the Cross of Christ acclaimed as the rood of salvation. In olden days, the service taking its origins in the veneration of the relics of the Cross in Jerusalem, the Cross displayed bare wood, perhaps encased in a precious reliquary. It was recognizable as an instrument of ignominy, but it was bared of the disfigurement of the abased Christ. Today it is more likely to be a cross with the figure still displayed, elegantly or crudely according to taste. Whatever the manner of display it is always a reminder of weakness, of the suffering and abandon of the Son, of the lowliness to which he descended before the powers of the world. Yet we hail the one who hung upon this cross as a Holy Strong One, who chose the power of weakness to reveal that he and his Father are nothing but love, all together love, and are lovingly present in the power of the Spirit poured out.

There is elsewhere in our doctrinal sources so much talk of God's power and might and reign that we tend to be caught up short by such an affront to our ideals of beauty and lordship. There is the theological temptation to translate this abasement and abandon into paradigms of justice in which God's dignity and honour are duly acknowledged and satisfied. When Christ Crucified is honoured as King it is often in terms of a right acquired that allows him to dominate the world through powers spiritual and temporal, wearing crowns and serving his rule.

But the strength of self-lowering asserts itself and exacts redress. We are even forced to take measure anew of the language of divine rule. When we do so, we see that I AM WHO AM was always looking for lowly, earth contradicting, ways to reveal the strength of this name. A wandering Aramean, a princeling shepherd, a slave people turned lose on the desert, a prophet yelling from a cistern, a barren wife, a maid from a remote and even despised village, an uneducated fisherman, an outcast publican, a tent-maker, were his allies. Nor was it a case of raising them above their station in life so that by power IT revealed itself. God worked through them by keeping them in their place, by putting the divine self in their place. When speaking, God constantly put aside the trappings of wealth and power, dissociated the divine from any kind of human ways of rule, and found a voice in and through the poor. Other testimonies forestall the testimony of the resurrection: the strength of love and the power of its justice lies in showing that among the weak of the earth, the force of a divinely emptying love, an outpouring of life and grace prevail where sin and oppression abound.

A clue to where this love survives and even abounds today is found in listening for the voice that speaks from within the circles of hell. When we think back from there, under the shadow of the Cross or within its light, to all that is said of creation and lordship and divine names, rather than see the power that rules by might we hear the breathing of the forces that yearn and cry out and remain lively in their quest for true life. The Word and the Spirit are the paradoxical pair that are sent out from the Father's maternal womb and breath the strength of hopeful yearning and of self-giving love over the face of the earth, so that even the crooked paths of ugly human behaviour are made straight.

The realization that the Church is both holy and sinful, not only in its members but even in its self-conceptions and structuring, offers in faith a fresh vision of how God gives divine life through weak forms. When we say that the Church is the Body of Christ we mean first of course that Christ grafts the baptized as members into his own crucified and risen body, sacramentally present and given so that they in turn may live the Pasch. But we also have to say that it is through this lowly form of a Church holy and sinful that Word and Spirit are present in and to the world. It is an abasement, a self-emptying of divine love to so give itself and the gift is totally gratuitous.

In the course of its history, even with the memorial of the paschal sacrifice before its eyes and the fire of the Spirit in its breast, the Church has found it difficult to identify with or to entertain this God and this Christ. Whether in government or in doctrine, it has turned its eyes higher and looked for things "from above" or tried to act "from above." Called to a purification of memories and engaging in this piecemeal, offense by offense, it is finding out that it has to purify its naming of God at the heart of each and every offense and infidelity. To be the Church of the Poor as it is called to be, bidden to follow Christ, Son and Word, into the depths of *kenosis* and to learn anew the meaning of being poor itself, according to the Gospel, it must needs be carried forward in the wind of the Spirit moving creation from its depths.

In this slight book I have written in various ways on this divine abasement and generous descent, seeing what it tells us of Christ, of Church, and of the God to whom they witness. Having dared to embark as on an immense ocean imaged for me by the waters of the South Pacific, now, like Pablo Neruda leaving Easter Island, I look back, as a trespasser, and see only the blue silence. Gazed upon, let us pray.

Notes

Foreword

1. While I did not have it at hand in Tahiti, on the history of the Council one may well consult *History of Vatican II*, edited by Giuseppe Alberigo, English version edited by Joseph A. Komonchak (Maryknoll, N.Y.: Orbis, 1995).

2. John Paul II, Encyclical Letter, *Redemptoris Missio*, no. 52. In its English edition, *Mission of the Redeemer* (Boston: Pauline Books and Media, n.d.).

3. Interventions of members of this group, including Cardinal Lecaro, may be found in Paul Gauthier, *Christ, the Church and the Poor* (Westminster, Md.: Newman Press, 1965). We also know that in his preliminary address to the Council, John XXIII singled out the Church's "option for the poor." On the theme in the Pope's addresses to the Council, see A. and G. Alberigo, *Giovanni XXIII, profezia nella fideltà* (Brescia: Queriniana, 1978). Mention of the group is found in Alberigo/Komonchak, *History*, vol. 3.

4. For example, Paul VI, Apostolic Exhortation, *On Evangelization in the Modern World*, 1975, nn. 30-32. (English translation, Washington, D.C.: United States Catholic Conference, 1976).

5. English edition, John Paul II, *Faith and Reason*, no. 93 (Boston: Pauline Books and Media, n.d.).

6. Lucien Richard, *Christ the Self-Emptying of God* (New York/Mahwah, N.J.: Paulist Press, 1997).

Part One

1. See his work *The Crucified God* (New York: Harper & Row, 1974).

Chapter One

1. There are of course many commentaries on this text, but I would mention in particular, Frank J. Matera, *New Testament Christology* (Louisville, Ky.: Westminster John Knox Press, 1999), 120-33.

2. The text here considered may be found in English translation in *Prayers of the Eucharist: Early and Reformed,* edited by R. C. D. Jasper and G. J. Cuming, 3d

ed. (New York: Pueblo Publishing Company, 1980), 114-23. It is one of the important Eastern sources for the compilation of prayers III and IV in the current Roman liturgy.

3. St. Germanus of Constantinople, *On the Divine Liturgy.* The Greek text with translation, introduction, and commentary by Paul Meyendorff (Crestwood, N.Y.: St. Vladimir's Seminary Press, 1984).

4. Basic information is available in volume IV of *The Church at Prayer*, 34-61, edited by A. Martimort (Collegeville, Minn.: Liturgical Press, 1992).

5. This homily is read every year in the liturgy of the hours. A critical edition of the text is found in *Melito of Sardis: On Pascha and Fragments*, ed. Stuart George Hall (Oxford: Clarendon Press, 1979). Melito as noted mentions the burial of Christ as part of the mystery. This is found later in the anaphora of the Byzantine liturgy, which also commemorates the burial at the annual Pasch.

6. See Joseph A. Fitzmyer, *The Biblical Commission's Document, "The Interpretation of the Bible in the Church."* Text and Commentary (Rome: Pontificio Istituto Biblico, 1995), 170-76.

7. *Egeria's Travels to the Holy Land*, translated John Wilkinson (Jerusalem: Ariel Publishing House, 1981).

Chapter Two

1. No historical reconstruction of the use of this title is intended here. It is being used simply as found in the Marcan narrative.

2. *The Last Supper,* in Rainer Maria Rilke, *The Book of Images,* a bilingual edition translated by Edward Snow (San Francisco: North Point Press, 1991), 52-53

3. For a discussion of the origin and meaning of this article of the Creed, see Hans Urs von Balthasar, *Mysterium Paschale: The Mystery of Easter* (San Francisco: Ignatius Press, 2000), 148-52.

4. See Matera, *New Testament Christology,* 138-43.

5. See ibid., 200-213.

Chapter Three

1. It is not without significance that the Catholic Church has recently been able to join with Christians who honour Nestorius in professing a common faith in Christ. See "Common Christological Declaration between the Catholic Church and the Assyrian Church of the East, November 11, 1994," *The Pontifical Council for Promoting Christian Unity: Information Service* N. 88 (1995/1): 2-3.

2. See Matera, *New Testament Christology,* 147-49.

3. For a survey, see Lucien Richard, *Christ the Self-Emptying of God* (New York/Mahwah, N.J.: Paulist Press, 1997), 73-83.

4. This question is reviewed in David N. Power, "Priesthood in Christian Tradition," *The New Catholic Encyclopedia*, rev. ed. (Washington, D.C.: Catholic University of America, 2003), 11:690-707.

5. The epistolary text is from Letter 28.3, *St Leo the Great. Letters*. Fathers of the Church, vol. 34 (New York: Fathers of the Church, Inc., 1957). For the sermons on the Passion, see *St Leo the Great: Sermons*. Fathers of the Church, vol. 93 (Wash-

ington, D.C.: Catholic University of America Press, 1996). Leo quotes the text from Phil 2:6-11 on the form of a servant in sermons 51.6, 52.2, 54.2, 65.3, 69.3, 72.4. The sermons were given in the course of Holy Week and may well indicate that the Roman Liturgy already attached Phil 2:6-11 to the reading of the Passion.

6. Letter to Ferrandus, in *Fulgentius, Selected Works,* translated by Robert B. Eno, *Fathers of the Church,* vol. 95 (Washington, D.C.: Catholic University of America Press, 1997), 476-565. The citation of Phil 2:6-11 is on page 548f.

7. There are helpful considerations on Gregory in John Milbank, *The Word Made Strange: Theology, Language, Culture* (London: Blackwell, 1997), 194-208.

8. As illustration see Athanasius, *Against the Gentiles,* nos. 40-42. This reading is given in the Office of Readings for Thursday of the First Week of the Year, where it goes with Ecclesiasticus (Sirach) 42:15–43:12.

9. See the foundations in Johann Baptist Metz, *Faith in History and Society* (New York: Seabury, 1980).

10. Jon Sobrino, *Christology at the Crossroads: A Latin American Approach* (Maryknoll, N.Y.: Orbis Books, 1978).

11. It may be found as Letter 165 in PL 54:1163ff., or *Decrees of the Ecumenical Councils,* ed. Norman Tanner, 1:77-82. (London and Washington, D.C.: Sheed & Ward/Georgetown University Press, 1990).

12. *Theodramatik,* or the drama of God, is the title that Balthasar gives to the second part of his major theological treatise. A liturgically based and accessible presentation of his thinking may be found in Hans Urs von Balthasar, *Mysterium Paschale: The Mystery of Easter* (San Francisco: Ignatius Press, 2000). Looking for the *Theodramatik* recently in a library I found it classified and shelved among books on stage drama!

13. "The Migration of Powers," in *The Complete French Poems of Rainer Maria Rilke,* translated by A. Poulin, Jr. (St Paul, Minn.: Graywolf Press, 1986), 334-35.

14. See E. Mveng, "Christ, liturgie et culture," *Bulletin de théologie africaine* 4 (1980): 247-55; "A la recherche d'un nouveau dialogue entre Christianisme et traditions africaines," *L'Afrique dans l'Eglise; Paroles d'un croyant* (Paris: L'Harmattan, 1985), 71-92.

15. One could consult the postsynodal apostolic exhortation, *Ecclesia in Asia,* chapters two and four, available on the Vatican Web site, and the Asian theologians' statement, "A Vision of Mission for the New Millennium," *Mission Today* 2 (2000): 253-54.

16. Aloysius Pieris, *Love Meets Wisdom: A Christian Experience of Buddhism* (Maryknoll, N.Y.: Orbis Books, 1988). Pieris specifies how the Trinity is invoked on pp. 129-35.

17. Augustine, *Confessions,* 9.10.23-25.

18. Bernard McGinn, *Visions of the End: Apocalyptic Traditions in the Middle Ages* (New York: Columbia University Press, 1998).

Chapter Four

1. John Paul II, "Apostolic Exhortation *Pastores Gregis,*" *Origins* 33 (2003/22): 353-92. What is given here is the translation published in *Origins,* but the Latin in fact says "under persecution."

2. Ibid., no. 20

3. Reference is to Eugene de Mazenod's Preface to the original *Constitutions and Rules* of the Missionary Oblates of Mary Immaculate, which is always reprinted in later editions and revisions of the Rule.

4. Briefly stated presentations of these insights may be found in *Mysterium Liberationis: Fundamental Concepts of Liberation Theology*, ed. Ignacio Ellacuría and Jon Sobrino (Maryknoll, N.Y.: Orbis Books, 1993), especially in the essays by Gustavo Gutiérrez, "Option for the Poor," 235-50, and Ignacio Ellacuría, "The Church of the Poor: Historical Sacrament of Liberation," 543-63.

5. Pontifical Council for Christian Unity, *Information Service* 1982, no. 50, 138-49.

6. For example, one sees the struggle with the question of poverty in the WCC Ecumenical Affirmation on Mission and Evangelism, 31-36, in *New Directions in Mission and Evangelization*, vol. 1, *Basic Statements*, ed. James A. Scherer and Stephen Bevans (Maryknoll, N.Y.: Orbis Books, 1992), 46-48.

7. Gianni Vattimo, *Belief*, trans. Luca D'Isante and David Webb (Stanford: Stanford University Press, 1999).

8. John D. Caputo, *On Religion* (London & New York: Routledge, 2001).

9. Eavan Boland, "A Habitable Grief," *The Lost Land: Poems* (London and New York: W. W. Norton, 1998), 32.

10. Thomas Aquinas, *Summa Theologiae* III, q.48.

11. Though this was written at an earlier date, a description of sacrifice along these lines is given in the 2003 encyclical letter of John Paul II, *Ecclesia de Eucharistia*, n. 13 (*On the Eucharist in Relation to the Church* [Boston: Pauline Books and Media, 2003]). The approach is of course found in a number of contemporary theological writings.

Chapter Five

1. John Paul II, " Tertio Millennio Adveniente," *Origins* 24 (1994/24): 401-16.

2. The two documents may be found in *Decrees*, ed. N. Tanner.

3. For recommendations on how to speak of them, see Commission for Religious Relations with Jews, "Notes on Correct Way to Present the Jews and Judaism in Preaching and Catechesis," *Information Service of the Pontifical Council for Promoting Christian Unity* 57 (1985): 16-21. Also the 2001 document of the Pontifical Biblical Commission, "The Jewish People and Their Sacred Scriptures in the Christian Bible," Section II, nn. 1-11. From the Vatican Web site www.vatican.va.

4. John Paul II, Bull of Indiction for the Jubilee, "Incarnationis Mysterium," *Origins* 28 (1998/26): 445-52.

5. *Fioretti*, chapter 8.

6. John Paul II, Encyclical Letter, *Ut Unum Sint* (Boston: Pauline Books and Media, n.d.).

7. This is the Irish way of putting the question whether the country should ally itself more with America or with the European Community. Rightly or wrongly, it is also meant to express a choice between seeking economic and political power or a communion of peoples who want justice for all parts of the earth.

8. For an Orthodox perspective on the *kenosis* of the Spirit, see Sergius Bul-

gakov, *The Bride of the Lamb* (Grand Rapids, Mich.: William B. Eerdmans Publishing Company, 2002), 387-428, where the *kenosis* of the Spirit is related to that of Christ.

Chapter Six

1. Since writing, I have found an excellent summary of the thought of the members of the World Council of Churches on Religions and Dialogue in Jutta Sperber, *Christian and Muslims: The Dialogus Activities of the World Council of Churches and Their Theological Foundation* (Berlin/New York: Walter de Gruyter, 2000), 216-88. For a Catholic perspective, a summary of conciliar and papal teaching may be found in Jacques Dupuis, *Christianity among the Religions: From Confrontation to Dialogue* (Maryknoll, N.Y.: Orbis Books, 2001), 45-73.

2. Pontifical Council, *Pastoral Attention to Traditional Religions.* On the Vatican Web site www.vatican.va.

3. See John Paul II, "Encyclical Letter *Ecclesia de Eucharistia,*" *Origins* 32 (2003/46): 754-68.

4. John Paul II, "Message for World Peace Day 2002, " *Origins* 31 (2001/28): 461-66.

5. "This Day," in Denise Levertov, *Oblique Prayers* (New York: New Directions Books, 1981), 80-81.

Chapter Seven

1. See Emmanuel Levinas, *Totality and Infinity,* trans. Alphonso Lingis (Pittsburgh: Duquesne University Press, 1969).

2. A good introduction to Greek thought is found in Boris Bobrinskoy, *The Mystery of the Trinity: Trinitarian Experience and Vision in Biblical and Patristic Tradition,* translated from the French (Crestwood, N.Y.: St. Vladimir's Seminary Press, 1999).

3. Ghislain Lafont, *God, Time and Being,* trans. Leonard Maluf (Petersham, Mass.: St. Bede's Publications, 1992), 242-53.

4. Walter Kasper, *The God of Jesus Christ,* trans. Matthew O'Connell (New York: Crossroad, 1984), 223-29. In Papeete, this was available to me in French translation.

Chapter Eight

1. "The Separate Rose XIX: The Men," in Pablo Neruda, *Late and Posthumous Poems 1968-1974,* bilingual edition, edited and translated by Ben Belitt (New York: Grove Press, 1988), 139.

2. This switches from the Pacific to the Atlantic Ocean, but the reference is to the poem by Elizabeth Bishop, "The Sandpiper."

3. The seminary in Papeete provided a French version of a book written in German by Claus Westermann and available in English as *Elements of Old Testament Theology,* translated by Douglas M. Stott (Atlanta: John Knox Press, 1982).

4. Hans Urs von Balthasar, *Glaubhaft ist nur Liebe* (Einsiedeln: Benziger, 1963).

5. Rainer Maria Rilke, *The Book of Images*, bilingual edition, trans. Edward Snow (San Francisco: North Point Press, 1991), 108-10.

6. James Dunn, *Christology in the Making: A New Testament Inquiry into the Origins of the Doctrine of the Incarnation* (Philadelphia: Westminster, 1980), 190.

7. I have since found the original Spanish and an English translation in *The Collected Works of John of the Cross*. Revised Edition. Translated by Kieran Kavanaugh, O.C.D., and Otilio Rodriguez, O.C.D. (Washington, D.C.: ICS Publications, 1991) but will stick with the above hybrid and unscientific rendering.

Chapter Nine

1. Eberhard Jüngel is known to English-speaking readers from *God as the Mystery of the World*, trans. D. Z. Guider (Grand Rapids: Eerdmanns, 1982).

2. See David Power, "On Blessing Things," *Concilium* 178 (1985): 24-39.

3. As many readers will know, this is the designation given to a fifth-century Syriac writer, mystical and liturgical, who used the pseudonym of Denis the Areopagite of Acts 19, but whose own name is unknown to history.

Index of Persons

Scripture Index

Old Testament

Genesis
1-11	152-53
22	13-14
32, 22-32	123
49	165

Exodus
1:15-21	121
3	120
12	12-13
14	12
17	125-26

Deuteronomy
4-5	126, 127
26	151, 174

1 Samuel
8:10-18	34
15:16-23	127-28

Psalms
21/22	59
74	196
118	196

Ecclesiasticus
43	33

Isaiah
49-53	28
50:4-7	11
52:13-53	16

Ezekiel
36	16
37	15

Zechariah
9:9-10	10

New Testament

Matthew
5:3-11	130
8:31, 38	26
13:11, 13	27
19	73
21:1-11	10

Mark
1:11, 12	25, 26
2:10	26
8:31	26
8:38	26
10:45	26
13	109-10
13:26	26
14:12-31	26
14:62	26
21:41	26

Luke
1:46-55	130
6:20-23	130
9	66
19	30, 38

John
1:9	28
3:13, 31	30
3:14-15	140
3:34	2
6:60-69	28
12:23	196
13:8, 14-17	28
15:15	28

212

Index of Subjects

─────────────── ✿ ───────────────

OF RELATED INTEREST

BRUNO STEIMER AND
MICHAEL G. PARKER, EDITORS
THE DICTIONARY OF POPES AND THE PAPACY
The definitive work on the history of the popes!

"This volume is the first English installment of the German Lexikon für Theologie und Kirche, a world-renowned reference work in Christian history and theology. The Dictionary arrives on the American scene at a moment when speculation about the future of the papacy is at an all-time high. This book is sure to be a sought-after resource for laypeople and priests wishing to learn more about the history of this complex and fascinating institution."

—LIBRARY JOURNAL

0-8245-1918-3 $50.00, hardcover

BRUNO STEIMER, EDITOR
THE DICTIONARY OF THE REFORMATION

From the Lexikon für Theologie und Kirche, the second installment of the Encyclopedia of Theology and Church. Covers every important aspect of the Reformation, including the major Protestant branches, developments in England, and the causes of the counter-Reformation in the Catholic Churches.

0-8245-2119-6 $50.00, hardcover

*herder &
herder*

ALSO FROM
DAVID NOEL POWER, OMI

SACRAMENT
The Language of God's Giving

"In the second half of this century, there have been crucial turns in
Catholic sacramental theology. Rahner explored sacrament in light of
God's self-communication in Christ; Schillebeeckx in terms of shared
meaning through personal encounter. In this prophetic work undertaken in a spirit of serene scholarship, David Power takes up again his
abiding concern: How does language constitute the reality of sacramental experience? Power's understanding of sacrament as a language
event, as gift through and through, may well be sacramental theology's
high-water mark in the final decades of the twentieth century."

—Michael Downey

0-8245-1798-9, $24.95, paperback

THE EUCHARISTIC MYSTERY
Revitalizing the Tradition

"[An] engrossing and illuminating work on the Eucharist that will
surely become a standard text in the classroom, a primary reference for
liturgists and catechists, and a nurturing and challenging book for all
whose faith finds a primary expression in the celebration of the sacrament.

"Not only an extraordinarily clear theologian and teacher, Power is a
gifted artist as well.... *The Eucharistic Mystery* is satisfying and provoca-
tive in many ways. It not only historically situates the challenges of contemporary eucharistic practice, but . . . gently draws the reader into
deeper engagement with the very mystery it examines."

America

0-8245-1723-7, $15.95 paperback

*At your bookstore or, to order directly from the publisher,
please send check or money order (including $4.00 for the first book
plus $1.00 for each additional book) to:*

THE CROSSROAD PUBLISHING COMPANY
481 EIGHTH AVENUE, NEW YORK, NY 10001
1-800-707-0670 (toll free)

herder &
herder